EBL
£6

CHARLIE PYE-SMITH

THE
OTHER NILE

With illustrations by Eric Parry

VIKING

VIKING

Penguin Books Ltd, Harmondsworth, Middlesex, England
Viking Penguin Inc., 40 West 23rd Street, New York, New York 10010, U.S.A.
Penguin Books Australia Ltd, Ringwood, Victoria, Australia
Penguin Books Canada Limited, 2801 John Street, Markham, Ontario, Canada L3R 1B4
Penguin Books (N.Z.) Ltd, 182–190 Wairau Road, Auckland 10, New Zealand

First published 1986

Typeset in Monophoto Photina

Printed in Great Britain by Richard Clay (The Chaucer Press) Ltd, Bungay, Suffolk

British Library Cataloguing in Publication Data

Pye-Smith, Charlie
   The other Nile.
   1. Nile River Region–Description and
   travel
   I. Title
   916.2'0455   DT115

   ISBN 0–670–80204–2

Library of Congress Catalog Card Number: 85–052050

The author and publishers are grateful to the following people
for permission to use photographs;
Mick Jennings for 1, 3, 4, 6, 8, 9, 11, 14, 15, 16, 17, 18, 20–27;
Richard North for 2, 5; Eric Parry for 10, 13.

This book is for my mother
and in memory of my father

CONTENTS

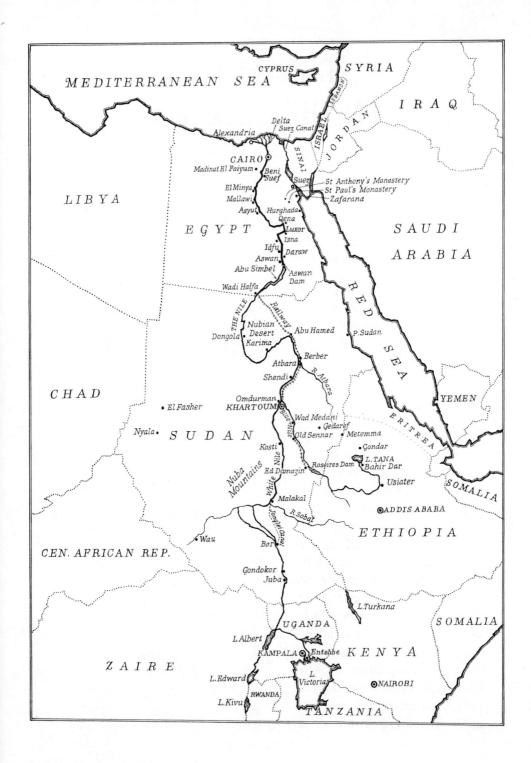

INTRODUCTION
BETWEEN THE BARBED WIRE

*There is no room for tourists in a world of
displaced persons . . . The very young, perhaps, may set out
like the Wandervogels of the Weimar period;
lean, lawless, aimless couples with rucksacks, joining
the great army of men and women
without papers, without official existence,
the refugees and deserters, who drift everywhere today
between the barbed wire.*

Evelyn Waugh,
When the Going Was Good

I had hoped to write about the changes over nine years; changes to
the river, to the cities and to the people who lived along the banks
of the Nile between Alexandria and Juba. And there were changes,
mostly for the worse. In 1975 Sudan was calm and the Sudanese
reasonably well fed. But in 1984 it was stricken by civil war,
drought and food shortages. Famine was lurking round the corner.
In 1975 I arrived in Ethiopia a little over a year after the revolution
which had brought down Haile Selassie. The country was turbulent
and wild, though it was still possible to travel through it if you kept
clear of Eritrea. But nine years later Ethiopia was in such a mess
that I knew, even before setting off, that I probably wouldn't be able
to cross its borders overland. However, to chart the more subtle
evolution of the Nile states would have required an intimate knowledge of their politics, their religions and, above all, their native
languages. I had none of these. Even if I had, my testimony would
have been unreliable, and for the most obvious of reasons. Africa
may have changed; but so had I. Travel is both an exploration

within and a journey without. The images that fall on the retina, though they be identical for each who sees them, are transmitted into the inner realms where mood, emotion, attitude and inclination all confer in judgement. And one man's meat can be the same man's poison – given a little time.

There were days when I despaired of understanding anything about life on the Nile. So I comforted myself with the thought that a Nubian from Wadi Halfa or a Dinka from south Sudan would have been equally baffled by the social (and antisocial) customs of people living in High Wycombe or Huddersfield. *The Other Nile* is my river, not theirs. It does not pretend to be a history or a treatise about modern times. It is simply an account of a journey which required a little time and a modicum of stamina.

It is now nine months since I returned from Africa, and some of what I have written in the following pages already seems dated. When I visited Omdurman there were no refugee camps on the edge of the city. Today the newspaper reports that 100,000 people are camped on the sand, many suffering from malnutrition. Sudan's President Nimeiri, about whom I have had quite a bit to say, has recently been overthrown, and though it is too early to predict in what direction Sudan's new political masters will take the country, it seems likely that the rule of Islamic law, which had such a profound influence on daily life while I was there, will be abandoned. However, I have told the story as it was then, not as it seems now. And where I was forced to rely on rumours to find out what was going on, I have not rewritten my observations to fit more closely with reports subsequently gathered.

A brief word about an unfulfilled intention. In 1975 I travelled through Africa with so little money that I invariably went third class on the trains and boats. Sometimes I rode the train roofs, not out of any great love of fresh air, but to avoid paying. This time I had intended to travel first class, not out of any yearning for comfort, but because I thought the contrast would be illuminating: I would step out of the overcrowded and filthy third-class carriage to be sucked into the slums of the unsewered back alleys; or I would saunter from first class and go to sit at the rich man's table, where I would eat exotic fruit and experience the voluptuous pleasures of his harem. Thus could I expose the enormous contrasts between rich and poor. Unfortunately, it didn't turn out like that. I was generally too mean to pay for a first-class ticket, even when I could afford it. And I regret to say that I have never been entertained in a harem.

My thanks go to the many people who provided me with help and entertainment. I am particularly indebted to Eric Parry, who did the sketches for *The Other Nile*. And were it not for Richard North I should never have visited the monasteries by the Red Sea. Both were old friends and their presence added greatly to my enjoyment of the early days of the trip. It would take many pages to list all those who helped me while I was in Egypt. Rather than do so, I will simply say that there is no country for which I have a greater affection. I miss Egypt still. That, in no small part, is a reflection of the kindness that I met with during my two months there.

Sadly, my memories of Sudan are not such as will carry me back there soon. Yet I owe a very special debt of gratitude to one group of people: the fifty or so refugees among whom I spent a month in Khartoum. I have written about them at length; and perhaps I owe them an apology for having done so, as I never told any of them that I was writing a book. More than that, I owe them whatever small message this introduction carries.

Some of the refugees became genuine friends, and all of them taught me a great deal. Their fortitude was remarkable, and I was unceasingly surprised by their lack of bitterness. I was a tourist in a world of displaced persons, yet they bore me no grudge for having those very fundamental things which they lacked, most notably the freedom to go wherever I chose and the fortune to live in a country where I could do and say pretty much as I pleased. In my hotel there were Ugandans who had survived the rule of Idi Amin but been driven north by Obote's undisciplined armies; there were men and women who had fought with the Eritrean Liberation Front; and there were opponents of the ruling regime in Ethiopia who would have been murdered had they not fled their country. They were all members of what Evelyn Waugh referred to as 'the great army of men and women without papers, without official existence, the refugees and deserters, who drift everywhere today between the barbed wire'. Every one had a story to tell. Some had survived famine, others war; a few imprisonment and torture. All nurtured a pathetic dream that one day they would escape to the West, where they would begin their lives anew. I say pathetic for two reasons. For one thing, most will never get the papers they need to come to the West. And for another, their vision of the West had little to do with the reality of how we live here. The West is not the Garden of Eden which so many supposed it to be: the fruit turned rotten on the tree long ago. We are not a charitable, loving people, ready to embrace the dispossessed from other continents. We are mean, self-centred and ruthless, and so are our governments. For those very few who do get to England or Canada or Sweden, a rude shock awaits them. They will not lead a life of happy, carefree rusticity, surrounded by the bounties of nature, as so many of them seemed to expect: they will probably find themselves, like Vietnam's forgotten boat people, trapped in the squalor of our inner city ghettos and subjected to the rancour of racism.

I didn't have to spend long with these men and women to realize that the famine was already widespread in Ethiopia, yet in the West we were taking not the blindest bit of notice. This could not be attributed to ignorance. Just before leaving London in January 1984, I went to a lecture in the Africa Centre and heard Mark Malloch Brown, a one-time UN refugee worker, tell the small (and mostly white) audience that a million or more people were starving to death in the Eritrean highlands. The British government knew this, yet it chose not to act. And our newspapers expressed not the slightest interest until July, when the full horrors of the Ethiopian famine were shown on our television screens. Western governments belatedly realized that they had to do something. There were debates in the House of Commons about sending food and aid, and eventually money earmarked for other countries was channelled to Ethiopia. 'From now on,' Andy Warhol once said, 'everyone in the world will be famous for fifteen minutes'; and we might equally well adapt his aphorism for the countries of the world. All a country needs to get its fifteen minutes is a good disaster. A famine, for example. Or better still, a war. Once Fleet Street realized that Ethiopia's time had come, everyone jumped on to the bandwagon, or in the case of Mr Robert Maxwell, the proprietor of the *Daily Mirror*, on to his hired jet – there's nothing like suffering to boost newspaper sales. I realize that we should be grateful for whatever coverage the Ethiopian disaster received, as it undoubtedly led to money and aid being sent to where it was needed. However, I found the orgy of self-righteousness which accompanied much of the coverage of the aid programme quite nauseating.

I often wondered, in the autumn of 1984, what my friends among the refugees were making of all this. I think they would have said what was fairly obvious. That our preoccupation with the Horn of Africa would be shortlived, not because life there would improve very much, if at all, but because we would get tired of hearing about it. Attention is already beginning to shift from Ethiopia to the Sudan, and by the time this book comes out, another country – perhaps Chad or Uganda – will be enjoying its fifteen minutes of fame.

I wouldn't dare to make any predictions about what the Sudan will be like in three or four years' time, except to suggest that most of the refugees I knew will still be there, and they will have been joined by many more. No Man's Land is getting bigger every year. And Waugh was right: it is no place for tourists. Nevertheless, I'm glad that for a little while I ventured between the barbed wire. If nothing else, it made me realize how lucky I was to have a country which I could call home.

London, April 1985

CHAPTER ONE
ALEXANDRIA: FROM RICHES TO RAGS

Alexandria, princess and whore.
The royal city and the anus mundi.
Lawrence Durrell,
The Alexandria Quartet

For reasons which escape me now, I never made my way down to Alexandria from Cairo – where I had flown to – in 1975. I have a vague memory of someone describing it as a maritime Wolverhampton; and perhaps that was enough to put me off. This time I sailed to Egypt from Piraeus on the SS *Egitto*, a grey, solemn piece of ironmongery, too big to register the swell of the March sea and too small to offer the sorts of entertainment which one would expect on a large liner, and which might have allayed the tedium of the crossing. It was run by a crew of Italians, notable only for their discourtesy and their complete lack of concern for the welfare of the passengers, of whom there were not many. A few years ago several companies ran regular services from Greece to Alexandria; today there is just one boat every couple of weeks, presumably because it is cheaper to fly. The journey took two days, and I had plenty of time to contemplate what I might find in Alexandria. Even a rudimentary knowledge of Mediterranean history suggests that Alexandria has had a remarkable career. The rollcall of the men and women who have lived in or passed through her is impressive: Alexander the Great, Cleopatra, Euclid, Ptolemy, Caesar, Mark Antony, Athanasius, Napoleon, Mohammed Ali ... I had a very definite image of what the city would look like when approached by sea, an image adapted from two paintings which hang side by side in London's National Gallery. One is a painting by Turner of Carthage; the other, by Claude, shows the Queen of Sheba setting off from a North African port (perhaps Alexandria) on her journey to the court of King Solomon. In both paintings monumental buildings of classical design dwarf the human flotsam strewn round the jetties. I was expecting a crumbling version of this, superimposed on which there would be queues of battered taxis, haggling taxi drivers and fraught tourists.

On the second morning out from Piraeus a thin jagged band appeared between sea and sky as we approached the city from the north-west. The horizon bristled like a sea urchin, thin metal chimneys gleaming brightly and pouring out wisps of nicotine-coloured smoke. A pilot boat came out to guide us through the bottleneck of cargo boats – some carrying wood from Russia, others weapons from America, more still wheat off the top of the EEC grain mountain – and soon we could make out oil refineries with their rows of squat cylindrical tanks, petrochemical works with their contorted mass of chimneys and pipes, and great warehouses with precarious gantries clinging to rusting sides. I once read that you could smell the north African coast before you could see it if a northerly breeze carried the scent of pine sap out to sea. For pine sap, read sulphur dioxide and burning tar. We edged our way along miles and miles of industrialized foreshore till we reached the harbour. Finally we came out from between two Russian boats – a lone sailor was jogging round the deck of one – to sight the gleaming silver dome of the mosque of Abul Abbass El Mursi surrounded by docks and cranes and dilapidated housing. It twinkled like a jewel in a scrapheap. The Queen of Sheba would have looked very out of place.

The western harbour is the back door to Egypt. Once across the threshold you step into a world of seediness, noise, dirt, milling crowds, wailing music, amplified mullahs, stumbling donkeys, clinking trams, terrible traffic. Everywhere, rich smells: of sewers, spices, perfumes, people and animals.

During my five days in Alexandria I spent a good deal of time asleep, seldom talked to anyone, and passed more of my waking hours drinking acrid coffee in street cafés than looking for what few signs of Alexandria's glorious past were still to be found. I had failed, idiotically, to bring with me a copy of E. M. Forster's *Alexan-*

dria: A History and a Guide; instead I read Evelyn Waugh's *When the Going Was Good*, or laid out across the dusty and unswept floor of my room in the Leroy Hotel a series of maps which stretched from the Nile delta south to Sudan's border with Uganda. I made plans about how I should progress up the river, but these were largely speculative. On my first trip I had travelled south as far as Khartoum, then headed east along the Blue Nile and up into the mountains of northern Ethiopia. Having traversed Ethiopia, I spent some time in Kenya before rejoining the White Nile at Juba in south Sudan. And from there I had headed north, by train and boat, back to Cairo. I didn't expect to be able to repeat the journey. The Ethiopian border would probably be closed, and there was civil war in south Sudan.

Every morning, a little after nine o'clock, an old Greek walked with slow and stiff dignity through Ramla Square. He carefully negotiated the trams which rattled back and forth outside the post office and avoided the cars which sped between the tram terminus and the Athineos tea-rooms. He would walk through the open door of the Athineos, remove his homburg and nod to the waitresses. He always sat at the same table, near one of the large windows over-looking the square, and every morning he would drink two bottles of Stella beer. With each he would take a ham sandwich. He was a large man with a bulging midriff, and the skin on his bald and blotched skull was stretched tight like polythene across a haggis. He was always immaculately dressed in a grey suit, and the cuffs and collar of his white shirt were starched and spotless. However, I probably wouldn't have noticed him if it hadn't been for a curious affliction which caused him to push out his bottom lip and wobble it between sips of beer, a sort of St Vitus dance of the lower mandible. He was a relic of prerevolutionary Alexandria, and one of the few foreigners who hadn't joined the mass exoduses of the 1950s (when Nasser nationalized commerce and industry over 80,000 Greeks left the city).

A further attraction to the Athineos came in the shape of the waitresses, with whom the old Greek was most familiar. There were three. Sometimes they worked the early shift; sometimes the late. They were fine tarty females, bow-tied in tight black suits. The eldest was lemon-shaped and her face was cheerfully painted with bright rouge and livid red lipstick. She looked like a tulip in drag. The other two were young, slim and very pretty, olive-skinned with large almond eyes framed by kohl and mascara. Whenever the opportunity arose they slouched against the cabinets of confectionery and chewed gum with exaggerated nonchalance, like aspirants to a bit part in an American B movie. The music of the café was Arabic though the sleazy jazz of Tom Waites would have suited it just as well.

The Athineos was one of four famous tea-houses in Alexandria. Pastroudis, set further back from the sea and just a few minutes' walk from the Leroy Hotel, had a finer interior with its dark-stained wood and curving art nouveau mirrors and screens. And the Trianon, a little way to the west of the Athineos, was more spacious and had a fine view past the Italian Consulate on to the bay. But the Athineos I liked best. By a slow process of cultural osmosis, the Arab world, here as in the streets outside, was reclaiming the European.

In 1977 Lawrence Durrell, one of the city's most famous expatriates, returned to Alexandria. He found that it had little in common with the Alexandria of his *Quartet*:

> The cafés still have their immortal names – Pastroudis, Baudrot, but no trade to set them twinkling with light and music. All foreign posters and advertisements have vanished, everything is in Arabic; in our time [he was there during the last war] film posters were billed in several languages with Arabic subtitles so to speak. Now a leaden uniformity rules. It is particularly exasperating to find that all the medicaments in the chemists are now known by Arabic names. Try and obtain some aspirin or throat tablets and see what happens!

I loved Alexandria precisely for those reasons which led Durrell, on his return, to hate it. Alexandria, like the Athineos, has gone to seed. The prima donna of the ancient world no longer sings but croaks. She has been ravaged by Romans, Arabs, Turks, French and British, and scarcely a trace remains of the finery in which she was decked by the Ptolemies, the dynasty which began with Alexander the Great in 331 BC and which ended three hundred years later when Cleopatra backed the wrong Roman horse (Julius

Caesar). Today she is an Arab diva in European rags. I loved the shabbiness of the streets and cafés, the melancholy which hung over the city late of an evening, the slow decay (not destruction, mind you) of what the Europeans had left behind when they fled. I don't know whether Durrell went into the Athineos – he was staying at the Cecil Hotel near by – but it would have depressed him if he did. There was still a hint of its former grandeur: original wrought-iron light fittings hung from the ceiling, though few had their full complement of bulbs; the frontage was still impressive with its great panes of glass, though now the squat and dilapidated post office opposite was covered by huge hoardings advertising in Arabic Lipton's tea and Coca-Cola; and the walls still carried long mirrors that created the illusion of great space. But bare hardboard, draped with lacy cobwebs, had replaced the pelmets, and the duster, here as elsewhere in Egypt, was a stranger to the establishment. Dust lay so thick on the plastic cheese plant beside the old Greek's table that someone had managed to scrawl graffiti across its leaves – in Arabic, of course.

I found Durrell's jaundiced view of his old city very sad. Maybe one shouldn't expect people to return to the mistress of their youth and ignore the wrinkles acquired over the passing years. But the truth, I suspect, was that Durrell was hankering after the lost Europeans of the city. Well, they have gone. And if you want some aspirin, ask in Arabic.

The billboards may be in Arabic and the cafés may be frequented by only a handful of Greeks, hanging on, like the old man with his wobbling jaw, much as the last dinosaurs must have as they watched the coming mammals usher in a new era, but this small corner of north Africa will retain its Hellenistic influence for some time to come. A Greek *taverna* still operates across the square from the Athineos; the food is characteristically dreadful. And the plaque on the Eastern Harbour breakwater, which encloses the lovely bay in front of the city, will carry for many years yet the names of the Europeans – Greek, English, Italian, French – who ran the Council when the long spit of stone was built in 1916: Barbaza, Bontoux, Casulli, Demetriadis, Interdonato, Swinglehurst . . .

Alexandria may be suffering from neglect, which has its own charm, but there is much of beauty which in a European city would have been swept away by what we euphemistically refer to as progress. There is a small chemist's shop in Ramla Square whose turn of the century décor remains unaltered. The walls are lined with cabinets whose drawers still carry the gilded names of old medicaments – tilleul, uva-ursi, gentian, valerian, chamomile . . . These drawers now hold pessaries and pills in place of petals and old potions, but I doubt if many such chemists have survived in Europe. Perhaps in Italy or Spain, but certainly not in England.

There is another shop worthy of special mention, Sofianopoulo's on Rue Ṣaad Zaghoul. It is on the ground floor of a four- or five-storey building. From the street you catch a glimpse of a large shining chrome coffee grinder as high as a man. It stands slightly to one side of a large room whose ceilings are supported by fluted wooden columns. The back wall carries dark wood shelving and before it is a counter; again, heavy and wooden. Two statues, almost life size, stand sentinel at each end. They are of an oriental style – there is a similar pair in Victor Hugo's house in the Channel Isles – wood with paint and gilt. Both women stand with one leg slightly forward of the other. One hand rests on the hip, the other holds aloft a platter, as though presenting the contents – unseen from the shop floor – for the approval of the gods. From a room behind the counter the aroma of roasting coffee drifts past the customers and on to the street, where it mingles with the smell of horse piss and perfume.

But for real Greekness you must go, predictably, to the Greek Consulate. The sun was high and a stiff, salty breeze blew off the sea when I took a tram from Ramla Square towards the east of the city. One of the guards on the consulate gates had taken his boots and socks off and he was smoking a cigarette in that marvellous leisurely way which comes so easily to an Egyptian soldier on duty. A janitor led the way up to the first floor and unlocked a door into a large room. The window blinds were down and he turned on the lights. The consulate calls this room a museum; but it is more like a shrine. On the staircase which winds up to it hang a dozen portraits, most in ink or pencil, of Constantine Cavafy, the Greek poet born in Alexandria in 1863. They show a man with a thin, austere face. The nose is slightly hooked and a thin mouth dips at the edges. Inside the room are many of his possessions. There is a photograph of a group of smartly dressed Greeks outside the Athineos, and another of Cavafy's grave. A third shows the ceremony which accompanied the erection of a brass plaque outside 10 Rue Lepsius, where the poet lived. Two flags hang limply on either side of the door, one Greek, the other Egyptian. Glass cabinets contain his notebooks, scraps of poems and letters. They are mixed, haphazardly it seems, with other odds and ends about his life: a faded copy of the *Listener* with an article about Cavafy by E. M. Forster, written in 1958, twenty-five years after the poet's death; and some reviews of his poems together with his notebooks. There is a bust of his head on a purple cushion – he looks ludicrous, like an effete emperor – and at one end of the room four chairs with low seats and high backs are arranged round a small table. The janitor signalled to me to come over to the bookcase, which stretched down one wall. He ran the back of his hand up and down the spine of one of the books. It was Gibbon's *Decline and Fall of the Roman Empire*, though I think the janitor was indicating his approval of the leather binding rather than of the contents. I would have liked to believe that he had read the chapter on the rise of Islam, but he spoke no English. The books, like Cavafy's poems, spanned two thousand years: Aristotle, Virgil, Macaulay's *England*, the works of Molière . . .

That afternoon I visited Rue Lepsius, a short, seedy street of nineteenth-century buildings. Like all the streets in Alexandria, its name had been changed. It has become Sharia Sharm el Sheikh; and, less easily explained, No. 10 was now No. 4. In Cavafy's day the ground floor was a brothel. Now the building housed a small pension, and the broad stairway was littered with rubbish. There were no whores to greet the visitor.

I had intended to write something to the effect of: I was sitting in the café downstairs from the Leroy, eating spiced liver served by a one-legged woman, when the book in front of me fell open at the following poem – 'Half past twelve. Time's gone by quickly . . .' This would have been dishonest, for although I frequently ate spiced liver at the café, and although I was invariably served by a one-legged woman, I didn't have a book of Cavafy's poems with me, and at the time I didn't know the poem 'Since Nine O'clock', which I began to quote. And it would have been disingenuous, too, as Gavin Young, in *A Slow Boat to China*, did roughly what I anticipated above, though in a posher café. However, one evening I was eating an omelette in the Cecil Hotel in the company of an Australian woman when she fished out Cavafy's collected poems from her handbag. On her instruction I read a poem called 'The City':

You said, 'I'll go to another country, go to another shore,
find another city better than this one.
Whatever I try to do is fated to turn out wrong
and my heart lies buried as though it were something dead.
How long can I let my mind moulder in this place?
Wherever I turn, wherever I look,
I see the black ruins of my life, here,
where I've spent so many years, wasted them, destroyed them
    totally.'

You won't find a new country, won't find another shore.
This city will always pursue you.
You'll walk the same streets, grow old
in the same neighbourhoods, turn grey in these same houses.

You'll always end up in this city. Don't hope for things
   elsewhere:
there's no ship for you, there's no road.
Now that you've wasted your life here, in this small corner,
you've destroyed it everywhere in the world.

The Leroy Hotel had three attractions. First, it was cheap and
virtually empty – the summer tourist season, when even the
government descends on Alexandria to escape the intense heat of
Cairo, had yet to begin. Second, I developed a particular affection
for the doorman. He was an ancient, bandy-legged character, chin
and jowls blurred by grey stubble, who lurked inside the vast ill-lit
porch of the office block on whose eighth floor the hotel was to be
found. He wore a heavy great coat, despite the warm spring weather, and a battered peak cap, around whose rim was written in
faded gold braid HOTEL LEROY. On my arrival he leapt forward,
bloodshot eyes shining brightly, and shook me warmly by the hand.
He grinned broadly to expose a mouthful of yellow and broken
teeth. They looked like the decayed piles of a rotten wharf poking
through red mud on a low tide. 'Hello! Everything all right?' he
asked. 'How are you?' He propelled me down a dingy corridor and
pressed a button to call the lift, gripping my arm while we waited.
'Hello! Everything all right? How are you?' he repeated three times
before the lift came. And we went through the same rigmarole
every time I came and went. The hotel's third attraction was its
elevation. My room had a magnificent view over the west of the
city. The roof-line was irregular and religious. The mosques poked
the horizon with minarets, some small and modest, others tall,
slender and ornate. And down there, far below my window, were
the city's alarm clocks, the bellowing muezzins and the crowing
cocks. The days would start with the muezzins telling the world
through crackling loudspeakers, 'There is only one God and
Mohammed is the prophet of God.' And the cocks, perched amid the
debris of Alexandria's flat rooftops, surrounded by old bicycles,
rabbit hutches, pigeon lofts and yesterday's washing, would reply
raucously, their crowing adding a strident confusion to the Muslim
call to prayer, as though to avenge the interrupted sleep of the city's
many Christians.

23

There is scarcely a street in Alexandria without a mosque or a church of one sort or another. There is the Coptic church, the Greek Orthodox, the Armenian, the Anglican, the Presbyterian, the Roman. There is even a synagogue. And the mosques, sucking the faithful in from the streets morning, noon and night, are as conspicuous and numerous as pubs in an English town. Before the coming of Christianity, the ancient Egyptians worshipped dozens of gods, and it was here, in Alexandria, that the cult of Serapis began. It was the Greeks who founded the cult, creating a hybrid from two Egyptian gods, Osiris and Apis. Then, soon after the death of Christ, Christianity was established in Alexandria, from where it spread south into Nubia and Ethiopia, where it still flourishes.

Three of us drifted into the Coptic Cathedral early one evening. A funeral had just finished. A deacon motioned to us to remove our shoes. We did so, and he led the way down red-carpeted stairs into a room with strip lighting. A modern mosaic depicting the life of St Mark ran round the walls. The deacon admired it, as he must have done countless times, and gave us a lecture in Arabic. The three of us understood not one word. He may have been telling us that we were looking at a great work of art, in which case he was wrong. Obscuring one chunk of the mural, and of much greater interest, was a large board, four foot square. At its centre was a reproduction of Leonardo's 'Last Supper'. It was printed on what appeared to be shimmering plastic of the sort which makes objects move when viewed from different angles, though unfortunately the disciples remained immobile as we passed. Each had been touched up inexpertly in bright colours and underneath the painting was written in large letters, 'Made in Italy'. The rest of the board was covered by pictures, cigarette-card size, depicting scenes from the Bible. There were sloppy-looking saints, an effeminate Christ with long blond hair, and improbable flocks of angels hovering over pastoral scenes more commonly associated with nineteenth-century England than first-century Palestine. Scattered among these cheap icons were plastic car-stickers of Shenouda III, the Coptic pope currently under monastic arrest in Wadi Natrun, a desert retreat midway between Cairo and Alexandria. (In 1981 President Sadat banished Shenouda for allegedly fomenting religious strife between Christians and Muslims.)

24

The deacon led us down to the newly renovated crypt. The walls were covered by blue tiling which gave it the atmosphere of a recently refurbished public convenience, and low down in one corner, behind a glass pane, was a recess with a pile of bones. The deacon knelt, peered in and made the sign of the cross. He invited us to do the same. Beside the bones were piles of crumpled notes – from the grey 10 piastre up to the purple pound – and scraps of paper with scrawled messages. They had been squeezed past the glass pane. 'Saint Marcus,' said the deacon emphatically, referring to the previous owner of the bones.

We padded back up the red carpet and into the main body of the cathedral, where we were taken to see more icons – one, to my Anglo-Saxon surprise, was of St George slaying what I had always taken to be an English dragon, but which here was unmistakably Semitic. We were shown a large Bible whose left-hand pages were written in the Coptic script and the right-hand in Arabic. (The Coptic language is still used in religious ceremonies but no longer spoken.) We then removed our shoes again and the deacon showed us into a room in which there was a baptismal vat large enough for complete immersion to be practised. A distraught and tearful woman prayed aloud, but the deacon ignored her and gave another lengthy exposition, presumably about the business of baptism.

Of Egypt's forty million inhabitants, about six million are Christian, and most of these are Copts (the word Copt is derived from the Greek for Egyptian). The Copts will tell you that they are far more numerous; the government and Muslims will say there are many fewer. Racially and in manner of dress the Copts are indistinguishable from the rest of the population, though many have a crucifix tattooed on the inside of the wrist. Occasionally they will lift the sleeve of their shirt or jellaba to afford you a glimpse of the tattoo, as if to say, 'you're one of us', which isn't true: there are fundamental differences of dogma between the Copts and other Christian churches. In the fifth century the Council of Chalcedon decided that Christ had two natures, the divine and the human. He was son of both God and Mary. The Copts asserted, in opposition, that Christ had only one nature, the divine. They are thus monophysites, as are the Christians of Ethiopia, whose bishops until recently were chosen by the Coptic patriarch in Egypt. However, I have heard some Copts say that they are not monophysites; and I for one have never quite managed to fathom the difference between the two schools of thought, and I certainly can't see why the schism should be so great that to this day Copts and other Christians are, if on speaking terms, not on praying terms.

The Copts claim that their church was founded by St Mark, who is said to have arrived in Alexandria twelve years after the death of Christ. It is also said that he suffered a gory martyrdom in AD 62, though it is thought (by scholars, if not by Copts) that Mark's gospel was written after AD 65. The city of Alexandria remained a Christian stronghold up till the Islamic invasion, and a fine city it must have been. When the Arabs invaded in AD 642 the leader of the cavalry wrote to inform the Caliph of Arabia of his conquest: 'I have taken a city of which I can only say that it contains 4,000 palaces, 4,000 baths, 400 theatres, 1,200 greengrocers and 40,000 Jews.' The magnificence of the city, incidentally, owed more to the work of the Ptolemies, and to a lesser extent to the Romans who displaced them, than to the Christians.

Outsiders have often been rude about the Copts. The Emperor Hadrian, who was obviously unsure what Christians stood for, had this to say:

Those who worship Serapis are Christians . . . As a race of men they are seditious, vain, and spiteful; as a body, wealthy and prosperous, of whom nobody lives in idleness. Some blow glass, some make paper, and others linen. Their one God is nothing peculiar; Christians, Jews, and all nations worship him. I wish this body of men was better behaved.

And Edward Lane, the Englishman who lived in Cairo in the 1830s and was the author of *An Account of the Manners and Customs of the Modern Egyptians*, was even more damning:

One of the most remarkable traits in the character of the Copts is their bigotry. They bear a bitter hatred to all other Christians, even exceeding that with which the Muslims regard the unbelievers in El-Islam . . . They are, generally speaking, of a sullen temper, extremely avaricious, and abominable dissemblers, cringing or domineering according to circum-stances.

Lane acknowledged his debt to one particular Copt, then proceeded to recount this man's opinion of his own people. 'He avows them to be generally ignorant, deceitful, faithless, and abandoned to the pursuit of worldly gain, and to indulgence in sensual pleasure. He declares the Patriarch to be a tyrant and a suborner of false witness . . .' And so he goes on.

I woke up early on my fourth and last day in Alexandria, reflected that I had yet to see the Nile, and set off to find it. I consulted the *Blue Guide* over a cup of coffee. On a geological time-scale I had arrived just too late. The Canopic branch of the Nile, which ran into the sea at Alexandria, had silted up over a thousand years ago. Rather than travel an hour along the coast to Rosetta, the Nile's nearest point of exit into the Mediterranean, I headed past Rue Lepsius to Tahrir Square, an oblong piece of concrete with a few clusters of scruffy palms. Donkeys, horses and mules, their carts piled high with vegetables, rubbish, gilded chairs and washing-machines, moved nose to tail with battered yellow taxis. It was infernally noisy. From the cafés came music; from the mosques, re-ligion. Just to the west of the square I was sucked with the vortex of human flesh into the markets. The Nile may have shifted eastwards but here it was reconstituted in edible form. A fantastic diversity of meats, vegetables and fruits, all reared on irrigated Nile water, were laid out across the stalls. Turbaned fruiterers shouted their wares over pyramids of oranges and grapefruit. Men in blood-drenched jellabas hacked away at whole carcasses of beef and sheep. The fishmonger was selling *tilapia* and perch from the Nile and a wealth of fish from the Mediterranean: black eels, brown and mottled squid, silver fish with blunt heads, pink ones with long beaks, fish with rainbow stripes. There were crates of lobster and crab, and hessian sacks full of misty blue shellfish. A man sat crosslegged on the ground plucking tiny brown songbirds, and down a dark alley veiled women were selling rabbits and pigeons and chickens. Customers fingered the live birds, testing the breasts, thighs and bellies like clumsy gynaecologists. A bird was chosen, killed and plucked. It was a crude, honest way of selling food. Beyond the food market the crowds ebbed and flowed through the draping multi-coloured foliage of the silk and cotton bazaar; and in dark alleys where the sun never shone the shop windows were weighed down with gold bangles, heavy and intricate silver earrings and blue scarab necklaces. The city here was almost untainted by European influence, though across the faces of the men and women was written its chaotic racial history. Alexandria, wrote Durrell in the *Quartet*, 'would never change so long as the races continued to seeth here like must in a vat'. Alexandrian blood is an extravagant cocktail: mostly Arab, but with a dash of Syrian and Greek, of Jew and Berber, of white sailor and black slave.

I wandered down the back streets and into some slums, then retreated to a café for lunch, after which I walked along the seafront and out towards the breakwater, past the fishing harbour and on to Fort Kait Bey, where I looked in at the remarkable Museum of the Institute of Oceanography and Fisheries, whose exhibits must be the worst-labelled and most eccentric to be found anywhere. Pride of place was given to a pair of seacows. The male had been given a thick coat of ordinary blue-grey house paint, and his erect penis, like his protruding tongue, was painted bright red. The vulva of his companion had received similar treatment. Beside them was the skeleton of another seacow. It looked as though death had been caused by violent beating of the ribs.

The weather was perfect, sunny and warm with a slight breeze. Midway through the afternoon I climbed down to a thin strip of beach near the fishing harbour and joined the rusty shell of an old car, some wooden crates and a small armada of plastic cans and broken bottles. I fell asleep over Evelyn Waugh and didn't wake till dusk. The rod-and-line fishermen on the Corniche were reeling in for the last time and heading back past the colonial buildings on the sea-front to their homes in the bowels of the city. The markets had closed for the night and the shoe-shiners in Ramla Square were packing up. For a little while the streets crackled with electricity. Groups of young girls, walking arm in arm like links in a chastity belt, promenaded through the Western shopping centre, and the men of Alexandria, released from the day's work, flooded into the cafés. I stopped briefly to watch a furious argument between two taxi drivers who had managed to bump into each other. The walls of the long-closed billiards hall behind them were plastered with advertisements and its doors were hidden behind corrugated iron.

Cavafy used to come here to make the acquaintance of other men. 'Traveller,' says one of his characters, worn out by an excess of high living, 'if you're an Alexandrian, you won't blame me. You know the pace of our life – its fever, its absolute devotion to pleasure.'

But today there is little *joie de vivre* after dark, even in the red-light district. By midnight the narrow alleys are as quiet as monastic cloisters and prospective revellers as chaste as monks.

'Hello, everything all right? How are you?' asked the old man on the door when I left the Leroy early next morning.

'Fine,' I told him. We shook hands.

'Can I have some money?' he asked. I was taken aback, not by the request, but by the fact that he spoke any English apart from 'Hello, everything all right,' etc. I offered him 50 piastres.

'No! No!' he remonstrated. 'English money.'

I asked him why he wanted English money.

'Just for the memories,' he replied. 'Just for the memories.'

I emptied out the contents of my bag and searched the seams for stray coins. I found a 10p piece and some Greek drachmas. He refused the drachmas and took the English coin, grinning delightedly as he dropped it into the pocket of his greatcoat.

CHAPTER TWO

CAIRO: SIGNING ON

At one o'clock in the morning a large limousine pulled up outside the Balmoral Hotel and disgorged its contents on to the pavement: Richard North, two suitcases and a stick for repelling rabid dogs. From the crumbling balcony of room 112 I watched North haggle with the driver. Bats swooped erratically around the street lamps, picking off the mosquitoes which had taken flight from the river a stone's throw away. I went downstairs and helped North up to our room with his baggage. He opened his suitcases and spread their contents out for inspection. He had a small word-processor, a cassette-recorder with three Bob Marley tapes ('for the desert', he explained), a camera, a few clothes, a copy of Gibbon's *Decline and Fall*, and a bottle of duty-free gin. He mixed a Balmoral Cocktail (one part gin to two parts squeezed orange, preferably in a pint toothmug), lay back on a bed which suffered from subsidence (caused by a deathwatch beetle the previous night while I slept in it), lit a cigarette and took a long swig.

'Why no ice?' he asked. 'Now tell me: how have you been and what have you been doing?' He passed the cocktail across to me and I ran briefly through the events of the past ten days, beginning at Piraeus and ending where we now were.

'So you've not done much,' he observed drily. He had asked me, before I left England, to contact four people in Cairo. I told him I hadn't been able to get hold of them on the telephone, which was quite true as I hadn't tried. He grunted.

Richard had come to Egypt to research 'Fools for God', a book about Christian monks. He was going to spend ten days in the country and I said I would tag along with him on his visits to the monasteries. His time was precious whereas mine wasn't, so I agreed that we should leave Cairo as soon as we had signed on with the State Information Bureau. Later we would return to the city and see it at our leisure.

We developed a keen and amused affection for the Balmoral, which had been recommended to us by the Archbishop of Canterbury's special envoy to the Coptic Church. On paper (or, at least, in the Cairo Tourist Guide) it sounded rather a grand establishment. It boasted two stars, three telephone lines, an international telex, and a private bath with each of its dozen rooms. Richard had written from England a month earlier to make a reservation. On my arrival at Cairo station I had telephoned the hotel to check that a room was available. Two of the three lines were out of order and the third connected me to the Chinese restaurant next door. A waitress told me to ring back in ten minutes. I did. The hotel had never heard of us; but, yes, there were rooms. I climbed into a taxi and we edged through the dense traffic towards the Nile. A yellow sun peered blearily through the filter of dust and exhaust fumes which hung over the flyover leading west. It was midday when we crossed the Nile on to the island of Zamalek and pulled up outside the Balmoral. The driver demanded five pounds, so I gave him one – someone had told me before I left the station that the trip would cost a local 50 piastres, 'so pay double as you're a foreigner'. The foyer was dark, shabby and dusty. A wide-eyed, large-mouthed girl in a smart black and red dress led me into an office behind the reception desk. A large green parrot swayed back and forth on a perch in a bell-shaped cage and the manager, a diminutive Korean, sat in a wicker chair smoking a cigarette with a gold band round the filter. The girl was called Hebba Maurice. Her English was perfect and she was to become as indispensable to us as the *Blue Guide*. She introduced me to the Korean. He nodded, smiled, stubbed out his cigarette and left. The parrot screeched. Once I'd filled out the hotel forms I asked if there had been any telex messages from North. Hebba giggled: 'No.'

'But you do have a telex, don't you?' I asked.

'Yes,' she replied. 'But it's been a long time since we had a message.'

I asked how long.

'About three years.'

Why so long? I asked.

'Oh,' she replied breezily, 'we just don't have those sorts of customers.' We never did find out quite what sort of customers came to this musty pension. Before I left for Upper Egypt I spent over two weeks in the Balmoral, yet the only other guests were a couple of gentlemen who looked like Muslim imams. They stayed just one night. Maybe they were only in Cairo for a day; or perhaps they weren't keen to stay in a place where all the staff were Christian. (One of Hebba's uncles was a monk in the monastery where Pope Shenouda was confined.)

Hebba showed me into a large room with three single beds. The balcony looked on to a half-constructed flyover where a score of workers in ragged shorts and oil-smeared turbans were deploying pneumatic drills, concrete-mixers and picks. The noise was deafening. The W C didn't work and Hebba said she'd get a plumber in the next day. Until then I could use the communal W C in the corridor outside – in the mornings the waitresses from the Chinese restaurant would squat there sorting rice from the chaff – but that didn't work either. Later in the afternoon I had to ask for an electrician. A fantastic confusion of bare wires ran round the ancient skirting to the bedside lights, but none worked. By the time Richard arrived the Balmoral was back in working order. 'This is definitely my sort of place,' he announced enthusiastically as he lathered himself with insect repellant. Before we turned the lights out a mouse climbed into the waste-paper basket and set to work on the orange peel.

Next morning we ate the Balmoral's obligatory breakfast, stale bread and weak tea, dropped in at a small stall down the road and drank a glass of fresh squeezed oranges, then crossed to the Rob-aeiyat el Khayam, a slightly upmarket Arab café. It was a little after seven o'clock and still quiet, though the early-morning traffic of taxis, lorries and donkeys was already kicking up dust which drifted through the open front of the café. The day was fine and a breeze came in from the street and fluttered the red and white tablecloths, sending ripples through the design of palms and pyramids. A giant picture of a beech wood ran the length of one wall. It might have been somewhere in the Chilterns; a very long way from Egypt, wherever it was. A waiter set before us a slim brass-topped table and returned with an aluminium tray with two Turkish coffees and a glass of Nile water which tasted like dilute hydrochloric acid. The area behind the counter was tiled and along the shelves were ranged a dozen large *shishas*, the water pipes which cost about ten piastres a smoke. Two men opposite us were already puffing away with expressions of extreme happiness.

North, a wiry man of neat build and striking good looks, was looking quite extraordinary. Beneath a thick mat of metallic grey hair lay a strong nose, either side of which was a brown eye set in a bed of wrinkles. He was wearing an enormous pink bow tie in honour of a visit to the British Embassy. It was wrongly tied and it had assumed the motile properties of an aeroplane propellor. He quickly drank his coffee, arranged to meet me later and left. An old man took his place beside me.

'What do you do?' he asked.

I told him.

'You are very small for a writer,' he replied. 'And you have no beard.'

I conceded that I didn't have a beard but pointed out that I was six inches taller than he was.

'I am a sculptor,' he announced. 'And my name is Fayis el-Daif.'

He was a small, rotund gentleman. He wore a grey double-breasted suit which had seen better days, a white shirt frayed at the collar and the cuffs, though spotlessly clean, and a maroon tie. His face was round and it had the hue and texture of a ripening walnut. His chin and cheeks were covered by a grey stubble. He spoke poor English and dreadful French.

'Yes,' he continued, 'I do the *sculptures modernes*. When King Farouk is alive I do six statues for the Abdin Palace. You see them still in the gardens.'

He ordered coffee, then presented his hands for me to inspect. The fingers were slightly swollen, bunched together and splayed outwards, giving his hands the appearance of seal flippers. He had arthritis. 'If I hold a hammer now,' he explained, looking wistfully at his crippled hands, 'I tremble too much to work. I sculpt no longer.'

We talked of Rodin, whom he loved, and Rodin reminded him of the statue he had made for his art school certificate. 'All the students drew lots from a bowl and I got "Eve et Adam".' He raised a bent finger to presage a point of importance. 'I do it with no apples,' he said gravely. 'My "Eve et Adam" is strictly *moderne*.'

He fell silent and I ordered another cup of coffee. Fayis gazed absent-mindedly on to the street. 'What about the serpent?' I asked.

'No apples,' he replied. 'And no serpent.' He proceeded to explain the form of his statue. 'Adam, he sit like this.' The sculptor leaned back in his seat, but held his head bent forward. 'And Eve, she have her head here.' He slapped his knees. 'She take the hand of Adam and she puts it on her breast. Then she begs Adam to think of her and for their future.'

'How?' I asked, when he fell silent again.

'When Adam looks where his hand is he sees Eve's breast. This makes him want to drink her milk.' Thus the Fall, which seemed reasonable.

I asked him if he was a Christian. He said he was.

'A Copt?'

'No,' he replied, 'a Protestant like you.' He said he'd like me to meet the vicar. I never did.

I met up again with Richard at the Balmoral at mid-morning, and we set off on foot for the State Information Bureau. The Nile was eel-grey and greasy, the only colours on the water rainbow blooms where barges had leaked their oil. In the picture postcards of Cairo the river is a furious blue, a reflection not so much of the sky but of the touch-up artist's predilection for bright and unnatural colours. The east bank across from Zamalek carried a six-lane highway lined by an uncomfortable and ragged skyline of modern buildings: the Hilton, the Ramses Hilton, an old terrace of office blocks and some new skyscrapers, still clothed with wooden scaffolding, which towered over the TV building.

The very title, 'State Information Bureau', inspired suspicion. So did the TV building in which the Bureau was housed, a cylindrical, five-storeyed piece of concrete dumped beside the Nile and guarded by tin-hatted soldiers, heavily armed and protected from the outside

world by piles of sand-bags. My confidence in the quality of information which emanated from here had not been bolstered by the publications I had so far seen. The Bureau's *Egyptian Profile* claimed, for example, that Hosni Mubarek had succeeded Sadat in 1981 after 'popular election' (there were no elections); and that 'female emancipation is no longer an issue' (which isn't even true for the educated middle classes, let alone the vast numbers of women who are subjected to female circumcision). The Bureau is the state's means of furnishing foreign journalists with propaganda. The scene, when we walked past the sentries, through the bag check and on to the scuffed linoleum floor of the foyer, looked (as did so many things, if you thought in clichés, in the supposedly inauspicious

year of 1984) depressingly Orwellian. A flight of steps curled up to
the first floor, and we walked down a short corridor, past the gentlemen's WC with its split toilet seats and broken cisterns, into the
Bureau.

Much to our surprise, the Bureau was almost exclusively the
domain of women. The office was open-plan and about fifteen
women were ranged round the formica-topped desks. The sparse
décor reminded me of an English dole office. Alternatively, it might
have been a police-station typing pool in Raymond Chandler's Los
Angeles. Most of the girls were young and all were well-dressed in
smart Western clothes. We filled out some forms (seldom does a day
pass in Egypt when one doesn't) and waited on a leather sofa while
our press cards were drawn up. Once we'd got them, Richard left to
hire a car. I waited to see Mrs Fatma, who was engaged in a
fearsome struggle with a fountain-pen and a large raft of forms.
Periodically she battled with a telephone which was evidently out
of order. (Once I tried to telephone the Balmoral from here. Fatma
looked over the Nile to Zamalek. 'It's very difficult making calls in
that direction,' she said. Apparently the wires to the east worked
better.) I was intending to try my hand at a bit of journalism as
a way of raising some money once I got back to England, and I
was hoping that Fatma could arrange some visits for me. I had
decided, whimsically, to write one piece on the perfume industry,
another on Egyptian agriculture, and something on the Nile
fisheries.

While I waited, three middle-aged Poles spent ten minutes
haggling with one of the girls. They were sleazy-looking
characters, parodies of the middle-aged hack, pot bellies protruding
from leather jackets and cigarettes dangling from dry lips. They
were insolent and aggressive. I was joined on the sofa by a short,
handsome man with grey hair and the palest blue eyes, a Russian
who worked for a Moscow TV station. He was enormously
amused by the Poles' frustration, and he turned to me when they
left. He asked how long I had been waiting. About an hour, I
told him.

'Do you know this word *bokkra*?' he asked. I said I didn't.
'Then you haven't been here long. It's an incredible word, the
most important word in the Arabic language. Especially here in

Egypt.' His eyes glazed over as he reflected on the remarkable nature of *bokkra*. 'According to the dictionary it means tomorrow. But that's not strictly true. What it really means is "perhaps tomorrow". But the perhaps is a qualified perhaps: it is a "per-haps, but probably not" sort of perhaps. In Egypt it's always *bokkra*. I've been here six months now and I haven't been able to start work yet.'

I wondered aloud whether that had anything to do with his nationality. Sadat had kicked the Russians out of the country in the mid-seventies.

'No,' he replied. 'It's nothing to do with that. Nor am I planning to film anything which might be construed as sensitive. I'm here to make documentaries about Egyptian life. That could mean films about farming and irrigation, or about the antiquities or the Suez Canal. Nothing remotely sensitive. But here,' he said disgustedly, 'you have to ask permission for everything. You must have guides, you must do this, you must do that, etcetera, etcetera.'

He lit a cigarette and said something to his cameraman, a gaunt and restless man who had just joined us. Mrs Fatma sig-nalled that she would be with me soon, possibly sometime before *bokkra*.

'In Beirut,' said the Russian, who had spent three years there covering the civil war, 'we never had to ask permission for anything. You just went where you wanted to go, filmed what you wanted to film. If you were killed, then bad luck, you were killed.'

I suggested that he was better off in Cairo. He lived, like so many expatriates, in the relative calm of Zamalek, where there was a Russian school for his children.

He shrugged. 'I never got used to war. You never do. It's always frightening. But in many ways I preferred living – or sur-viving – in Beirut to Cairo. You've seen this city, haven't you? The pollution is so bad in central Cairo that you breathe in the equivalent of thirty cigarettes a day on top of what you already smoke. The overcrowding is chronic. There's terrible poverty everywhere. Do you know how much green space there is in Cairo for each inhabitant?'

I shook my head.

'Thirteen square centimetres – not enough to fill a child's hand!'

A girl came to fetch him. We shook hands. 'Remember *bokkra*,' he suggested.

I watched and waited. The theatre of the absurd was alive and well here. The laddered stocking, the miscreant and gushing fountain-pen, the spilt coffee, the telephone which connected up with no one: these were the props of the office drama. The most senior of the women, a heavy-set, handsome and austere female, sat to the left of the stage. Her desk was neat, she dispensed orders with severity and authority (to both journalists and press officers), and she had no time for idle chatter. Next to her sat one of the office's few males, a handsome youth with much charm and plenty of time on his hands. His main duty, as far as I could see, was to take pieces of paper from one desk to another, from one signatory to the next. Then, moving right, as seen from the sofa, came Fatma. She was beautiful and beautifully dressed. She had a habit of standing on one leg, with the other (in high heel) bent backwards to delicately jostle the edge of her chair seat. Then came a lascivious and seductive woman in a grey dress. She it was who suffered a laddered stocking shortly after the Poles' departure. And it wasn't long before I became familiar with the other ten press officers and the army of tea boys.

Eventually Fatma came and sat with me on the couch. I explained who I wanted to see and the places I wished to visit.

'Who do you want in the Irrigation Ministry?' she asked. 'The minister?'

No, I said, just someone who could explain how the water went round and round. A technician, I suggested. As far as the perfume industry was concerned, she said she knew just the place: the jasmine fields of the Faiyum. We could call in there on our way back from the desert monasteries. And she would arrange a visit to a perfume factory once she'd found one. I thanked her and said I'd phone her when we reached the Faiyum in a few days' time.

I was given another form to fill out, and a slight, bespectacled Englishman took her place. He worked for Reuter's and he'd recently been transferred from Beirut to Cairo. Like the Russian, he had preferred Beirut. 'It's so quiet here,' he claimed. 'The people in our office are going crazy for the lack of news.'

I asked what they wanted.

'Oh, a few assassinations,' he replied.

It was mid-afternoon when I left. I had rather enjoyed my first visit to the Truth Machine, though I pitied the journalists who flew in for a few days to cover a story for which they had a deadline. Sometime after dusk Richard and I charged up our spirits with a Balmoral cocktail and went out in search of a decent meal. We had no idea what we would get to eat in the monasteries – not much, suggested Hebba, who claimed that all monks suffered stomach disorders caused by their poor diet – and we decided to indulge ourselves with some fine Egyptian food; preferably a bowl of *hammam*, traditionally cooked pigeon. We ended up in one of Egypt's two Wimpys. It differed from the Wimpys in Europe in two ways. The food was considerably better and the waiters were supremely intelligent. Most of them were studying law, or medicine, or civil engineering. They were intriguing conversationalists but terrible waiters.

'*Vous parlez français?*' asked a tall waiter with horn-rimmed spectacles.

'*Oui,*' replied Richard, who was speaking, I presumed, on my behalf rather than his.

'*Et vous aussi?*' I inquired before we ordered.

'*Non,*' said the waiter with a grin.

So we ordered in English; Richard a dish which cost 120 piastres; and I something more substantial, a mixed grill, at 230 piastres. (There are 100 piastres to one Egyptian pound, whose value was rather less at the time than that of its sterling namesake.) A long while later the food arrived. My dish only differed from Richard's by the presence of one small and very pallid egg. ('All eggs in Egypt taste musty,' wrote Lord Cecil, who served in government here early this century, 'as if they had been laid by a mummy.') We called the waiter and explained that this egg could not, logically, account for the 110-piastre difference between the plates.

'Sorry,' he said. 'You're quite right.' He promptly imposed his own solution on the problem by switching plates. He disappeared and we called him back again. We pointed out that under this dispensation I was getting even less than North for my extra money.

He thought about it for a while, roared with laughter and left us. I expect he will make a very good lawyer. The mixed grill, by the way, had neither sausages or bacon. It was, I suppose, the *cuisine moderne*.

CHAPTER THREE
THE HEROES OF THE FAITH

If thou wilt be perfect,
go and sell all that thou hast and give
to the poor, and come and follow me.

A twenty-year-old orphan heard these words in the Sunday gospel, sometime around AD 270, in a small village by the Nile. Anthony gave away his money and entrusted his young sister to a community of virgins. Having dispensed with his worldly possessions, he left his house and went to dwell in a shed at the foot of his garden, where he lived alone for some years, making baskets, ropes and mats, just as many monks do today. His next move was to some nearby tombs, where he was constantly harassed by demons. Christ apparently answered his prayers by dispelling them. He was about thirty-five years old when he left the tombs, crossed the Nile and occupied an old fort on the edge of the desert. Here he lived alone for twenty years until his friends broke down the door and pleaded with him to entertain, once more, the company of his fellow men. But Anthony turned his back on them and the river and headed into the eastern desert, that great chunk of rock and sand wedged between the Nile and Red Sea. According to Derwas Chitty, whose *The Desert a City* traces the earliest beginnings of Christian monasticism, a monk out of the desert was like a fish out of water to Anthony. 'The desert is represented as the natural domain of the demons, to which they have retreated on being driven out of the cities by the triumph of the Church, and into which the heroes of the faith will pursue them.'

We pursued St Anthony, the Star of the Desert, Father of the

Monks, in an old and battered Fiat. It was six o'clock in the morning when we left the Balmoral. The road climbed slowly out of Cairo, into the rising sun, orange and blurred by dust, past the airport, past miles of grim army barracks where queues of soldiers, cigarettes dangling from mouths, waited outside small latrines, then on to the desert. We travelled for an hour through a scruffy, stony landscape devoid of any plant life. Dumps of rusty oil barrels and wrecked cars gave it the appearance of industrial wasteland. At nine o'clock we passed the factories and chemical refineries on the outskirts of Suez and searched for the town centre. It took us a quarter of an hour to find it: we had expected something more substantial than the small, bleak grid of shops and dreary blocks of flats which we found.

We drank some mint tea in a small café. The occasional car rumbled over the uneven and pocked street, and a horse and cart struggled by pulling a small tanker of oil – Mobil here was not forsaking low technology. Oil leaked from the brass tap at the back.

'The trouble with these piss-poor Arab towns,' reflected Richard, motioning to the dilapidated market across the road, 'is you can't tell if they've been bombed or not.' Suez had been. Three quarters of the town was destroyed in the 1967 war with Israel, and more damage was done in the 1973 war.

After a second cup of tea we bought a few provisions, including some tins of corned beef, which were inappropriately labelled 'Lucky Cow', then headed south along the Gulf of Suez. The road followed the sea, sometimes almost running into it. There were no beaches: the desert just came down from the barren hills to the west and ran straight into the water. We passed minefields protected by flimsy coils of barbed wire and notices telling 'foreigners' to keep out. Egyptians with any sense presumably did the same.

The road had never recovered from the last war, when long stretches were crushed into a fine tilth by tanks. Sometimes we had to slow down to walking pace; frequently we had to leave the track to circumvent a boulder or a gaping hole. Then out of the blue we would hit a stretch of gleaming new tarmac. But these never lasted for more than a few miles. Around eleven o'clock we rounded a corner to find a collective taxi – an eight-seater Peugeot – waiting in front of a pile of rubble. It was only the second car we had seen since leaving Suez. On the hillside above, a bulldozer was hewing a pipeline track out of the rock, and what it displaced was strewn across the road. Four more Peugeots pulled up, each with seven passengers. They were all heading for Hurghada, a small town far down the Red Sea. At one o'clock the road was cleared, and three hours later we arrived in Zafarana. Five battered old oil drums blocked the road into town, and a soldier in a leather Biggles helmet appeared from a small hut, from whose crest fluttered the national flag. He had a craggy, weather-beaten face and a large droopy moustache. After a quick glance at our papers he removed a couple of barrels and waved us through.

Zafarana would have made an ideal set for an Eastern spaghetti western. It consisted of a small white lighthouse, a watchtower, a single hand-cranked petrol pump and a scattering of small habitations like mud potting-sheds. Near the petrol pump there was a hut with a faded sign claiming it to be the Red Sea Resthouse of Zafarana. It was closed and it looked as though it had been for a long time. A little way to the south was the Paradise of the Desert. We went in. Three Arabs sat in silence drinking tea in one corner. They nodded at us and we smiled back. They too had large droopy moustaches. So did the café owner. It appeared to be a cult here. Half a dozen paintings clung at awkward angles to the lime-green walls. They were all Constables or neo-Constables. 'The Hay Wain', a great favourite in Egypt, was not among them. (There was a shop near the Greek Orthodox church in Alexandria which had more Constables on display than the V and A.) A hot wind blew in from the desert while we drank our tea.

Zafarana was also remarkable for its dogs, which far outnumbered the small indigenous population of humans. They were of medium build, mixed colour and indeterminate breed, and, like all Egyptian dogs, they were sleazy, amiable and indolent. Occasionally one would rise briskly from the ground, trot a few paces, then, remembering that here, in Zafarana, there was nowhere to go and absolutely nothing to do, collapse again. North, who had quickly come to terms with the Egyptian dog, hadn't even bothered to bring his anti-rabid-dog stick with him.

We filled up with petrol, wove round dogs and oil barrels, and headed west away from the sea. Twenty miles later we turned left on to a desert track. Ten miles away we could just make out the walls of St Anthony's monastery at the base of a spectacular ridge of cliffs. They were a livid orange in the crepuscular light. We passed a couple of gazelles nibbling at one of the few clumps of succulent in the desert and shuddered up to the massive walls.

We walked through the wooden gates and a monk with an enormous red beard and a large pot belly ushered us into the refectory. A bus-load of pilgrims had arrived from Cairo the day before and they were finishing their evening meal. We asked Father Zecharius if we could stay the night. He disappeared with Richard's letters of introduction, one from the Bishop of Cairo and another from Father Anthonius, a Coptic priest in London. One of the pilgrims, a delightful woman who spoke fluent French, gave us some bread and jam. We sat down beside a monk whose long black hair spilt out from beneath an embroidered cowl. I'm not sure whether he was simple or wild or mad. His piercing eyes were locked on to a light bulb which kept flashing on and off, and he reminded me of an El Greco disciple – simple, passionate and wondering; though here it was the vagaries of the monastic generator rather than the appearance of the Messiah which transfixed him.

It was dark outside when Father Cyrillos, another monk, retrieved us. Certainly, we could stay the night. He said he would take us on a tour of the monastery in a few minutes. We waited outside the refectory, lit cigarettes and were promptly asked by a passing monk to put them out. Tall date palms towered above vegetable plots and fruit trees, and an old vine snaked its way round the walls of the garden. I was looking at a huddle of small churches beyond when I caught sight of two elderly white men walking down a lane towards us. I gave Richard a sharp dig in the ribs and he muttered some profanity.

I had always imagined the afterlife to be like this: full of forgotten people turning up in the strangest of places. 'I've come two thousand miles to get away from people like you!' bellowed Richard as Max Nicholson approached. Richard knew Nicholson well and I had met him a few times. Both of us had written about him in the past as he was one of the grand old men of British conservation, a subject which we'd both dabbled in. Max introduced us to his companion, Peter Hollom, the author of some standard texts on European bird life; he immediately disappeared with a pair of binoculars and a tape-recorder in search of the monastery's ravens, which we could hear croaking in the night. Before we could interrogate Max about his reasons for being here – I recalled that he had said some harsh things about Christianity in his writings, so unless he had renounced his beliefs, it seemed improbable that he could be here as a pilgrim – Father Cyrillos whisked us off on a tour of the monastery. Max, hobbling with a stick, accompanied us.

I was too intrigued by Nicholson's presence to attend fully to what Father Cyrillos had to tell us as he led us into the tiny Church of the Four Creatures. It was the shape of a beehive, domed and windowless. The monk's torch played across the frescoes. They were faded with age but we could still make out in the swinging beam of light the vermillions, golds, blues and reds of the clothes of the saints. The creatures were of more sombre colours. We were quickly led through another church, slightly larger than the first, though candle-lit, where St Anthony is supposed to have been buried; then into another, larger still. The Father led us to the altar, on which lay a glass coffin. It was hidden under a piece of rough cloth. 'On 24 January 1824,' he explained, 'the monks came across the body which lies now in this coffin. They were burying another monk. St Joseph, though long dead, was in perfect condition. So his body was removed and each year we hold a ceremony in his honour. His body is perfect. His skin, his fingers, his eyes – they are all still in perfect condition. It is a miracle.'

Father Cyrillos led us past another church – we could hear the droning and chanting of monks inside – and escorted us past an olive grove to the monastery wall below the cliffs. Mineral water flowed from a crack in the groundrock into a system of small canals. 'This water has been flowing without cease,' explained the monk, 'ever since St Anthony came here and founded the monastery in the third century.' He implied that it was a miracle.

The tour was over and we were shown into a dormitory. There were a dozen or so beds beneath the vaulted ceiling. With the aid of a torch we unfurled our sleeping bags, carefully choosing our beds to avoid the infestations of red mites which thrived in some. I studied Max in the gloom. He was wearing well for his eighty years. His face was dominated by a predatory nose, twinkling eyes and a square jaw, in which was set a mouth that assumed the severe shape of a rectangle whenever he talked, which was often. He had a precise, aristocratic voice and his Ss were generally attached to an H, a disconcerting foible which meant that there was a background sound similar to a bicycle tyre passing over drenched tarmac while he talked.

'So what are you up to, Max?' asked Richard.

'We've been birdwatching,' he replied prosaically.

He and Hollom had been on an expedition over the border in Sudan, investigating the possibility of establishing a national park in the Red Sea hills. A chauffeur-driven Mercedes – the chauffeur, a Muslim, had to sleep outside the walls in the car – had taken them the eight hundred miles to Sudan. They had camped in tents for two weeks and they looked none the worse for wear. Max implied that their visit had had the blessing of President Nimeiri. They had dropped into the monastery in search of a bed and birds rather than religious inspiration.

Richard asked Max what he'd found in the Red Sea hills.

'A most interesting mix of Palaearctic and Ethiopian fauna and flora,' replied Max. He reeled off the names of the birds they'd seen. This was followed by some old gentleman's talk about whether or not they should wear pyjamas. Richard offered them a swig of brandy ('Fairly elegant spicy prune-like flovers moderate oak tan – nic-well balaced & very please,' said the label) but they declined and made ready for bed. Richard and I walked down the alley and out of the monastery. It was bitterly cold. Three soldiers were huddled round a radio listening to a football match. We sheltered behind the pilgrims' bus, drank sickly brandy straight from the bottle and had a smoke.

We were up early the next morning. Richard at four o'clock, for a service; Nicholson and Hollom at six, to investigate monastic bird life; and me at eight, for breakfast. I ate a lump of monastic bread – no wonder the monks had stomach disorders: it was like biting into a loofa – and went to sit on a wall overlooking one of the gardens. A donkey came past with a sack of cement, and some of the pilgrims were preparing to leave. Max appeared.

'We've been beating the olive groves,' he announced. 'It's really most upsetting for serious birdwatchers like us. All the birds are out of habitat and in the wrong place. You see the desert lark down there?' He pointed to a nondescript brown bird on the ground. 'You should never see these birds except at the foot of scarps and cliffs. Yet here they're in the olive trees!' He sounded disgusted, but he was kind enough to identify for me some of the other species in the monastery. There were Spanish sparrows and hoopoes in the garden. And blue rockthrushes and pied wagtails had dropped down from the sky to take a rest, like Nicholson, on their journeys northward towards the European spring. 'You see,' continued Max when Richard arrived, 'the desert lark likes to be next to a vertical surface. The lark would agree with O. Henry, who used to say, "I don't like scenery at 45° to the welkin." '

Richard, who had heard of neither O. Henry nor desert larks, looked bemused. As we accompanied Max out to his car he stopped to eye one of the pilgrims' bags. It had the word ASCOT written on the side. Max tapped it with his stick and addressed its owner. 'Have you been to the races?' he demanded. The pilgrim looked blank. 'You know,' continued Max tetchily, 'the place where the horses go round and round and round.' The pilgrim didn't know. Max chuckled, bade us a peremptory goodbye, and climbed into the Mercedes.

It was mid-morning when we began the ascent to St Anthony's cave. At first the incline was gentle but it gradually became steeper and more perilous. After twenty minutes we reached a rock face which was so sheer I was tempted to turn back. Wooden slats, weather-worn and rickety, had been fixed to the rock to make a flight of steps; and a fragile handrail beside them to give the illusion of safety.

Finally, dizzy and out of breath, we scaled the last vertiginous scree to come out a thousand feet above the monastery at a fissure which led to the saint's cave. Three rough wooden crosses were tacked on to boulders near the entrance. We sat on a shelf of rock outside and gazed north. It was a stunning view. The mountain dropped down to the walls of the monastery below, and beyond stretched the desert – brown, flat and featureless – to a ridge of hills some thirty miles away. Mount Sinai – where Moses met God at the Burning Bush – was just visible across the Red Sea; or so I fancied –

the faintest of thumb prints on the blurred horizon. The shadow of a vulture raced across the rocks below us.

I struck a match and we made our way into the fissure. There was only just enough width to pass through and we had to stoop to avoid hitting our heads on the roof. Twenty feet in we came to a tiny cave, so utterly dark that the light of the match penetrated only a few inches. We could just make out a rush mat on the floor. A small alcove in the wall contained a book; perhaps a prayer book, maybe a Bible.

For long periods St Anthony pursued his solitary life of devotion in this small cave, and he must have sat, as we did once we came out, to gaze at the same harsh scene. One of the pilgrims had told me that her visit to the cave was the most wonderful experience of her life. And she had jabbered about it in the most pious way for a good ten minutes. However, it was the topography rather than the cave's history which impressed me most. I found it difficult to focus seriously on the man whom I knew best from Flaubert's remarkable work, *The Temptation of St Antony*. Here, for example, is Flaubert's saint, suffering from the pangs of hunger. Outside his cave he searches for bread but all he finds is a crust. The jackals have made off with the rest.

In sheer fury, he flings the bread to the ground.

No sooner has he done so than a table stands there, spread with everything good to eat.

The byssus tablecloth, striated like a sphinx's fillet, produces its own undulating luminosity. On it are placed enormous hunks of red meat, huge fish, birds in their feathers, quadrupeds in their furs, and fruit of almost human coloration; while pieces of white ice and violet crystal flagons mirror each other's brilliance. Antony notices in the middle of the table a boar steaming from every pore, its legs under its belly, its eyes half shut – and the thought of eating this formidable beast gives him acute pleasure. Then come things he has never seen, minces quite black, jellies golden in colour, stews in which mushrooms float like water-lilies on a pond, and mousses like clouds in their airiness.

The aroma of it all brings him the salty smell of the ocean, the freshness of fountains, the strong scent of woods. He dilates his nostrils as much as possible. He drools. He tells himself that this will last him for a year, ten years, a lifetime!

As he lets his astonished eyes wander over the dishes, others accumulate, forming a pyramid whose corners crumble. The wines start to flow and the fishes to palpitate, blood bubbles in the platters, fleshy fruits come forward like amorphous lips; and the table rises to his chest, to his chin – bearing one single plate and one single loaf, exactly opposite him.

Anthony – tempted, naturally – reaches for the loaf of bread, then draws back. More loaves appear: it must be a miracle, he thinks. But realizing, disgustedly, that it is the work of the devil, he kicks at the table and the banquet vanishes into thin air.

Flaubert's Anthony is a most endearing character ('cantankerous, bitter, envious, greedy, sadomasochistic', as Kitty Mrosovsky remarks in her introduction to the book). And it was this Anthony, rather than the mild, patient and humble saint of Athanasius' biography, that had stuck in my mind. Athanasius was the bishop of Alexandria and a contemporary of Anthony. He described the saint's endless tussles with the demons of the desert and the lonely and comfortless life of an anchorite. Anthony is considered to be the first of the long line of monks who lived as hermits. There may well have been others before him, but he was the most famous, the most adored of his time. By the time he was born the Christian church in Egypt had already suffered its first bout of persecution, which took place at the end of the second century under the rule of Septimus Severus, but an even greater wave of persecution occurred during his lifetime. The Egyptian Church claims that the persecutions under the Emperor Diocletian led to the martyrdom of 144,000 Christians, and the Coptic calendar is dated not from the time of Christ's birth but from the Era of Martyrs (AD 284).

Despite the cruel treatment meted out to the Christians by some Roman emperors, the church continued to grow. By AD 320 there were over a hundred bishops in north-east Africa and in the fourth and fifth centuries Alexandria fell under the rule of the Coptic patriarch and his monks. The monks, according to E. M. Forster, who traced the history of the church in his guide to Alexandria, had some knowledge of theology (one of their heroes being St Anthony), 'but they were averse to culture and incapable of thought'. The monks had had no compunction about persecuting the pagans. An eye for an eye was the rule. Christianity gradually spread further south, into Nubia, the great expanse of desert between Aswan and modern Khartoum, and east into Ethiopia. (Historical evidence suggests that the Ethiopian church was founded on the Red Sea coast in the latter half of the fourth century; more romantically, the Ethiopians consider their church, like their royal family, to have begun with the Queen of Sheba's liaison with King Solomon, and they believe that the Ark of the Covenant was taken to their country by the Queen herself.)

I had come to St Anthony's monastery with the vaguest knowledge of monastic life and with my own stock of cliché-ed prejudices. I had seen the monks' retreat – into the desert, into the monastery, away from women – as an act of escapism. For some it may be just that: obsessions, with religion, politics, scholarship, whatever, often are. But it can also be the opposite: a running towards, not away from. Was Anthony retreating from some trauma of childhood? Or was he pursuing the demons, vanquished in the cities, to harass them further in the desert? Perhaps. I wonder, incidentally, what became of his sister? It would be nice to know whether she went willingly into the community of virgins. And whether she stayed once there.

Travellers' tales from not long ago paint a none too complimentary picture of the desert monks. They were likened to wild animals and savages, and the milk of human kindness was curdled if not absent for those who dropped in for succour at many monasteries. One gets the impression that the monks of the last century were generally ignorant, ill-versed in theology, bigoted in outlook and aggressive to outsiders. In contrast, the monks today are mostly well-educated, very refined and fully cognisant of the goings on in the outside world. Father Cyrillos, for example, who chatted with us on our return from the cave, had qualified from university with a degree in chemical engineering and for sixteen years he had worked for a fertilizer company. And many other monks had taken to the monastic life after spending some time in one of the professions. Father Cyrillos was happy to explain to us the workings of the monastery: where the food came from (the monks had a farm at Beni Suef on the Nile); and how each of the thirty-odd monks was allotted a particular task (Cyrillos was re-

sponsible for PR, others for looking after the bakery, the poultry and so forth). But the question we most wanted to ask, 'Why have you become a monk?' prompted the answer, 'To devote myself to God,' which told us nothing we didn't know already.

That afternoon we drove round to St Paul's monastery, which lay over the mountains to the south. From the outside it was much more beautiful than St Anthony's. The stone walls surrounding it were irregular, and their outline was broken by turrets coated with mud. A few small paneless windows looked out on to the barren and undulating landscape. We didn't get inside. 'Closed for Lent – no visitors please' said a sign tacked on the wooden gateway. We climbed on to a ridge and glimpsed cowled monks going about their business. A rubbish tip beside the main gate was largely made up of empty Lucky Cow corned-beef tins.

On our way back to Zafarana the rear end of the exhaust-pipe broke from its mountings. We clattered up to the petrol pump and asked the boy who worked it if anyone could mend it for us. He shook his head. We drove the car on to a concrete ramp and I scoured the ground for bits of wire. The boy watched as Richard crawled beneath the chassis. He burrowed under to join him. Another man came and he wiggled under as well. We stuck the exhaust back on and offered the man and the boy a small sum of money. They refused it.

We had originally planned to spend three or four nights at the monastery. But once there our enthusiasm for such a long stay evaporated. We decided that we would leave after the second night. On our last evening we were invited to dine with a family of pilgrims in a small room off the main refectory. We ate an okra stew and the whole affair was very jolly. Richard produced the bottle of brandy and was greeted with some severe finger-wagging from an old lady, so he put it away and we stuck to water. He seemed to enjoy himself but I felt uneasy – the atmosphere was much too pure and prelapsarian for my liking – and I retired to bed as soon as the meal was over. The next morning we got up at four o'clock and stumbled wearily into the early-morning service. Eight monks stood in a row facing the altar, each with a song-book before him. The novices were in white, the others in brown. We watched from behind a wood and ivory screen with a dozen pilgrims, some of whom, from time to time, would fall to their knees and pray, pressing their heads to the ground just as praying Muslims do. In the gloom – the only light came from the candles in front of monks and two very poor oil lamps – we could see the dark outline of the monks' cowls and the fuzz of their beards (I think all of them were unshaven). The liturgy lasted for four hours, though I lasted less than two and returned to bed. It had a mesmeric quality, but I found it slightly unnerving, listening on an empty stomach to the ecclesiastical droning, occasionally interspersed by the discordant jangle of a metal triangle and the clash of cymbals. I recognized the 'Kyrie Eleison' but nothing else. I was particularly intrigued by the way the monks came and went. One would suddenly peel out of rank and disappear. At one point only four remained to continue the service. One didn't even bother leaving the church; he simply sat down in one corner and had a sleep. Before leaving Cairo, I had read a passage in *When the Going was Good* in which Waugh described his visit to an Ethiopian monastery in the 1930s. (Waugh travelled in enviable style: rather than turning up at a monastery with a few tins of Lucky Cow corned beef, he took with him a Fortrum and Mason's hamper. Tinned grouse, etc.) 'At Debra Lebanos,' he wrote, 'I suddenly saw the classic basilica and open altar as a great achievement, a positive triumph of light over darkness consciously accomplished ... I saw the Church of the first century as a dark and hidden thing; as dark and hidden as the seed germinating in the womb ...'

The mass at Debra Lebanos which Waugh described was infinitely more riddled with secrecy, obfuscation and hidden ceremony than the one we witnessed. Yet here too the whole ceremony, performed in half darkness, seemed as alien to me as the ceremonies of the pagan religions further up the Nile. An English church service today (and I imagine a monastic one too) has little in common with the rituals brought to our country by the early saints, yet one felt that this scene at St Anthony's could not have been much different than that which took place every morning, in the cool hours before dawn, a thousand or even fifteen hundred years earlier. The monastery has had its traumas. It was attacked by bedouin in the eighth and ninth centuries. It was razed in the twelfth and restored in the thirteenth. In the fifteenth century the servants revolted and massacred the monks. Despite all this, the primitive church was alive here. There hadn't been any great schisms or reformations, and none was to be expected.

CHAPTER FOUR
PEASANTS AND PIGEONS

It was exactly 8.12 a.m. when Richard joined a group of peasants outside the monastery walls. I know this because that is what it says in his notes – a curious *mélange*, largely illegible, of fine detail and general comment. The peasants – being Muslims they'd had to sleep outside the monastery – were huddled round a fire. Richard drank tea with them and agreed – by sign language, presumably – to take two of them down the track to the main road. He returned to wake me and pack. We said thanks and goodbye to the monks, and the four of us got into the Fiat and set off. When we reached the main road we stopped to let the peasants out. However, they indicated that they wished to travel west with us towards the Nile.

The desert, at first sight so alien and tedious, develops its own fascination. Its texture, its colour, its contours and its backdrop are continually changing. Around St Anthony's it was gravelly with sporadic clumps of thorny succulent and desiccated shrub. To the west the gravel thinned out and we drove through an undulating, sandy landscape, in places covered by a thin veneer of grey vegetation which awaited a few drops of rain to give it temporary life again. We passed the occasional cluster of shabby army tents, which were no more than telephone outposts, and one sizeable camp. An officer flagged us down outside its gates and asked for a lift. He squeezed in beside the two peasants.

They made an odd trio. The officer was clean-shaven, fresh-faced and unmistakably middle class. He wore a smart uniform; and, unlike the peasants, he spoke a little English. Of the peasants, Mahmood Salaama was the elder. He was a thin, wiry man with a fine oriental face, his skin stretched so tight that one could see all the contours of his skull. Abla Azim Mohammed was younger, perhaps thirty-five, larger and fatter in the face. He, too, was a handsome man. He had a large moustache and from under his *emma* – the swathe of white cloth which Arabs wrap around the head – sprouted curls of jet black hair. Whenever addressed (and when we gave him some Bob Marley to listen to on the cassette) he would reply with an enormous smile of flashing white teeth. Both peasants wore jellabas, waistcoats and ragged tweed jackets, although the temperature was well into the eighties.

Soon after we dropped the officer we caught sight of the Nile valley, a thin green line shimmering in the distance. The road wound down towards it and the desert ceased abruptly where the date palms began. We were back in cultivated land. There was no intermediate: on one side of the line, lifeless desert; on the other, the verdant richness of cropland.

We stopped at a small café where the peasants enlisted the help of half a dozen others to convince us that the ferry we intended to take across the river at El Wasta wasn't running today. It was Friday, the Muslim holiday. If we wanted to go to the Faiyum, whose perfume fields we were to visit, we would have to follow the east bank of the Nile north as far as El Tubbin, where we could cross by bridge. We set off again, dazzled still by the richness of the country. Not an inch of the irrigated land was left uncultivated. We passed groves of date palms, young crops of barley, strips of purple-flowering *berseem* – the staple diet of donkeys, camels and horses – and plots of vegetables. In every field there were peasants hoeing, scything, harvesting and planting.

At midday Mahmood motioned to Richard to drive off the road and we entered a village. We shuddered along its dirt roads, turning first left, then right, then left again between the mud dwellings and along a thin canal where women and children squatted in rows, laboriously washing the family clothes. We passed two men on donkeys with wide loads of newly cut sugarcane and another piled high with *berseem*. Finally, we came to a halt in a small yard and Abla Azim led us into his house. It was still in the process of completion, and like the rest of the village it was a single-storey affair. Nine hundredweight bags of calcium nitrate fertilizer were stacked in the middle of the main room, and in one corner there was an old TV on a wooden box. Bolsters and cushions lined one wall and we removed our shoes and sat crosslegged on the carpet. A young girl appeared – she was slim and very pretty – and took orders from Abla Azim. She disappeared through a door in the back of the room and we waited. Behind the house a hoopoe called incessantly, like a one-note oboe. *'Hoyt-hoyt,'* explained Mahmood.

With the help of a phrase book the peasants told us about their families. Abla Azim had a wife – busy now cooking our food – and five children; Mahmood, a wife and four children. He proudly produced a photograph of his eldest son, an engineering student. Richard replied with a wife and three children.

The young girl reappeared with two large dishes, one with goat's cheese, the other with mashed eggs in olive oil. She placed them on a low table and we scooped the food into our mouths with lumps of bread and our fingers; the cheese was so strong it burnt the roof of my mouth. We followed these with dates from Abla Azim's plot of land and mint tea. When we had finished eating the peasants asked us to write our names for them. We did so and Mahmood carefully folded away the piece of paper in his wallet. They then said they would write theirs. Mahmood wrote his very slowly, but Abla Azim gave up after much effort and many aborted squiggles. He summoned his young son, who competently performed the task for him.

Not so long ago many people in our own country lived in close proximity with animals which they intended to eat once fattened for the slaughter. Crofters in the Shetlands, for example, used to let their chickens and geese into their bedroom at night, and they slept in beds like large wardrobes. They could keep the animals out of their beds by closing the bed doors. And well into this century the miners of northern England kept pigs in their gardens. Such commensalism is rare now, not least because we have ridiculous laws stipulating that pigs must sleep and eat a good distance from where humans live. But in Egypt the peasant still rubs shoulders with his animals. We had just begun our meal when a large white rabbit lolloped into the room. We admired it, and our praise very nearly led to its death – we had great difficulty persuading Abla Azim not to kill it in our honour. When we had finished eating, and while we waited for tea to arrive, Richard wandered into the back room. He found Abla Azim's wife lying beside a donkey. The streets of this village, like those of every village I was to visit, were as much the feeding grounds of animals as the thoroughfares of humans. Peasants returning for their midday meals parked their donkeys and camels outside the front door. Goats scavenged on the rubbish tips and buffalo lumbered by on their way to the fields.

After a second cup of tea our hosts suggested we should lie down and sleep until the heat of the day had passed. We declined and made ready to leave. We wanted to thank Abla Azim's wife for the meal, but she remained out of sight.

These peasants were full of grace and dignity. When they wished to be dismissive – we looked to them twice on our journey through the desert to see if we should pick up individuals waiting for lifts – they would hold out a hand a little distance from the waist, palm facing inwards, then flick their fingers contemptuously outwards, their eyes averted from the offending person and their lips curled in an expression of disdain. When we left Mahmood, who accompanied us back to the road, he stood very straight, tapping his long fingers against his breast and then bringing his hands together as though in prayer. But the debt of gratitude really lay with us, though we expressed it less eloquently.

An hour later we crossed the Nile and headed south along the west bank; past groves of palms, each standing on a pedestal of mud, a testimony to the sinking level of the land; past water buffaloes and donkeys circling round and turning irrigation wheels; past flocks of white cattle egret trailing in the wake of ox and plough; past pigeon houses of gothic grandeur; through mud villages where donkeys, mules, goats and horses milled across the roads; occasionally we caught a glimpse of a felucca's white sail through the trees. At Tamiya we stopped at a market to buy oranges and a few miles further south we turned away from the river. The Necropolis of Maidum, a pyramid with a crumbling apex, towered over the palms to the south. Within five miles we were back in desert but soon the Faiyum appeared before us.

Magnificent eucalyptus trees lined the road into Madinat, the capital of this large heart-shaped oasis. We swerved round a dog, half-dead but still twitching, which the lorry ahead of us had hit, and cruised into the centre of town, which was sliced in two by a canal. It was nearly dark when we found a hotel. The Montasa was clean and dull, and our patience was sorely tried by the exceptionally unpleasant little man who ran it. He was a Copt, though in saying so I do not suggest he was representative of the species. We ate well – a half-chicken each – in a café by the canal. Its veranda ran round a pool where three large water-wheels creaked, groaned and whistled. Richard fancied that they sounded like souls grumbling in purgatory.

Next morning I phoned Fatma at Cairo's State Information Bureau. There was such a din outside the post office that I aborted the call the first time I got through to her. I just managed to make out what she was saying the second time. The Madinat branch of the Bureau was expecting us.

Madinat's annual feast day had begun with a spectacular procession along the canal. It was led by an army jeep in which sat four officers in tin hats. They looked like something out of a Second World War film set. They were followed by four Peugeot vans full of armed soldiers, a fire-engine, and a bunch of twenty-odd soldiers, most with cigarettes clamped between lips, who made no attempt to march, either in time or out, with the brass band which came after them. This may have been because the music they played was drowned by wailing sirens and honking horns. The band was pursued by thirty small boys in army uniform, making some attempt to march in time and each holding a coloured balloon. Two tractors came next, their trailers transporting various bits of greenery, including three small trees in pots, and behind them came two enormous ditch-digging machines. The rear end of the procession was brought up by three tractors with gleaming three-furrow ploughs, two JCBs and the fire-engine, which had broken ranks, nipped down some side-streets and reappeared at the back.

It was a splendid occasion, full of good humour and watched over by the assembled populace – veiled women with bags of shopping balanced on their heads, droves of small boys who ran alongside giving advice and passing comments whose nature appeared to be derogatory, and old men in the street-side cafés, breaking off from games of backgammon and dominoes to puff meditatively at *shishas* and observe the procession through a silky screen of blue smoke. Everything was spotlessly clean. The ploughs looked as though they had never turned a furrow. The trumpets had been polished. Boots were freshly blacked and hair was recently combed.

It was a little after nine o'clock when we entered Madinat's State Information Bureau. 'I am chief here,' announced the man behind the desk. We shook hands, explained who we were, and sat on a leather sofa by the window. The windows were open and the weather was fine. A few small fleecy clouds floated over the Nile Valley some way off to the east, and the early-morning traffic raced round two granite obelisks outside.

We waited. Five minutes ... ten minutes ... fifteen minutes. Nothing happened. The chief sat motionless, an unread paper, at which he never once glanced, spread out in front of him. He was a solidly built man in late middle age. He had small, dark eyes set in a chubby face of waxy pallor, and a small black moustache. His nostrils were enormous and flared and these, combined with his dress – black pinstripe suit, white shirt and black tie – gave him the appearance of a smartly dressed Etruscan horse bound for a funeral. A couple of times he summoned up enough energy to swivel his eyes in our direction and deliver what appeared to be severe looks of disapproval.

For want of anything better to do I studied his office. There was a large black and white photograph of Cairo Tower on one wall, and there were two others, one of a petrochemical works and one of Madinat's obelisks. Inevitably, there was a photo of President Mubarek on the wall behind the chief. After twenty-five minutes I asked him if he had a W C, not because I needed one but to create a diversion. When I returned, North was experimenting with his clothes. He had removed his sleeveless red windcheater and his khaki overshirt and was replacing them the other way round, with the shirt over the windcheater.

'Does this look ridiculous?' he asked. 'I don't want to look ridiculous.'

The chief gazed at him with an expression of utter astonishment; but he remained silent. However, the episode unnerved him enough to make him remove a pack of cigarettes from his pocket, take one, light it and smoke it.

'We've come to see the perfume fields,' explained Richard, just in case there was any doubt about the purpose of our visit.

'Yes,' said the chief. 'Man coming.'

After three quarters of an hour, a small and delightful character called Mr Said turned up. He presented us with two blank sheets of paper and asked us to write our names, our passport numbers and the purpose of our visit. He scrutinized our answers. 'Sorry,' he said. 'There aren't any perfume fields in the Faiyum. Just a few perfume trees scattered around peasants' allotments. Is there anything else you would like to see?'

We settled for a fruit farm, and we said we'd like to drop in at one of the spectacular pigeon houses common in this part of Egypt. Before following Mr Said out of the office we went over to the chief. He stood up and shook hands with us. We were surprised not only by the speed of his movements but by the broad and generous grin which accompanied his wishes for a happy day.

'What's your position in the office?' I asked Mr Said as we climbed into the back of a van.

'Chief,' he replied.

The van had two drivers and a public-address system. 'We use it for things like family-planning talks,' said Mr Said. Richard suggested we blast the countryside with some Bob Marley. Mr Said smiled nervously.

Two miles past Fidimin we pulled into the village of Sanhur and rolled up to the gates of Gorgi Farm. It was a 28-*feddan* (about an acre) labyrinth of trees, bushes and flowers. Mr Farak, the manager, led us round.

We had come at a perfect time. It was spring and everything was in bloom. The tall hoof-of-the-camel trees were covered with purple blossom, the malalucca hedges were hazy pink, and yellow flowers sprouted along the edges of the prickly pears' fleshy leaves. The grapefruit and orange trees were weighed down with fruit, and beneath the heavy boughs of the great fig trees the ground was dappled with sunlight. There were small plots of olive, date and mango, and wherever space allowed there were beds of flowers. Some, like the rose, were grown for commercial reasons: at least we had seen a plant used in the perfume trade. Turtledoves cooed in the branches of the taller trees and goldfinches twittered in the bushes. The scene was as verdant and colourful as a Rousseau painting. 'A little paradise,' Richard told Mr Farak.

On our way back to Madinat we stopped at the first pigeon house we came across. It was the size of a two-storey house, made of mud and whitewashed. Pigeons flew in and out through scores of small holes round the sides, and half a dozen children raced out from a nearby village to join us. One or two little boys asked for baksheesh. Our drivers shooed them away but one little girl – she looked like a dusky urchin in a cheap Woolworth's print: enormous eyes, wild hair, thin limbs pushing through ragged clothes – lingered just out of chasing distance. She wanted to be photographed in front of the pigeon house, but sadly the drivers sent her running with a barrage of insults.

It was early afternoon when we left Madinat. On the way back to Cairo we stopped at Lake Qarun. Hoopoes picked through the grass at the water's edge and bee-eaters decorated the telegraph wires with their flashy blue and orange plumage. By the roadside children were selling live turkeys, geese and ducks. They advertised their wares by leaping into the road and waving the fowls in front of passing cars. It looked a very perilous occupation for all concerned.

CHAPTER FIVE
CAIRO: A VERY PUBLIC CITY

This is indeed a funny country. Yesterday,
for example, we were at a café which is one
of the best in Cairo, and where
there were, at the same time as ourselves,
inside, a donkey shitting and a gentleman
who was pissing in the corner.
No one finds that odd.
Gustav Flaubert (1850)

There is nothing in the annals of European weather that quite prepares you for the *khamasin* (which means fifty, the number of days the storm is supposed to blow each spring). The sun appeared briefly at dawn – I was smoking a cigarette on our balcony at the Balmoral – but by eight o'clock it had been swallowed up by clouds of dust that rolled over Cairo from the deserts to the south. I ate breakfast and went to sit on the east bank of Zamalek, from where I watched the city on the other side of the river fade in the storm. The stark outlines of the skyscrapers became blurred and ghostly and then disappeared completely. The wind gained force and the side of my face grew sore as the sand and dust scratched the skin and clogged my eyes. Before long the palms in front of the TV building went the same way as the buildings, and all that was left in front of me were the grey waters of the Nile. I struggled across to the city and spent the morning being buffeted and battered by the debris of the streets as it took flight before the hot winds. Cairo's refuse problem would be Alexandria's by the evening. In mid-afternoon the wind dropped and the light outside the café where I sat on Talaat Harb Street turned from a lustreless and dirty grey to a ghastly yellow. This garish piece of melodrama signalled the end of the storm, though it was another day before the dust settled.

When clouds of dust swallowed whole streets, when the sinking sun shimmered through exhaust fumes, when the jabbering and the wailing and the shouting in the markets fused with the roar of engines and the honking of horns, the city was possessed by her own demons. It was as though here, in this vast overcrowded slum, high technology and all it had spawned had come together to play Russian roulette. It was just a matter of time before the twentieth century blew its brains out – and Cairo was where it would do it.

In 1975 I passed through Cairo twice. The first time I stayed just long enough to get a visa from the Sudanese Embassy and to see the pyramids. I remember little apart from the constant battle against hustlers and beggars on the streets. Many months later I was in Cairo again, having returned from the Sudan, and I spent a week there. I forget where I stayed, but I remember the evenings well. I found a club where even a card player as inept as I was couldn't fail to win money. I played blackjack every night and I won every night. The proceeds from my gambling were very welcome as I had been next to broke when I arrived. I left the city firmly convinced that there could be few madder places to spend one's time than Cairo.

I returned to Cairo in 1984 anticipating my reactions of nine years earlier. In short, I fully expected to dislike it and I was prepared to rush through my business as fast as possible. As it turned out, I spent two weeks in Cairo and could happily have stayed two months. On reflection, what attracted me most to Cairo was that, compared to London, where I have lived before and since, or the other north European towns which I know well, it is a very public city. I have not quoted Flaubert to be disparaging. There is something healthy about a country where a man can piss openly, even if one disapproves of him doing so in a café. Cairenes live as much on the streets as in their homes, and the contrast with our own cities is striking. With us alienation has reached its peak. Our streets are no longer places to be lived in but routes to pass along on our way from one building to another. We cocoon ourselves behind concrete and the tighter we cram ourselves into our cities the more we seem

1. A dank and smoky back street in Cairo

2. The bakery at St Anthony's monastery.
The monks are cowled; the three in white jellabas are workers
who live in the desert outside

3. Frequently one comes across shepherds in desert
which appears devoid of fodder

4. A morose child watches his mother weaving on the doorstep

5. Lunch over, two of Abla Azim Mohammed's children
join us for coffee. His wife and daughter remain out of sight.
Mahmood Salaama sits smoking on the right

6. Soldiers munch raw sugarcane in a third-class carriage

7. A passenger ferry heading at dusk for the west bank of the Nile at Luxor

8. A box maker at Kom Ombo working with the ribs of date-palm leaves

9. Asleep in the desert

10. Isna temple. The size of the hieroglyphs
can be gauged from that of the owl which stands on the lotus-sculpted
capital of one of the temple's massive columns

11. A buffalo-driven *saqia*, a water-lifting device first used during Ptolemaic times; *saqias* are gradually giving way to diesel pumps

12. Peasants and cattle in Daraw market

13. Feluccas glide round Elephantine Island.
There is no stretch of the Nile more beautiful than this one at Aswan

to shun one another. Everything we have done to our cities over the past half-century has been calculated to brutalize. We have cleared away Dickensian slums and erected in their place high-rise blocks in the idiotic belief that people will somehow be happier perched hundreds of feet above the ground rather than on the ground, which is where we belong.

Not that Cairo is learning from our mistakes. In fact it is making just the same ones, but even more recklessly. What redeems the city is the way in which the people react to the follies of modern planning.

The town planners, the road builders and the engineers are having a wonderful time in Cairo. They are driving huge flyovers, indiscriminately it seems, wherever it suits them. If a bazaar, a public park or a tenement is in the way, no matter – knock it down! Across the city – and Richard and I spent days doing little other than walking, often just where the fancy took us – you come across great pillars awaiting yet another overhead road. They are sprouting like weeds. And more roads will breed more cars, and with more cars will come more noise and more fumes. Of course, the architects of this madness can escape at night, into their air-conditioned flats in Zamalek or Garden City or Docci, where there is just enough peace and quiet to let them dream of next year's devastation.

'I loved Cairo ten years ago,' said the Russian film-maker. 'It was quiet, at least by comparison with today; the streets were fewer and less crowded. You could even find somewhere to park when you came into town.'

I know of no other city where culpability for ruining areas which were once harmonious blends of living quarters, markets and factories lies so indisputably with the motor car: here it is celebrating its apotheosis. There are parts of Cairo, for example around Tahrir Square and along the Corniche, the road which runs along the Nile, where the construction of new flyovers and motorways doesn't matter much, at least not from an architectural point of view. There is nothing much to spoil. But some districts have been ruined, or are about to be ruined, by new roads. In April 1984 a couple of miles of pillars marched from downtown Cairo west through the edge of Khan-el-Khalili, a market area of great beauty. It was awaiting a flyover which would (and doubtless by now does) carry traffic at *piano nobile* height past such beautiful mosques as al-Azhar and al-Husayn. Near by is Atabah Square post office, a fascinating place, both architecturally and as a paradigm of commercial inefficiency. It is an Italianiate building of the last century, its facade topped by delicate cupolas. You walk through the main door not into an enclosed space but into a courtyard. Twenty or so officials sit behind grilles like monkeys in cages. Its poste-restante service is reputed to be the most unreliable in the world. All in all it is a place of great character, and in April you could admire it from a distance. Not so, three months later, when I returned to Cairo. The planners had been good enough to leave the building intact, but they had wrapped a one-lane flyover round it. I returned on the day the flyover was opened. I went into the post office, picked up a letter which, by the admission of the post office's own stamp, had taken seven weeks to travel from London to the pigeonhole marked P, and returned to the street just in time to see a large limousine full of officials honour the scarcely dry tarmac of the flyover with its first customers. They wore weary expressions as though this was a familiar chore, which it probably was.

'You'll find that much has changed since you were last in Cairo,' a representative of the government had told me before I left England. He was a sleek, olive-oil sort of character who spoke faultless and colloquial English. He was sitting in a leather armchair smoking a long cigarette, in a very plush, very peaceful office just off Oxford Street. You could hardly hear the traffic. 'Cairo's a wonderfully modern city now,' he told me. 'Full of new motorways, new flyovers, new underpasses. You'll be terribly impressed!' And I was in a way. But what impressed me was not the ludicrous network of concrete ribbons which the planners had imposed upon the city, but how the people of Cairo made the best of their dreadful lot. For a couple of dozen Egyptians the flyover in Atabah Square was open long before the limousine rolled over it. Between the concrete piles merchants had already set up stores selling books, writing paper, gaudy nylon scarves, jellabas and plastic toys. Under another flyover near the Ramses Hilton the concrete wasteland has been turned into a football pitch. Egyptians have a genius for using space that elsewhere might be left redundant.

When I arrived back from the Faiyum I went to see Fatma. She was looking, as usual, thoroughly alluring, and she greeted me as though I was an old friend. She was eager to learn whether I had enjoyed my visit to the perfume fields of the Faiyum. I said we'd had a marvellous time, which was true, but I didn't have the heart to tell her that if there were any perfume fields in Egypt they were not to be found in the Faiyum. While I was at the Bureau Fatma explained the other meetings which she had arranged: one to see the chief advisor to the Minister of Agriculture; and another to see the Irrigation Minister. I was astonished that she had arranged a meeting with the latter, partly because I had specifically asked to see a technician, but more because the minister had consented to give me an audience. He had asked for a list of questions to be sent before the meeting. Richard arrived and we put some together. We borrowed an ancient typewriter and presented Fatma with the finished product.

'Oh dear,' she exclaimed. 'I think the minister would prefer it if the questions were hand-written.' We asked why, and for an answer she smiled charmingly. So I wrote them out by hand.

Fatma said that she had found a perfume factory at Hawamdia, and she gave me the address. I was to visit it the following morning.

There is a marvellous scene in Flaubert's *Temptation of St Antony* when the hermit is visited by the beautiful and lascivious Queen of Sheba. 'The possession of the least place of my body,' she tells Anthony (his teeth are chattering) 'will give you sharper joy than the conquest of an empire. Offer your lips! My kisses taste like fruit ready to melt into the heart! Ah! how you'll lose yourself in my hair, breathing the scent of my sweet-smelling breasts . . .' The hermit crosses himself. The Queen of Sheba, scorned, leaves with her slaves, her dromedaries, the women servants, the little negroes, the monkey, and the green couriers, each with a broken lily in the hand. Anthony is left alone. In the reader's imagination a gorgeous and indefinable smell lingers through the following pages, the intangible mixture of essences and perfumes that must have trailed in the wake of the Queen of Sheba, Cleopatra and all the other legendary and lesser women of ancient Egypt.

The Egyptians were renowned for their heavy perfumes, and the archaeologists who opened the tomb of Tutankhamun in 1922 were greeted by the oily smells of embalming unguents which had lasted four thousand years. The Egyptians grew many of the raw materials needed for the manufacture of perfumes, and those they didn't, like myrrh, opoponax and lavender, they imported from elsewhere. Much of the kingdom's wealth derived from the taxes imposed on traders bringing spices and perfumes from the orient through to Europe. Even the poor in Egypt would use perfumes like musk and civet, and Lane reported that in the last century Egyptians still fumigated their homes with frankincense and aloe wood. A rich man would sprinkle his guests with orange-flower water before they departed, and the very rich would burn ambergris, the wax from a sperm whale's intestine.

The Egyptian's love of perfumes has not diminished, and in the bazaars in Cairo one is continually pestered by perfume-sellers. They tell extravagant tales (lies, in other words) and charge extravagant prices. I had warned Richard about this, but he ignored my advice and allowed himself to be taken in by someone he met on the street. The someone happened to be the manager of Groppi's, the smartest café in town, and in return for £E10 Richard procured a small vial of vulgar-smelling liquid, with which, curiously, he seemed quite pleased.

It took me an hour by collective taxi to get to Hawamdia, which was twenty-odd miles upstream from Cairo. From outside, the industrial estate looked stereotypically Victorian – dark and satanic. Smoke billowed out from factories behind the high stone walls which ran round the estate, and men on foot and bike were being sucked through the main gate by the magnet of economic necessity. I was early – it wasn't yet eight o'clock – so I crossed a canal and walked into the main town. The streets were mean and muddy and so was the café which I went into. The music was so loud that none of the customers could talk. I drank a tea. The boy who ran the café refused to let me pay, yet I imagine I had more money in my pocket than he earned in a month. One often heard tourists complaining about Egyptians trying to wheedle baksheesh out of them. Seldom, which was a pity, did they have much to say about the Egyptians' generosity.

From the café to the sugar and distillery factory it was nearly a mile's walk, the last stretch beside the river. At the gate of the factory I was asked for my press card and my passport. Nobody was expecting me, I was told. After ten minutes or so I was led into the factory and directed round the corner of a warehouse. In the middle of a square five men were waiting. They stood in formation, legs straddled and hands in pockets. They might have been Yorkshire mill-owners of the last century. Mr Gazar, a small man with pebble glasses and a round face, asked what I wanted. I said I'd come to see him. He replied that he had never heard of me and told me to wait in his office. One of the factory engineers, Mohammed, waited with me. Gazar joined us and telephoned Cairo. 'Sorry,' he said when he put the phone down. 'That was head office. They hadn't told me you were coming. Now that they have, you are very welcome.'

Coffee was ordered. An official came in and asked if I had a camera. I had. He wanted to confiscate it but Gazar waved him away.

'How can we help?' asked Gazar. I said I was interested in the manufacture of perfumes.

'We don't make perfumes,' he said.

'What do you make?' I asked.

'Fodder yeast, bakers' yeast, ethyl alcohol, vinegar, glacial acetic acid, CO_2 . . .'

I said I was interested in those too. Gazar gave me an old-fashioned look and briefly explained the workings of the factory. Sugarcane cultivated in Upper Egypt was turned into molasses. The molasses were transported by barge down to Hawamdia. Here they were converted to yeast, vinegar and so on. Gazar asked if I had any questions. I hadn't, so Mohammed took me on a tour of the factory. We scaled up ladders to stare down into vats of liquid and we inspected engines and generators. We looked at pipes, fermentors, flues and chimneys; it was a complete mystery to me what went where and why. In one shed were two rows of enormous wooden vats full of vinegar, the newest of which had been designed by Mohammed. He was justifiably proud of it. It was twenty feet high, twelve feet in diameter and beautifully made of English oak.

The tour over, we returned to thank Mr Gazar. He asked Mohammed to take me along to the Chemical Organic Factory a couple of hundred yards up river. Once there, we were led into the office of the vice-chairman, Dr Mamdouh Fahmy. We shook hands. 'Let me finish dealing with all these people,' he said. Mohammed and I sat down while a steady stream of workers passed through the office to see Fahmy.

I asked Mohammed how many workers there were here. Four hundred, he thought. I asked if Dr Fahmy knew them all. Naturally, said Mohammed. But he wouldn't tell me how much they were paid.

'The factory is like a family,' he said. 'Fathers are followed by their sons. Every worker gets a house and the factory provides virtually everything he needs. The factory has built mosques, churches, cinemas, a school for the children and workers' clubs. Medicine is free for all the employees and the factory even has a bus to take the workers and their families into Cairo to do their shopping in the evening.'

'Now,' said Fahmy, his business over, 'do you want me to speak?'

'Yes,' I said.

'Fine! I will do.'

Fahmy was a charming man with a shock of wispy hair rising from the back of his head like smoke from a volcano. He was constantly amused and amusing, and he had the ability to make the processes of chemical engineering interesting if not intelligible. He talked very fast for ten minutes, about fermentation, filtration, bacteria, acetone and something called n-butanol, which was apparently of great importance here.

'I like people who ask questions,' he said. 'Even if they are stupid questions, it means they want to learn.'

I took the hint and asked him a question. It was undoubtedly a very stupid one.

'Let's go round the factory,' he said. We passed a pile of rice bran. 'This is a paradise for the mice and the *oiseaux*,' announced Fahmy.

A large man in a boiler suit came across to shake his hand. 'This old man is sixty,' said Fahmy, 'and he is married to a girl of twenty. I respect him very much.'

We passed some large steaming tanks. 'This is where we do the cooking,' he said. He wasn't going to blind me with any more science.

Everywhere we went the workers came to greet him. With each he bantered and chatted. It was a remarkably friendly place. We bumped into a group of girls. 'I like the girls very much,' he said. And they liked him.

By the Nile we looked down into a barge full of molasses. A pipe near by was discharging some factory waste. Fahmy was amused by the recent plans, much discussed in the Egyptian press, to clean up the Nile. 'The molasses are very good for the fish,' he suggested.

He wondered whether I'd like to see the fire-fighting equipment. I said I would. There was an old red fire-engine in a small shed. 'This is no good,' he announced. 'The only ones that are any use are the ones with cannons which fire water or powder. This is the good thing.' He led us to a small box by the door. 'When I turn this switch,' he explained, 'the pressure of water changes everywhere in the factory.'

He turned the switch. We looked round but saw nothing.

'What's happening?' I asked.

'Nothing,' said Fahmy. 'It's broken.'

The tour ended in the scientists' laboratory. We looked down a microscope at some bacteria. As far as I could gather the scientists were constantly searching for some particular strain of bacteria vital to the process of fermentation. 'It could take an ignorant man a day to find,' said Fahmy, 'and a clever man ten years. *Inshallah!* God willing!'

It was after midday when I left. I thanked Mohammed and Dr Fahmy – they had been remarkably forbearing considering my ignorance – and walked back through the factory housing estate. The manager's house was set in a spacious garden with a swimming-pool. The others had pleasant flats, each with a small garden, and some had coops for hens and ducks. I passed the workers' club with its watered lawn and beds of geraniums, the open-air cinema and a small mosque. Children were returning from school. The girls wore smart blue dresses and head-squares.

I left the industrial complex none the wiser about perfumes or chemical engineering but pleasantly surprised by the working conditions in the factory and the relationship between the managerial staff and the workers. I said as much to the young man who sat next to me in the taxi back to Cairo, a teacher of English in a secondary school.

'It's only the technicians who get the nice houses,' he said. 'The rest of the workers live in the surrounding villages like poor Egyptians.'

I asked how much the workers were paid. Between £E40 and £E70 a month, he thought. The teacher earned £E40 a month for a thirty-hour week. He paid £E25 a month in rent. To make ends meet he had to teach rich pupils in his spare time.

Next time I saw Fatma she asked whether I had enjoyed my visit to the factory. Very much, I told her; but what had happened to the perfume factory? 'Oh,' she replied airily, 'it's broken down.' Apparently it hadn't made a drop of perfume for months. Hebba thought that a good thing. 'Egyptian perfumes are revolting,' she said. 'I wouldn't dream of wearing them.' She liked the French stuff. I never did write an article about perfumes.

Richard pursued journalism in Egypt with much greater success than I did. He too was interested in smells, but of a very different nature to those I had been after. One morning we breakfasted early, crossed the Nile over July 26 Bridge, then headed north-east up 6 October Street. Mr Jeremy Goad was already at his office near Ramses Station when we arrived at eight o'clock. He worked for Ambrit, a consortium of British and American engineers who had the immense task of modernizing Cairo's sewage system. Goad was tall, fair, Cambridge-educated and suspicious of journalists. He had made clear to Richard over the phone his reluctance to see us. Richard had two techniques for getting information out of wary individuals: one was to 'word-bomb' them (a form of verbal battery); the other involved 'love-bombing', whose meaning is self-evident; he deployed this technique now, but it didn't work with Goad, who was pleasant but cagey. I glanced round the office while we waited for tea. There were two desks, one at which Goad sat, another strewn with maps and plans; and there was a Midland Bank calendar on the wall, a painting of Suffolk sheep grazing in rich pasture.

When Lane lived in Egypt in the 1830s he estimated the population of Cairo to be about a third of a million. In 1947 the population was just over two million. In 1984 it was twelve million, and it continues to rise at the rate of about a thousand people a day. At least two million people live in dwellings which aren't connected to the city's ancient and overworked sewage system and their excrement is dumped in vaults beneath their houses. A mafia-like association of families carts the sludge away and dumps it wherever it can, down manholes into the existing system, or – though the authorities won't admit it – into the river, whose waters are drawn for drinking. The unsewered areas are dotted throughout Cairo, but, predictably, it has been the frequent appearance of raw sewage rising from manholes and flooding the streets in the wealthier suburbs that has spurred the authorities to act in recent years. Goad laid a map out before us and traced the line of a massive tunnel which Ambrit was building and into which the existing system would be plugged when completed.

It requires either remarkable faith or great foolishness to believe that the urban decay and squalor in Cairo will be effectively countered in the near future, if ever. The problems are enormous and sewage disposal is just one of them. Since the 1952 revolution, when General Naguib and a handful of other officers overthrew the monarchy of King Farouk, the government has played a prominent role in virtually every sphere of Egyptian life, nationalizing banks and industry, and establishing price controls for a whole range of basic goods. But it has ignored rubbish, which is urgently in need of nationalization. While the provincial governates and city councils have responsibility for cleaning the streets, which they sometimes do, refuse disposal is strictly private enterprise. It is left to the *zabalene*, who one sees with their donkeys and carts, combing the town for rubbish early in the mornings and late at night. But the *zabalene* – many are children – just nibble at the problem, taking the rich pickings from the wealthier suburbs and the restaurants and leaving the poor to dispose of their garbage as best they can. 'The concept of regular refuse collection,' observes the World Bank drily, 'does not appear to have taken root in Egypt. Most people dispose of their refuse by dumping it on sidewalks, in sewer manholes, and other

73

places where it breeds insects carrying diseases and constitutes a serious health hazard.'

In the same report the World Bank claims that a quarter of all urban households in Egypt and a third of all rural households live below the absolute poverty line. A measure of quite how acute poverty is in Cairo can be gauged from public reactions to government attempts to increase the price of food (which is heavily subsidized and a considerable drain on the country's economy). Not long after I left Cairo, President Mubarek announced a one-piastre rise in the price of bread. Riots followed. People are that poor.

In 1975 I wandered, unthinkingly, into one of the slums to the east of July 26 Street. I was repelled by a fusillade of rocks thrown by small children. Few outsiders spend much time in the slums, and those who do come away with a shocking picture of what it is like to be poor. Unni Wikan, a Swedish anthropologist, spent eight months in the slums of Giza. Here is her entry for 7 August 1972: 'My God, I'm sick and tired of this life. Quarrels everywhere, gossip and slander, hypocrisy and self-praise – the stench, the piss and filth and garbage, kids fighting and screaming voices penetrating absolutely everywhere.'

It would be wrong to suggest that one is met by aggression whenever one strays into the poorer quarters of town. After we left Goad we spent the day wandering round the streets. (Goad informed us on parting that he was acting in the Cairo Players' production of *Noises Off*, which we went to see that night: he spent most of the first act, appropriately for someone in his profession, with his trousers down.) We decided to walk to the City of the Dead, which lay about five miles to the south, on the other side of town. I thought I knew a short cut and I led Richard down a promising-looking side street. We walked for half an hour without getting out of the maze of narrow, winding streets, and eventually we ended up where we had begun. The quarter we were in was not conspicuously poor, though statistics would probably have put it in the slum category. We saw no other Westerners and the occupants of the area looked at us in such a way as to suggest that white men there were about as common as negroes in the House of Lords. We were greeted with amusement and interest, not aggression. The ground floors of most buildings were given over to small workshops; the other five or six were residential. Every imaginable form of small industry was present and many spilled out on to the crowded streets. Everybody was doing something, whether it was mending cars, fixing sewing-machines, running up shirts, selling fruit or driving donkeys through the streets. Even the blind and limbless were occupied. One man without legs sat on the ground selling cigarettes and matches. One with no eyes was selling metal washers. They were old washers, such as might have been collected from the floors of garages or repair shops.

One's natural inclination is to argue that the poor of cities like Cairo should have a similar system of social security to our own. Yet one wonders how areas like this would function once their inhabitants were subjected to a formal economy, where fixed wages, organized labour and institutionalized unemployment rearranged the social system. I do not suggest that it is better to be poor in Cairo than Hackney (materially it is so obviously worse), but where the poor organize themselves, where a scavenging economy flourishes and the state's immediate influence is small, people do exhibit an ingenuity and spiritedness which is markedly lacking in the organized ghettos of Western cities. What struck me most about the people in the poor quarters in many Egyptian towns was that they did not appear to be suffering from lethargy, boredom, Godlessness, hopelessness; for want of a better expression, from the poverty of affluence. Cairo never depressed me, even though some of its slums disgusted me; whereas I know large swathes of London – for instance, the high-rise flatland round Canning Town, or Tottenham, or Stockwell – that fill me with despair.

At least the poor in Cairo are fed. The same is not true for huge numbers in other parts of the continent. The misery I saw in Ethiopia nine years earlier (and which I was half-expecting to see again this time) had nothing in common with the poverty of the Egyptian slums. The poor there were in the extremity of suffering, debilitated by lack of food, and fearful of both the law, as administered by a repressive regime, and, paradoxically, of lawlessness, the rural villages being constantly subject to the depredations of the raiding bandits, the *shifta*. Unlike the Egyptian poor many Ethiopians had no certainty of survival.

We found our way, eventually, to Khan-el-Khalili. An intricate

75

web of alleys, culs-de-sac and dead-ends wound like a confused mass of tendrils through an area of small factories, workshops, cafés and mosques. We passed goldsmiths peering through hand lenses, blacksmiths sweating over anvils, and joiners chiselling away at half-complete tables. Barbers were scraping off stubble with cut-throat razors and tourists were capturing the market's medieval and crumbling atmosphere on celluloid. The streets were choked with cars, flocks of sheep, horse taxis, women from the country with boxes of rabbits and chickens on their heads, barrow boys, and men in purple robes selling coffee and *felafels*. One minute you whiffed a goat or a sewer; the next, frankincense or cinnamon.

I have always had a passion for cemeteries, but none I had ever seen matched the scale and grandeur of Cairo's City of the Dead. We dashed across the motorway which ran over the crest of the hill above Khan-el-Khalili and followed a *zabalene* into the cemetery. The streets through the cemetery were wide and paved and traffic passed through on its way from the city to the modern housing estate at the foot of the Muqattam Hills beyond. Even the smallest of the tombs was the size of a peasant's shack and the largest looked like medium-sized mosques. I don't know how many corpses were buried here – a huge number, I imagine, as the cemetery stretched for over three miles from where we were now to the Citadel, whose silver domes and needle-thin minarets we could see gleaming in the distance. But 'City of the Dead' is really a misnomer: it is the Middle East's greatest squat, with a population of over 500,000 refugees. Some tombs remained empty but many had been converted into rough habitations. Through an open door we glimpsed a home-made charcoal stove, an old sideboard and a table with a few chairs. A woman sat at the table, her back facing the door, and three children played on the stone floor. One came out to wave as we passed. In other tombs the squatters had set up small businesses, making boxes out of cardboard or the ribs of palm leaves, or selling fruit and bread.

Compared to many of the slums in the inner city, the City of the Dead seemed spacious and airy. Nevertheless, it is a measure of Cairo's population problem that one out of every twenty inhabitants must live in a cemetery. I had forgotten to ask Goad what was to be done about the human waste of the City of the Dead. Whatever else

the dead require it is not clean water and piped sewers. Cemeteries are not the ideal place to squat.

I had been about a week in Cairo before I realized that I hadn't seen a single beggar. This was extraordinary, as nine years ago beggars were to be encountered everywhere, in the modern town round Talaat Harb Street and Tahrir Square, in the alleys of Khan-el-Khalili, at the railway stations and outside all the mosques. My mind turned to beggars when Richard returned one evening to the Balmoral with two books he'd bought for me from a second-hand bookstall. One was Trollope's *Barchester Towers.* The other was a collection of seventeenth-century English verse. It included a sonnet which described a beggar woman (she had blonde hair, full lips, sensual eyes and slender hips, which reminded me of Julie Christie) and the gist of the poem was that she proved irresistible to everyone who saw her (which rather begged the question of why she was a beggar). As a piece of outrageous romanticism it could not have been bettered. On this visit I saw only two beggars in Cairo, one outside a church in Babylon, the other outside a mosque in Khan-el-Khalili.

In 1929 Evelyn Waugh visited Babylon, the old Roman fortress which became a Coptic centre after the Arab conquest of AD 641. 'In this constricted slum,' he wrote,

there are five medieval Coptic churches, a synagogue, and a Greek Ortho-dox convent. The Christians seem to differ in decency very little from their pagan neighbours; the only marked sign of their emancipation from heathen superstition was that the swarm of male and juvenile beggars were here reinforced by their womenfolk, who in the Mohemmedan quarters maintain a modest seclusion.

We took the tram from Bab al-Luk south to Babylon. Turn right out of the station and you walk into the riverside slums; turn left and a flight of steps dips beneath the solid walls of the Christian city. The alleys which wound round the churches and the cemeteries were cobbled and quiet. Babylon had been cleaned up for the tourists. Bearded patriarchs no longer rubbed shoulders with ascetics and paupers amid the stench and jostle of overcrowded and unsewered slums. Which was doubtless a good thing. A few women were selling souvenirs and plastic icons, and there was a desiccated old hag begging outside the Church of Sergius. We gave her a small note, which she held up against the light like a banker checking the watermark. There was nobody else begging up there in the city. After we had looked in at some of the churches we nipped into the Coptic museum.

'I don't know how you feel about museums,' said Richard as we paid the entrance fee, 'but I like to go round them at a fast trot.' This we did. We soon found ourselves back outside the walls, and we took the train back into town, where we parted company. I went to look at the mosque of Sayyidna al-Husayn. Rows of thick marble pillars rose from a carpet of rich green. They were ringed with gold leaf, and those who weren't praying sat round the square pedestals. There were students browsing through Islamic texts, businessmen with briefcases, and huddles of small children who appeared to have been dumped by mothers out on shopping expeditions. At the back was a tramp with no legs, asleep and snoring rhythmically. The mosque was opulent, calm and very beautiful. When I left I went to where a crowd had gathered outside. On the ground writhed a man in rags. He was blind and very black. He held an enormous bone, perhaps the femur of a bullock, from which he was tearing cartilage and shreds of raw meat. He made a grotesque gargling sound as he ate, and some of the crowd responded by laughing and jeering.

It would have been nice to report that beggars were now so few in Egypt because those unable to support themselves were looked after or helped. And there may even be some truth in this; I was told that beggars had been cleared off the streets and put in 'social institutions'. One man told me that the beggars were fed and housed decently. But another claimed that the institutions were 'concentration camps', their main purpose being to hide away people who might upset the tourists, whose contribution to the economy is so important. On the whole, however, Egyptians were reluctant to talk about the beggars' fate.

Gradually we got to know the city better, and before we left we could venture out without a map and be fairly sure of finding what we wanted. And it didn't take long for us to establish a regular circuit of watering holes, where we would retire, at frequent intervals and on most days, from the heat of the streets. We became regulars at the Robaeiyat el Khayam, where I had met the sculptor, and most days we lunched at either Felfela, just off Talaat Harb Street, or Café Riche, which was right on it. The Riche's claim to fame had more to do with politics than its cuisine. It was said that it was while they were having a drink here that Naguib, Nasser, Sadat and a handful of other officers planned the *coup d'état* which overthrew King Farouk. A large canopy cast its shade across the tables on the pavement and we would sit sipping beer with shabby-suited businessmen and students. We also became frequenters of the two Brazilian Coffee Houses in the centre of town. These cannot be too highly recommended. The coffee was superb and the till girls delightful. A cantankerous shoe-shiner passed his time doing business in either one café or the other. A refusal to have one's shoes cleaned was taken as a personal insult, although trying to keep your shoes clean in Cairo is futile – no sooner are they done than dirt gathers on them like scum on a millpond.

One of the great advantages of visiting a country with the purpose of writing about it is that you can get into places which for the tourist are out of bounds. The Ministry of Agriculture and the People's Assembly, for example.

The Ministry was an impressive building with a classical facade in the suburb of Docci, twenty minutes' walk west from Zamalek. Half a dozen gardeners were watering the geraniums and nasturtiums outside the columned portico when I arrived. I was led into a large, high-ceilinged office which housed a diminutive secretary, three solid wood tables and some handsome filing cabinets. On one wall hung a large portrait of President Mubarek – a serious, fleshy-faced man with large eyebrows and a heavy, spread-out nose; not an unattractive face, but lacking the striking good looks of Nasser and Sadat, his two predecessors. The secretary explained that Dr Osman el-Kholi, whom I had come to see, was with the Minister. He would be a little late.

I sat down on an enormous leather sofa and a gnarled old man brought me Turkish coffee. The secretary sat down beside me and we chatted until Kholi was ready to see me. After a while I was led into a room the size of a small barn. Seven men sat on comfortable chairs round a low table in one corner. It was a long walk across to them. Three of them rose to shake hands and I was directed to a high chair which was placed before an enormous desk on the other side of the room. Dr Kholi, the technical advisor to the Minister, left the meeting, which continued without him, and we sat facing each other across the desk. He was exceptionally wide and very short – built from the ground upwards, as Damon Runyon would say. He wore an expensive brown suit, a white shirt and a beige tie. His fingers were small and fleshy, and one, the second of his left hand, carried a large purple stone set in a ring of ornately sculptured gold. We talked for half an hour about Egyptian agriculture, which is to say about the Nile. Less than 4 per cent of the country is cultivated. The rest is desert. The narrow strip beside the Nile and the wedge-shaped delta must provide the food for over forty million people. At the moment they don't, and self-sufficiency is one of the government's main goals. Dr Kholi seemed optimistic. 'In five or six years we should be self-sufficient in everything except wheat,' he suggested.

Two thousand years ago the Nile Valley was Rome's granary. Today the country has to rely on massive imports and aid to feed itself. The heavy subsidization of basic foodstuffs is also a heavy drain on the economy. In 1983/4 the government spent £2,000 million on food subsidies alone.

'If my food is in the hands of others,' said the Irrigation Minister the next day, 'then so is my freedom.'

I was sitting with Minister Samaha at a small blue-and-white-tiled table in his office in the People's Assembly. The room was slightly smaller than Dr Kholi's but it had the same high ceilings, heavy furniture and air of fading grandeur. An ancient wooden clock told the wrong time above a large door padded with green leather. On the table before us a small china vase held a bunch of sweet peas and lilies of the valley.

Minister Samaha was a slight, sallow-skinned man who spoke faultless English and chain-smoked. He was courteous, charming and helpful, and he treated all those who entered during our meeting, from government advisors to tea boys, with the same friendliness and respect. Whatever the strictures on democracy in Egypt, ministers evidently do not feel the need to hide themselves behind the armies of civil servants and henchmen as do their counterparts in Western Europe. An Egyptian with journalistic credentials as meagre as mine would have little chance of seeing a minister's secretary in Britain, let alone a minister.

It is vogue among Egyptian officials to exude confidence in the future prosperity of their country which few independent analysts would share. Samaha did not follow suit. He was honest, though not unduly pessimistic, about the problems of feeding the people, about which more later.

While in Cairo I tried to find out as much as possible about what was happening in Sudan and Ethiopia. I visited the Ethiopian Embassy, where I was told that I could either fly to Addis Ababa from Khartoum, or make my way into the country overland – if, that is, I went via Kenya, which would be like travelling from London to Paris via Istanbul. Once in the country, they said I would be able to travel wherever I wished, except in Eritrea. I had good reasons for not believing this. But my immediate concern was with the Sudan. There was a civil war in the south and the Sudanese Embassy in London had been unable to tell me how this affected travel from Khartoum to Juba.

I was in the State Information Bureau one day when I learnt of a most bizarre event. Richard was sitting at a typewriter in a small room off the main office while I observed with interest the reams of news which were spewing out of the Reuters and Agence Presse machines in one corner. Also in the room was a man in his fifties with grey hair, green eyes and sharp features. He was the political correspondent of the Italian paper *La Republica* ('very heavy potatoes,' as Richard said later) and he wore an expression of sly amusement. 'Here,' he announced gravely as he folded away his notes, 'you must wait and wait and wait.' He was having little success in fixing up a meeting with some Egyptian politicians. He had recently arrived from Khartoum, where he had been covering the visit of the Italian Foreign Minister. 'But I left before the bombing,' he added.

'What bombing?' I asked.

He was surprised that I hadn't heard. Apparently, a plane had flown over Omdurman, Khartoum's sister city, and dropped a few bombs, leaving behind some flattened buildings and five dead. I asked who was responsible. 'That,' he replied, 'depends whose story you believe.' The Sudanese government had taken the line that the bomber had been Libyan and that the attack had been carried out on the orders of Colonel Gadafi. Others said that it had been flown by two disaffected Sudanese pilots. Whose side, I asked, was the Italian on? He shrugged. 'Nimeiri and Gadafi are both mad,' he announced, 'completely mad!' He didn't think I would be able to get much further south than Khartoum.

The *Egyptian Gazette*, the country's English-language daily, blamed Gadafi for the bombing. This was quite predictable. The *Egyptian Gazette* will blame Gadafi for virtually anything. And the Italian showed me a piece about the Sudan in his copy of the *Guardian*. It had been written before the bombing, and it concentrated on the country's present woes, which were many. There was rebellion in the south and many soldiers had defected to join up with the guerrillas fighting Nimeiri's government. Kidnappings and killings had forced Chevron to stop its oil operations in the south and the French company CCI to halt the excavation of the Jonglei canal. Both projects were vital to the Sudanese economy, which was bankrupt. The recent declaration of *sharia* – the Islamic code of law whose punishments include hand amputation for theft, flogging for alcohol consumption and stoning to death for adultery – had not only upset the Christians and animists of the south but many Muslims in the north, including Sadiq el-Mahdi, the great-grandson of the man who defeated General Gordon and the British exactly a century ago, and a prominent Muslim leader. Nimeiri had had him imprisoned for protesting against *sharia*.

I found this news very depressing, and I was overtaken by the illogical notion that I might even have problems getting into the Sudan. Accordingly, I decided, as a safeguard, to buy a ticket for the boat trip from Aswan to Wadi Halfa, the northern point of entry to Sudan, while in Cairo. The Nile Navigation Company had a small office in the railway station. I arrived at 3.15 to be told that it was closed.

'Come back before three o'clock tomorrow,' said a man in the office.

A young Egyptian waylaid me on the way out. He asked if I was going to Sudan. I said I was and he asked why. I didn't answer. 'Don't go,' he suggested. 'Sudan's at war with Libya.' He said he'd read it in the papers.

Next day I returned at 2.30. 'The office is closed,' announced the man I'd seen the day before. 'Come back before two o'clock tomorrow.' I protested but he escaped through a door in the back of the office.

The next day I arrived at 12.45. The office was open. I asked for a first-class ticket to Wadi Halfa. 'That will cost you £E21.50,' said the ticket man. He asked when I was going. There were two boats a week, he said: one on Mondays, the other on Thursdays. I said I'd go on 5 April.

He consulted a ledger. 'On 5 April, second class full, first class OK, third class OK.'

I counted out £E21.50. He disappeared into a back room and reappeared five minutes later with another man. 'Come back in a week's time,' suggested the new arrival.

'No,' I said. 'I want to buy a ticket now.'

'You can't,' he replied. 'You can only book one week before sailing.'

'But if second class is full,' I protested, 'that means some passengers must have booked more than two weeks in advance.'

'Yes,' he replied.

'So I'll do the same,' I said.

'No. Come back on the 28th.'

I told him I couldn't. I was leaving Cairo the next day.

'Then book in Aswan,' he suggested.

'There won't be any first-class tickets left by the time I reach Aswan.'

'OK,' he said. 'Go third class.'

That evening, our last in Cairo, Richard and I set off for a farewell meal. Outside the Balmoral we bumped into the man I'd met from Reuters, and we took him for a coffee in the Robaeiyat el Khayam.

I introduced him to Richard as a man who preferred living in Beirut to Cairo.

'I've changed my mind,' he said. 'Our Beirut office was bombed last week.'

He asked me if I'd read *The Times* recently. It had carried a report which added a further twist to the mystery of the Omdurman saga, claiming that the bombing was carried out on the orders of Nimeiri. The target: Sadiq's house, which was hit. Reuters, surprisingly, were relying on rumours as much as everyone else. 'We used to have a stringer in Khartoum,' said our companion. 'But we don't know what's happened to him. It's months since he's been in touch.'

Our meal was a very poor affair. We had made the mistake of consulting an American guidebook, and on its recommendation we visited three restaurants. The first was closed. The second was deserted, which seemed the strongest possible testimony against it. And the third, at which we ate, was remarkable only for its soup. It was called simple soup, which was quite true. It consisted of hot water with a dash of mutton stock, but not enough to disguise the taste of chlorine.

Richard departed for St Catherine's monastery on Sinai at four o'clock the next morning. He left me a Bob Marley cassette, half a bottle of cheap gin and a tin-opener. I met the Korean manager on my way to the station. 'I'll see you in a couple of months,' I said.

'I doubt it,' he replied sourly. 'People who go to places like Sudan and Ethiopia don't always come back. Don't you read the papers?'

CHAPTER SIX
HADRIAN'S RIVER

This chapter belongs more to history than to the present day. There are two reasons for this. First, I saw very little of its subject, Middle Egypt, the transition band which lies between the country's Nubian and Mediterranean extremes. This was not planned: I simply fell asleep shortly after leaving El Minya, where I passed the first night on my way south, and failed to wake up until my train reached Upper Egypt. The second reason I shall elaborate shortly. Suffice it to say that one man passed this way who for me remains one of the most interesting Europeans to have visited the Nile Valley.

I arrived at Cairo's Ramses Station an hour before my train was due to depart. I bought a second-class ticket and parked myself in the shade of a pillar on the platform where the Asyut train was due. Every ten minutes or so, small, dusty trains with only third-class carriages pulled in, and through their paneless windows and doorless doorways the passengers would spill out and rush from the station. Many were peasant women, up for the day from the country to sell the produce of their fields. Some carried boxes of rabbits and pigeons; others sacks of vegetables. One had an enormous bunch of gladioli and a huge bottom. I studied a map while I waited, and determined that I would stop at regular intervals up the Nile Valley – a night or two at El Minya; others at Asyut, Jirja, Qena, Luxor, Isna, Idfu and Aswan. The train left at midday. I was glad to be on my way: I'd been in Egypt over three weeks and I felt as though I had hardly seen the Nile. The landscape when we pulled out of Cairo was broad, green and flat, rather like Holland with palm trees. But once past Beni Suef, a small town on the same latitude as the Faiyum oasis, cliffs and hills rose behind the cultivated strips of land on either side of the river. It was mid-afternoon when I arrived in El Minya. I found a hotel not far from the station and wandered round the town. It was asleep.

The Nile was very wide here, almost half a mile across, and a stiff breeze from the north roughened the water. Now and then a felucca drifted past, its sails a brilliant white against the green palm groves and beige cliffs on the far bank. There was scarcely any activity on the riverside. A couple of fishermen were lying in their small boat on a pile of nets. One slept; the other read. Near by, half a dozen goats browsed on a lush strip of grass by a government building and hoopoes picked through the rubbish at the water's edge. I left the river and headed past a mosque where a huddle of veiled women sat in the shade munching sugarcane. In the main square I found a café with marble tables and heavy wooden chairs. Huge rotating fans hung from the high ceiling, in one corner of which a pair of swallows was building a nest. Two men were playing backgammon and another two were staring across a chessboard at one another. I drank a coffee and watched the soporific scene outside. Under some palms three horses browsed in harness, while their cabbies sat on the ground and passed the time smoking, spitting and chatting.

At five o'clock there was a downpour. It was the only rain I saw in Africa on this visit. It lasted for no more than ten minutes but it turned the streets to slithery mud and left huge elliptical puddles outside the shops and houses. Two dogs rose very deliberately from under the palms and went to lie in a puddle. They gazed attentively at their reflections until a battered black Buick rumbled towards them, ploughing ephemeral furrows of water as it approached.

As the sun dropped, so did the wind. At dusk the river turned a soft grey-blue, and the cliffs behind were tinged delicate pink. The muezzins called the faithful to prayer, though they did so surprisingly quietly; perhaps in deference to El Minya's large Christian population. I watched two soldiers down their rifles, kneel on the wet paving and bow towards Mecca. Not to be outdone, and for want of anything better to do, I decided to go to church. It was Sunday and time for evensong, or its Coptic equivalent. But the main church – or perhaps it was a cathedral – was closed.

There was a recent copy of the *Egyptian Gazette* in my hotel room.

I skimmed through it while I drank a Balmoral Cocktail, and my attention was caught by an item of news which came from one of the gulf emirates (I forget which). It was a small, po-faced piece of news, reporting, without comment, that the ruler had selected a group of eminent historians to rewrite his country's history. Their task was to rectify the 'errors' made by previous histories. In twenty or thirty years' time the *Gazette* may well carry another piece, announcing that another ruler has ordered a further history to be written, in order to correct the mistakes of the one which was about to be embarked on.

At first this all struck me as farcical. Yet when I thought of the books which I had pored over as a child, books about Africa and explorers, I realized that this ruler was following in the noble tradition of the Victorian historians, whose interpretation of the events in Africa was outstanding more for its racial bigotry, its presumption of white superiority, and its disinterest in the fate of Africans, than for any erudition or accuracy in recounting what really happened out here. I grew up thinking of the Nile simply as a geographical conundrum (there was no children's equivalent of Alan Moorehead's excellent studies of the river's history) and the heroes of my books were men like Baker, Speke, Stanley, Livingstone and Burton. It was Speke, as far as my histories were concerned, who had discovered the source of the Nile – no mention was made of the Arabs who for centuries had known where it was (near Lake Victoria), let alone the Africans who actually lived there. This history, written by Europeans and for Europeans, had a certain flavour of romance to it when I was young. Now it bores me profoundly, since the main characters are interesting not for their vision of what might have become in Africa (few had any), but only for their idiosyncrasies. Burton, for example, was a linguist of genius, and among his many achievements must be counted the first English translation of the Kama-sutra. This endears him to me. But for the most part these explorers – there were exceptions like Livingstone – went to Africa for self-aggrandizement and for whatever kudos they could attract by their adventures.

However, there is one man who shines like a beacon of enlightenment among the many who made the journey to the Nile from Europe. The Emperor Hadrian, who arrived in Alexandria some sixty years after the martyrdom of St Mark, may have played a minor role in Egyptian history, but he didn't treat the Egyptians as a colony of barbarians. On the contrary, he embraced many of their ideas and ended up worshipping some of their gods.

Before I left Cairo I had bought a copy of Forster's *Alexandria: A History and a Guide*, and I browsed through it in my hotel room. For Forster, the golden age of Alexandria was the time of the Ptolemies, that 'rare and fragile chain' which linked Alexander the Great, who founded the city, and Cleopatra, 'the last of a secluded and subtle race . . . a flower that Alexandria had taken three hundred years to produce and that eternity cannot wither'. He recounts, lovingly, the life of this 'voluptuous but watchful' queen, her affairs with Caesar and Mark Antony, and her eventual downfall. The Roman era (which lasted from 30 BC to AD 313) began inauspiciously with the arrival of Octavian, 'one of the most odious of the world's successful men'. Having devoted a long chunk to the Ptolemies, Forster disposes of the Romans in a page and a half, noting simply that things improved after Octavian's death and that the rule of imperial Rome brought happiness to the Mediterranean and to Alexandria for the next two hundred years.

In the early years of Roman rule, Alexandria was not a peaceful city. There were frequent battles between the Greeks and the Jews, and these were brought to the attention of Hadrian while he was in Britain directing the construction of the wall which carries his name. He sent the protagonists stiff letters of reproach, and for a while the trouble subsided.

Hadrian was a remarkable traveller, spending twelve of his twenty years as emperor visiting all corners of his vast empire. A few years after he left Britain he arrived by sea at Alexandria, accompanied by Antinous, the Greek boy who had been his constant companion for nine years and whom he loved more than his wife (not altogether surprisingly: she was a hard and unloving woman). She also came along on the trip.

Much of Hadrian's day-to-day life remains obscure but Marguerite Yourcenar, in her *Memoirs of Hadrian*, has decked the bare skeleton of historical and recorded knowledge with an imaginary flesh. She portrays Hadrian, disease-ridden and near death, reflecting from his villa outside Rome on his own life and that of the empire. He recalls his time in Egypt. In Alexandria he built nothing of note, but as always he was accompanied by architects and craftsmen, intellectuals and poets, a retinue capable of not only building cities but of injecting into their stones the poetic and religious foundations without which no great city could exist. Yourcenar's Hadrian spends his time in the empire's third city (the second was Antioch) visiting the sites with Antinous. He would have gone to the great lighthouse of Pharos, where the Fort of Kait Bey now stands, and he would have taken in the tombs of Alexander and Mark Antony. He would also have seen that famous obelisk, Cleopatra's Needle, which now stands beside the Thames, but which then stood, one of a pair, outside the Caesareum, the temple begun by Cleopatra as a tribute to Mark Antony, but which their vanquisher Octavian later appropriated for his own deification. And we can be sure that Hadrian visited that great centre of scholarship, the Mouseion. It had been established by the Ptolemies and those who had worked there included Euclid, the father of modern mathematics, and the great geographer Eratosthenes. Hadrian may have been a great soldier and adventurer; but he was also a lover of the arts and a noted scholar. He was the architect of magnificent buildings – some, like the Pantheon in Rome, survive to this day – and he was even said to fancy himself as a singer and flautist.

There were also the affairs of state to deal with in Alexandria, and squabbles to settle between Greeks and Jews. One of Hadrian's outstanding achievements was to retain peace in the empire, though he did treat the Jews appallingly. In Alexandria he sided with the Greeks, and while elsewhere he ordered the destruction of Jerusalem, in whose place he planned the erection of a city to be named after himself. After Hadrian left Alexandria he headed south up the Nile. The scenes along the banks today must be much as he found them – the vineyards hemmed in by groves of palm north of Minya; the plots of wheat, fruit and *berseem* surrounding mud villages; fat men on donkeys trotting past peasants working wood shadoofs on the water's edge; women beating clothes on the banks; and flocks of cattle egrets wheeling after the plough.

We do not know – and nor should it matter to us – whether Hadrian and Antinous were lovers. But it would be no exaggeration to say that Hadrian lived for Antinous. Whether Antinous died for

Hadrian is a moot point – some claim it was suicide – but just south of El Minya he drowned in the Nile. From the vantage point of today's modest and monotheist times, Hadrian's reaction to his friend's death seems extraordinary. He deified him and in his memory he founded the city of Antinoopolis. I didn't visit the site as nobody in Minya could tell me where it was. In any case, nothing of it remains today. A little over a century ago the ruins of the theatre, the triumphal arch and the colonnades were turned into cement or carted off to nearby towns to be used as building material. Hadrian left his mark on Egypt, but more importantly Egypt left her mark on him. It was the gods of the Nile, as much as any others, that held sway over him and the inhabitants of Rome, and on his return he constructed within his villa his own memorial to the Egyptians. Before the first stone of Antinoopolis was laid, Hadrian continued south to Thebes with Plotina, his dreadful wife.

About the time when the last stones of Antinoopolis were being filched, Amelia Edwards made her way up the Nile from Cairo to Wadi Halfa. Her adventures were recorded in her book, *A Thousand*

Miles up the Nile. She took a very dim view of El Minya, where she found large numbers of one-eyed people.

Not being a particularly well-favoured race, this defect added the last touch of repulsiveness to faces already sullen, ignorant and unfriendly. A more unprepossessing population I would never wish to see – the men half stealthy, half insolent; the women bold and fierce; the children filthy, sickly, stunted and stolid.

I liked the place. It had a pleasant atmosphere of sleepiness, it was passably clean, and the inhabitants seemed well fed and cheerful. During my brief period here I was not once asked for baksheesh or pestered by little boys, and in the villages along the Nile that is rare. I did, however, meet a bold woman.

After supper I went to the post office to make a call to Cairo. The man working the phones was besieged by a dozen prospective callers, and for ten minutes I hovered around on the edge of the scrum – orderly queuing is an anathema to the Egyptian – during which time my progress was away from the counter rather than towards it. Acknowledging defeat, I headed for the exit, but before I got there I was accosted by a girl in her mid-teens.

'Why are you leaving?' she asked in French.

I told her why.

'Come with me,' she said, and I followed her.

Young girls in Egypt seldom have the confidence (or perhaps the desire) to acquaint themselves openly with a European. This girl wore a tee-shirt and a pair of shorts, a combination most Egyptian mothers would consider immodest if not immoral. She was slim, leggy and quite stunning: almond eyes, aquiline nose, sharp chin, dimpled cheeks and wavy black hair. She asked me what number I wanted to call and wrote it on the inside of her wrist with a biro. She then proceeded towards the counter. Once into the crowd I followed her progress by the jerking of heads which belonged to bodies that had received a sharp nudge sideways. A couple of minutes later she reappeared and escorted me to a kiosk in which I waited for my call. Unfortunately, she was gone when I came out.

The next morning I missed the early train to Asyut and took the first one going south. It went so slowly and stopped so frequently that I got off at the first town of any size and waited for the next express. Here I had a curious meeting with the stationmaster, a handsome man with a silver moustache, immaculately dressed in a tweed jacket and cavalry twills. 'Perhaps you wish to come to my house,' he suggested after we had exchanged a few pleasantries. 'It is only an hour away.' He spoke good, though ponderous English. I thanked him and declined.

'I have many European youths in my house,' he continued. 'I have only one bed. A very small bed.'

I wandered off down the platform. It was a lovely day. The sky was blue and clear and small breezes eddied through the flowerbeds. The stationmaster followed me.

'What is your sexual position?' he asked.

'Heterosexual,' I replied. This answer pleased him enormously.

'Good!' he said. 'So you like boys.'

I said I didn't.

'Yes! Yes! Yes!' he chanted enthusiastically.

I proceeded to award myself a wife and three children, hoping this would finally convince him otherwise. He asked me the names, ages and genders of the children. I made them up. This seemed to satisfy him, and for the next ten minutes he told me of all the antiquities which I should visit. I affected a keener interest in archaeology than I have ever felt before or since.

'What did you say your children were called,' he asked, once he had dispensed with the monuments of Middle Egypt. I had forgotten.

'Aha!' he exclaimed excitedly, grabbing my hand. I withdrew it and left the station. My train wasn't due for another hour.

Fifty minutes later I returned. The stationmaster came over and produced some coins from his pocket: one from Iraq, another from Italy, and an old English florin. 'From my friends,' he explained. 'I have an album full of addresses of European boys. I have one friend from Hertfordshire in England. He lives in a village called Bananas. Do you know it?'

He wrote his address on a piece of paper as the train pulled in. 'Send me an English magazine from England,' he said.

'About sex?' I asked wearily.

'No! No!' He sounded aggrieved. 'About driving motor cars.'

I climbed on to the train and he waved goodbye. 'I help European boys so much,' he said as we pulled away. 'When they come to my house I cover them with kisses.'

Some time later – before Mallawi, I think – I fell asleep and I didn't wake up until we were well past Asyut. I got off at Qena.

Amelia Edwards's book about the Nile was a labour of love. She was here to see the temples and the artefacts of ancient Egypt, and her enjoyment derived from her discoveries rather than from what she saw of modern life, of which she seemed to disapprove. She was a prim and very proper English spinster, and I imagine she went among the villages and villagers with an expression of distaste fixed firmly on her face. She would have been shocked by Flaubert, who travelled up the Nile with the archaeologist Maxime du Camp in the 1850s. 'The Egyptian temples bore me profoundly,' he wrote in his notebook. 'Are they going to become like the churches in Brittany, the waterfalls in the Pyrenees?' Du Camp, who comes across as rather a tedious and pedantic man, noted Flaubert's apathy: 'He would have liked to travel, if he could, stretched out on a sofa and not stirring, watching landscapes, ruins and cities pass before him like the screen of a panorama mechanically unwinding.' Flaubert's interest in the country lay not so much in the dead, in whose honour so many temples had been built, but in the living. He noted that there were no good brothels left in Cairo (although he indulged in a little sodomy – 'Travelling as we are for educational purposes, and charged with a mission by the government, we have considered it our duty . . .'), but he found them virtually everywhere else, including Qena, where I had just arrived. He wandered through the whores' quarters, but he abstained – in order, he said, 'to preserve the sweet sadness of the scene and engrave it deeply on my memory'. This was out of character.

My stay was brief. I made a tour of the cheap hotels – five in all – and each was full. I decided to continue to Luxor and returned to the station. The next train was in three hours' time so I took a *hantur*, a horse-drawn cab, to the collective taxi rank. If you hang around the tourist traps in Egypt it's easy to think that these vehicles are just for the tourists. They aren't, and in many small villages they are the only means of public transport. The *hantur*'s two wheels reach to shoulder height and you sit across the axle on a small seat beneath a leather canopy shaped like a Victorian bonnet. The driver, who perches on a bench in front of you, wields a long leather whip with which he beats the horse, or, if the horse is lucky, its harness. Some *hanturs* are beautifully kept. Their brass footplates are polished, the upholstery is clean and the horses well cared for. Others have axles without wheel bearings, torn canopies, threadbare seats and horses so ill-treated that they can barely move the cart. Mine fell into the latter category.

It was late afternoon when our Peugeot pulled away from the taxi rank. The streets were all in dusty shadow, but the sky above was full of a glorious end-of-the-day luminosity.

CHAPTER SEVEN
LUXOR: DEATH AND DELUSION

On condition that we respect ruins,
that we do not rebuild them, that, after having
discovered their secret, we let them
be recovered by the ashes of centuries, the bones
of the dead, the rising mass of waste
which once was vegetation and races,
the eternal drapery of the foliage – their
destiny may stir our emotion. It is through them
that we touch the depths of our history . . .
Élie Fauré

It was past eight o'clock when we reached Luxor. There was a power cut and I felt my way into town along gutters and broken kerbs. The sky was black and the streets even blacker. In sunken doorways candles flickered and faces leered like Bosch ogres. There was a rich mix of medieval smells – of rotting vegetables and fresh orange juice, of burnt coffee and grilled lamb, of hashish and sandalwood, goats and donkeys, drains and the Nile. The streets were full of people laughing and cursing and shouting; and cyclists, with a wonderfully Egyptian disregard for safety, hissed like adders to warn of their approach. It was like walking through a shanty on the banks of the Styx; then all of a sudden the lights were switched back on and I found myself standing in the centre of town, gazing at the massive columns and giant statuary of Luxor temple.

I spent the night in a cheap hotel overlooking the station. I went to bed early under a filthy sheet on a filthy mattress and slept until four, when the muezzins woke me with their chant of 'Prayer is better than sleep! Prayer is better than sleep!' I dabbed cream on the night's flea bites.

96

In 1975 I had travelled with so little money – I tried to live on the equivalent of £2 a day – that I stayed in the worst and cheapest establishments, of which there was no shortage. I accepted fleas, bedbugs, poor food and sometimes thieves as part of the package. This time I had no wish – nor were there any financial reasons why I should – to accept the same discomforts. After an early breakfast I walked through the sprawling souk in search of another hotel. I looked in at three, and I chose the Venus, not because it possessed any advantages lacking in the other two, but because the sales patter of the manager was unusual, if not unique.

'The other day,' he announced as I made inquiries, 'I saw an old man in the street. He had shaggy grey hair and he was walking very slowly. I said to him: "Are you William Golding?" He said he was; so I invited him into the hotel and gave him a Coca-Cola.'

I asked how he recognized him. 'By his deep, deep voice,' he replied. 'Yes, a Nobel Prize winner came to drink Coca-Cola here in the Venus!' The hotel was Christian, clean and quiet, and my room had a fine view over a small square, where I could observe, day after day, without ever losing interest, the dramas of commerce, and, on one occasion, of death.

I was woken one morning by a tremendous hullabaloo. I threw open my shutters to see sixty or so women, all dressed in black and veiled, rushing through the square and wailing as though it was the end of the world, which it apparently had been for someone. I jumped into some clothes and rushed after them. They congregated outside a small mosque down a back alley. There was plenty of wailing still, and some sort of dirge was in progress. It was a later phase of a funeral whose beginnings I had witnessed the previous night. I had been sitting outside a café near the station around midnight when a solemn and silent procession of men, again numbering about sixty, passed through the main square. A battered and apparently much-used coffin was carried shoulder high and the pall-bearers changed every few minutes, presumably to let everyone have a go at carrying the deceased. The women's vigil the following day must have lasted some time, for having found where they had gone I went for breakfast and they were still carrying on outside the mosque when I returned an hour or so

later. By chance, I saw the coffin once more that evening. It was the men's turn again, but this time the atmosphere was very cheerful. Those following the coffin were cocky and jaunty, chattering away to one another, smoking cigarettes and greeting bystanders. I imagine the dead person was buried soon afterwards: it does not do to keep bodies around too long in a hot climate, and the midday temperature in Luxor was now in the upper nineties.

With me in the café was an English girl who proceeded, once the coffin had passed, to recount a peculiar story about a recent encounter which she had had with death. It had been near the pyramid of Sakkhara, which lies a little way upstream from Cairo. After she had looked over the pyramid, a tout asked her if she wanted to see a dead body. Such an offer is by no means extraordinary in Egypt, and tourists spend a good deal of their time inspecting mummies, or bits of them, and studying the designs of funerary shrouds or the forms of stuffed animals which accompanied the dead on their burial, and whose spirits possibly pursued them into the afterlife. The girl decided it would do no harm to see another dead body and she followed her guide down a ravine and behind a clump of bushes. And there, sure enough, was a dead body. 'It was a man,' explained the girl. 'I could make out all his features, though his eyes had gone – dried up or pecked out, I suppose.' Once she'd inspected the body the guide demanded some baksheesh.

Few other cultures have devoted as much time and energy to giving their dead a good send-off as did the ancient Egyptians. They built pyramids the size of small mountains and temples which dwarf the greatest of our cathedrals. Yet during the past couple of centuries the dead have been subjected to some dreadful treatment. The Victorian public may have been scandalized by the robbing of graves to supply corpses for dissection but they delighted in the tomb-robbing of Egypt. We even gave our archaeologists knighthoods rather than prison sentences. The finest mummies were shipped back to the museums of the West, where they still excite a macabre interest and gather dust; but many more were put to more practical uses – by, for example, I. Augustus Stanwood, the owner of an American papermill. During the civil war his Maine mill ran short of wood pulp and rags, the raw material needed to manufacture paper. The ancient Egyptians came to his rescue. He imported mummies from the Nile Valley, stripped them of their cloth (a good mummy yielded up to 30lbs of linen), and turned the cloth into paper. Several shiploads of mummies kept him in business until the war ended. Surprisingly, his main competition came not from arch- aeologists but from Egyptian Railways, who, for a ten-year period, used no other fuel than mummies.

Luxor's prosperity today owes everything to tourism, and the tourists come primarily to see the wealth of tombs and temples, many of which have only been unearthed since the beginning of this century. The temples are crowded with digging archaeologists, swarms of tourists, Coca-Cola sellers, guides, and urchins flogging fake scarabs and objects which may or may not be mummified flesh. But although tourism here has a history which stretches back to Roman times – when Hadrian visited the town his wife was said to have inscribed a poem on one of the Colossi of Memnon – it was only when Thomas Cook started his boat tours that the local people found their lives being rearranged to suit the foreigners.

Vivant Denon, the French artist who travelled up the Nile after the Napoleonic invasion of 1798, tried to enter the galleries of Luxor temple and was repelled by the ruin's inhabitants. Seventy years later, Amelia Edwards found the temple teeming with human life, its great walls towering over mud hovels and sheds of buffalo, camel and donkey – 'the sordid routine of Arab life', she called it. Shortly after her visit, the fellahin were bribed out of the temple or driven from it. A great pity! It has been reduced to a museum piece. Much finer if the peasantry had continued to breed, die, worship and trade among the columns, pylons and statues of gods and kings. I cannot believe that the inhabitants of these ruins were untouched by the great battles, the sacrifices to river gods and the kites and vultures and jackals depicted in the bas-reliefs which were their city walls. The living history of Luxor temple began with the pharaohs. It ended abruptly – having survived and adapted to the dynasty of the Ptolemies, the Roman conquest, and the supplanting of the river gods by Christianity and Islam (there is still a mosque within the walls) – with the evictions of the last century. But perhaps it is churlish to rail against the inevitable. Tourism is one of Egypt's biggest earners of foreign currency, and were it not for the 400,000 foreigners who visit Luxor every year the town would be much poorer.

On my first visit to Luxor, I did the 'stones trail'; that is, I hired a bike and made a tour of some of the temples. This time I set myself the task of visiting just one site, the Ramasseum. From the point of view of solitude, I chose the perfect time: two o'clock in the afternoon with the temperature nudging a hundred. I took the ferry across the river, climbed through a small village where I stopped for a cup of sweet mint tea, and trudged slowly west. For the first mile the road curled through fields of sugarcane and barley. The barley was just turning and within a month or so it would be harvested. Most of the sugarcane had been cut and neat bundles awaited carriage to the river beside a narrow-gauge rail track. I passed under the shade of an avenue of eucalyptus and spent what seemed an interminable time approaching the two Colossi of Memnon, whose great size made the peasants passing along the road beside them look like levantine Lilliputians. Once past these two great statues (originally they guarded Amenhotep III's temple, of which nothing remains now) the road bent sharply to the right and ran up towards the Valley of the Kings. I was sweating profusely when I reached the Ramasseum, where the only sign of life was the ticket collector, who was staring moodily at a dead dog which lay outside his cabin.

The object of my visit was not so much the temple, as the remains of a statue whose existence I had first learnt of when, along with twenty other ten-year-olds, I had been set the task of memorizing Shelley's *Ozymandias*.

> I met a traveller from an antique land
> Who said: 'Two vast and trunkless legs of stone
> Stand in the desert . . . Near them on the sand,
> Half sunk, a shattered visage lies, whose frown,
> And wrinkled lip, and sneer of cold command
> Tell that its sculptor well those passions read
> Which yet survive, stamped on these lifeless things,
> The hand that mocked them, and the heart that fed.
> And on the pedestal these words appear:
> "My name is Ozymandias, King of Kings:

Look on my works ye mighty and despair."
Nothing beside remains. Round the decay
Of that colossal wreck, boundless and bare,
The lone and level sands stretch far away.'

I asked the ticket collector to point out where the statue of
Ozymandias lay. He thought about it for a while, scratched his
head, and announced: 'No smoking please.' I found the statue without too much effort, and I was particularly taken by Ozymandias's
granite feet, which were neat, of pinkish hue and rather effeminate,
with long slender toes. His body had fallen over into the temple
behind but it was impossible to make out the features of the face.
The Ozymandias of Shelley's poem was considerably more impressive than the real thing. The ticket attendant was still contemplating the dead dog when I left.

I fell into a very pleasant and idle routine while in Luxor, winding
down from the weeks in Cairo and gently preparing myself for
the rigours which lay ahead in Sudan. I didn't look at any more
temples (with the exception of Luxor temple, which stood conspicuously in the town centre) and on most days I did little more than
read a book or take short walks in the countryside across the river.
These I particularly enjoyed, and I would watch the peasants scything sugarcane, or moving their goats along the mud lanes. Often I
came across young children of no more than five or six years old
skilfully herding flocks of sheep. Otherwise I spent much of my time
in cafés, chatting, drinking, smoking *shishas* and watching games
of backgammon.

There were four cafés in the small square outside the station, and
on my first visit, back in 1975, I stayed in a hotel above one of
them. The café was still there now, but it had changed beyond all
recognition. The New Karnak used to be a lively, disorganized place
full of Egyptians in jellabas. It spilled out into the street, and men
would drift in from the markets, or the fields, or the station, sometimes on foot, sometimes on donkeys. It was earthy and unpre-
tentious, and when one night a female donkey, chased by a sturdy
male, charged through, upsetting tables, waiters and customers,

nobody seemed in the least surprised. In the evenings the travellers going south to Sudan would meet here, but they were few compared to the locals. Now the New Karnak was exclusively the domain of young tourists. The food was Western, the tables were clean, the waiters spoke English, and most of the tourists were on two- or three-week holidays. Even the square outside had been given a clean-up, and the *hanturs* which waited by the station were pulled by horses which looked much healthier and better fed than they used to be.

It was in the New Karnak that I first met Jacques, an individual whom I remember from 1975 with a slightly perverse affection. He had a broad, beaten-about face and a nose which had been broken in a couple of places. His eyes were humorous and clear blue, and his hair blond and curly. He had left France a few months earlier and, like me, he was heading for Ethiopia. When I asked him where he came from, he replied, with admirable simplicity, 'from the slums of Paris'. Over the next couple of months I bumped into him several times – in Khartoum, on the Ethiopian border, and in Gondar. I was always pleased to see him, though the stories I heard about him from other travellers were not encouraging. He had next to no money, and it was claimed, with some justification probably, that he kept himself going by stealing from other travellers. He wasn't particular about where he slept or what he ate or how he travelled, as long as it didn't cost him much. The last time I saw him was in a whore house in Ethiopia. He had his arm round a girl and he was getting drunk. As usual he was garrulous and charming. We spent the evening together, and a week or so later, when I arrived in Addis Ababa, I asked around to see if he was there. Someone said he had been and gone, having stayed just long enough to steal some money from two Americans. Apparently he had headed for Djibouti, from where he intended to take a boat to India.

Sometimes Jacques was accompanied by another man from Paris, a particularly nasty piece of work – dishonest, lecherous and foul-mouthed. I did my best to keep clear of him, but once I had the misfortune to ride on the same lorry in northern Ethiopia. It was a long journey and we broke the trip in a small village where the choice of accommodation was limited to one hotel and one brothel. We chose the brothel. The lady who ran it brought us a bottle of *tej*, a yellow wine made from honey, and then lined up six whores for our inspection. The youngest was in her teens, sad-eyed and delicate. I think her price tag was the equivalent of about £2. The brothel-keeper progressed down the line until she reached an ancient female with few teeth, not much hair and a large amount of blubbery flesh. Her price was about 20p. I'd seen enough of Jacques's friend not to be surprised when he took her.

The other traveller whom I first met at the New Karnak, and whom I still recall vividly, was a New Zealander. He was an exceptionally boring individual, but symptomatic of the times. He had been travelling for seven years, and he had covered Asia, both Americas, Europe and most of Africa. He had returned once to New Zealand and tried to settle down, but without success. He travelled simply because he felt compelled to keep moving, and whenever I saw him he expressed little interest in where he was. The last time I met him he was in Addis. 'I've got $7,000 on me,' he moaned. 'I could fly to Peru tomorrow, or Goa, or Alaska. But what for? I don't want to be here; and I don't want to be there.' He had lived through the era of the great hippy trails, when all roads led to the East, to the mystics and the dope havens; and he'd taken a long time to discover that you couldn't just hitchhike to paradise.

I think many of the long-term travellers of that time suffered from excruciating boredom. They were bored not only by what they saw, but with themselves. Some, like the New Zealander, had set out with the naïve belief that somewhere they would find their promised land. They had cobbled together, from what they had read and seen, a system of ideas and ideals which they mistook for a philosophy, and which they could explain only by recourse to a sort of hippy jargon. There was much talk of freedom and anarchy, but few knew what either meant, confusing spiritual freedom with physical motion, and anarchy with the renunciation of responsibility to others. The road had not only spawned its own jargon, but its own literature. The guidebooks were written not by Michelin but by Miller, Kerouak, Burroughs and Wolfe; and you'd meet people who talked about Buddha and Zen and nirvana as though they were some sort of beneficial medicine, to be swallowed twice daily like cod-liver oil. The New Zealander claimed that he was escaping from the society in which he had been raised. It didn't seem to occur to him that he might be escaping from himself, or trying to. Not that we should denigrate him for that. Men like Rimbaud and Gauguin and Lawrence did just the same. And what did they find? Cancer, syphilis and the white plague, according to Henry Miller: 'No desert isles. No paradise. Not even relative happiness.'

One supposition about travel which is commonly held to be true is that it broadens the mind. I saw little evidence for this, either in myself or others. Indeed, the conversations most frequently to be had were to do with money. Where was the cheapest hotel in Nairobi? How much were the whores in Mombasa? How little could you live on in Sudan? What's the black-market rate in Aswan? Parsimony, not paradise, was our real obsession.

Despite all this, I found myself looking back to those times with some nostalgia when I visited the New Karnak in 1984. And what I missed most was the air of waywardness that attached to so many of those who were wandering around a decade before. The New Karnak was packed every night with youngish tourists. The vast majority were away from home for just a few weeks. All were reasonably well-shod, and all seemed well-informed about where they had been and where they were going. Most of them were extremely sensible and rather serious.

So far I'd only met three people who had been away for any length of time. There were two Swiss brothers – a bricklayer and a typesetter – who had taken six months to get from Switzerland to Luxor and were heading for India. They remarked on how few people they had met who were away for more than a short time. The other traveller was a most laconic character, a thin-faced and droopy-moustached American. Over a beer by the river he produced from his shoulderbag a postcard which was covered with hairline cracks and frayed around the edges. It looked as though it had been ironed a few times. It was a picture of a small town, built on a grid pattern and surrounded by steep mountains whose tips were covered with snow. 'Silvertown, Colorado,' he explained. 'That's where I live. A little Victorian mining town, 9,000 feet up in the Rockies. Very quiet place.' He was a gold assessor in the town's small mine, and it was difficult to tell whether he loved the place or hated it. Apparently it was a wonderful place for skiing and fishing. 'But,' he reflected wistfully, 'it's no good for women or growing vegetables.' All the same, I think he missed it, and there was something about him that reminded me of myself and many others I had met the first time. He simply couldn't decide whether he was going to carry on travelling because he wanted to, or because he felt it to be his duty.

It was while I was in Upper Egypt that Eric Parry turned up. He had already spent a week in Cairo, dividing his time between sketching the city and trying to get a visa from the Sudanese Embassy. Although he was armed with letters from his bank, from the British Consul and from a Cambridge professor confirming that he was (a) financially solvent, (b) British and of sound character, and (c) going to Sudan for professional reasons (which meant illustrating this book) the Embassy had so far refused to give him a visa. They hadn't said they weren't going to give him one; but neither had they said they were. In fact, their behaviour was entirely consistent with everything I knew about Sudanese bureaucracy. Eric had broken off negotiations to keep our rendezvous. We spent an evening together in Luxor and Eric sketched in the cafés. He was particularly impressed by one with a television. It was rather like a small cinema. The lights were turned off, and wooden seats were arranged in straight rows. He decided to give the Embassy one more try, and he took the night train back to Cairo. We arranged to meet three days later, and I filled in the time by taking a short holiday beside the seaside.

CHAPTER EIGHT
A SPAGHETTI TOWN

*A man-made jewel in the tropical paradise
of the Red Sea, one of nature's
last unspoiled fairylands . . . The fragrant,
unpolluted air and transparent gem-blue waters
set the tone . . .*
The Hurghada Sheraton on itself

Anna toyed unenthusiastically with dry chunks of overcooked barracuda, pushing them back and forth across a plate of stodgy rice. She stared disconsolately down the scruffy street outside the café, downed her fork and pushed the plate of food away. 'Hurghada is like spaghetti without the sauce,' she groaned. 'No meat. No peperoni. No tomatoes. Nothing! It's just a plain spaghetti town!'

Anna was a tall Italian brunette with large brown eyes and a sensual mouth. The mouth had been trained to sing opera; but it didn't like it, so now it made a living in a rock band. It was on a fortnight's holiday in Egypt. It asked me if I'd found the beach. I said I hadn't.

'Well, it won't be a proper beach,' announced Anna with admirable prescience. She turned to the café owner, a large, surly man much given to praising his cuisine, which was dreadful, and Hurghada, a miserable gathering of shacks and tourist chalets beside the Red Sea – it looked as though some architects had been playing Lego with breeze blocks. 'What's the use of a beach without palm trees?' asked Anna.

The café owner shrugged: 'Ees bootiful place, Hurghada.' Anna shook her head.

The bus from Luxor had taken four hours to cross the Eastern Desert. We had hit the copper-sulphate-blue Red Sea at Safaga, a long, thin industrial settlement dominated by an enormous phosphate works. Hills like lumps of dead coral hung over the town. We dropped a few passengers off there and headed north, past Magawash tourist village, whose barbed-wire perimeter gave it a jackboot-and-doberman ambience, past the Hurghada Sheraton and a smattering of offshore oil rigs, and into Hurghada. The bus driver stopped on the outskirts and a man climbed on board.

'My hotel is best hotel in Hurghada,' he announced, motioning to a grim concrete building beside the road. It was called Hotel Cleopatra. The five Europeans declined his offer of rooms. The bus continued, and five minutes later we arrived in a dusty and rutted square. A maroon dusk had settled over the hills behind. Like the rest of the town it looked like an abandoned building site: none of the houses rose more than one storey from the sand, but nearly all sprouted reinforced concrete pillars awaiting the next.

I got off the bus and watched the reactions of the others. I had imagined a little tropical paradise: a whitewashed Arab village clinging to steep russet cliffs; dhows gliding round coral atolls; waving palms; jetties piled high with cinnamon from Madagascar and cloves from Zanzibar. I think my four companions had been thinking along similar lines.

Anna came over to me. 'What happens on the road further north?' she asked.

I looked at my map. 'There's Zafarana,' I said, adding that it was a hundred and fifty miles north. I described the Paradise of the Desert, the army blocks and the dogs. I told her I didn't think there was anywhere to stay.

'Maybe I'll go to Suez,' she said. She lapsed into Italian for the benefit of her girlfriend, Assunta, who could speak French, but no English, then flagged down a passing taxi and asked the driver if he was going to Suez. He thought it was a bad joke. I was glad he didn't take her. I picked up her bag and the five of us – the two Italian girls, a heavily tattooed Englishman, Alan, his lightly tattooed Dutch girlfriend, Mirjam, and me – set off in search of a hotel. Before we left the square, a thin and rather handsome young man accosted us. He spoke perfect English and very passable Italian. He claimed to have a bungalow by the beach and we followed him.

The bungalow had three bedrooms, a kitchen and a WC that didn't work. There was a German couple in one room. The man had dysentery. In another room there were two English girls. We were shown into the third room. It had three beds. We said we needed five. Alan and Mirjam were taken into a bungalow next door. The Italian girls said they'd risk sharing a room with me.

I spent twenty minutes searching for the beach, but I never found it, and I met up with Anna and the other three in the café which our solicitous landlord claimed to be the best in town. He had come along too, though I noticed he didn't risk eating anything. There were no Egyptians eating there, only young foreigners. After we'd paid for the meal we hunted the back streets for an Arab café. We soon found one and over strong coffee Anna gave a fine parody of a muezzin calling the faithful to prayer. It sounded like a chorus of lecherous tom-cats and went down badly with the other customers.

It was just before midnight when we went to bed. Our early evening despair had been transformed into a curious state of euphoria. The five of us had made an unspoken pact, or so it seemed, that we would enjoy our short stay in Hurghada. I think every one of us would have left first thing in the morning had we not met each other.

In the few hours between our arrival and our going to bed, the girls, despite the presence of Alan and myself, had already been subjected to some blatant sexual harassment. The café owner had done his best to chat up both Anna and Assunta, and our landlord had performed an obsequious prelude to the overture which he was composing to ensnare Anna, and which was to gain tempo over the coming days. I climbed into bed fully aware that I was obliged to act decently, despite inclinations to the contrary. I fervently hoped I wasn't going to snore, but that proved the least of my problems. Around two o'clock I needed to relieve myself. I stole quietly out of bed and gently turned the door handle, which came away in my hand. I rattled the door but it stayed shut. The windows were covered with mosquito mesh, so there was no way out there. I decided that I would have to hold on until morning. This proved impossible. Anna awoke at three o'clock to find a naked man removing various instruments of destruction from his bag: a knife with a long curved blade, a kitchen fork and a tin-opener. Much to her credit, she didn't suspect the worst, and together we attacked the door. Afterwards we couldn't close it.

The Egyptian government has great hopes of attracting tourists to the Red Sea. The coral reefs – which I didn't see – are reputed to be particularly fine, and they are the main attraction for visitors to Hurghada and the coast. Hurghada, however, has absolutely nothing else to recommend it. There is not one building of the slightest interest, and there are no monuments or temples. It is drab, stark and ugly. There wasn't even a decent souk, or a single street which one could happily stroll down. When I think of Egypt, I think with my nose as much as with my eyes and my ears. It is a wonderfully smelly country. One's nose is continually twitching. Cairo smells, Luxor smells, Qena smells, everywhere along the Nile smells. But Hurghada was as bereft of odours as it was of trees (we never saw a single one). Nor could I eulogize about the sea here. Certainly it was a marvellous colour. It was warm to swim in. It was cleanish. But the real beauty of a sea is a reflection of the land which backs into it. The landscape south of Hurghada was tedious in the extreme.

Early on our first morning we hired bikes and cycled out of town. After a few miles we passed a small tourist village called Moon Valley, which I had failed to notice on the bus ride in the previous evening. In the hills behind it anti-aircraft guns faced Israel and the north-east. We rode past the Sheraton and half a mile later we pushed our bikes down to the sea. We spent the best part of the day here, occasionally flopping into the water to cool off; otherwise chatting and eating sandwiches of cucumber, processed cheese, chili and sand.

I took a what-I-did-on-my-holidays photograph. It has a surreal quality to it. The sand lay not flat and golden, as it would have had there been tides to sweep it twice daily, but rutted and dimpled, like a carelessly iced Christmas cake. My four companions made up the foreground. On the left, Mirjam, bronze and blonde, and austerely pretty in a sparse bikini. Beside her, Alan. He was sprawled on a white towel in a pair of denim shorts. ('Been wearing denim for twenty years,' he confided *à propos* of nothing that evening. 'Can't see myself ever changing.') I liked him. He was an ex-hippy in his late thirties, and good-looking in a rough, stubbly way. He had lived in Holland for the past five years and kept himself going by doing odd jobs. He and Mirjam had spent the winter working on farms in Israel, and they were leaving Egypt soon to find fruit-picking jobs in Crete. He was carefree in a way which many say they are but aren't, and I found his complete lack of ambition – in terms of work or material gain – thoroughly refreshing. Assunta sat on his left, swathed in a small towel. She was a small, rotund girl with a delicate face encased in straight fair hair. By trade she was a professional photographer, but her camera remained idle in Hurghada. Anna, almost a foot taller, and an Identikit of what an Englishman (or I, at any rate) imagines an Italian woman should look like, had her chin resting on jack-knifed knees. The foreground is completed by a couple of shoulderbags, some discarded clothes and shoes, two bottles of mineral water and some abandoned rounds of bread.

Four bikes stand in the sand behind the sunbathers, and beyond them two cars are traversing the middle distance, drawing the viewer's eyes off to the right of the celluloid and towards Hurghada. They are driving over the sand. A hundred yards or so behind them there is a thin strip of tarmac with two lamp-posts and no traffic. Behind the road low and irregular hills nudge the skyline. By any standards, it is a dreadful photograph: the composition is awful, there are no shadows, the sky is under-exposed and the faces are over-exposed. But it does capture the scruffiness of the desert. Even if the human flesh were removed, along with their belongings and the bikes, and if the cars had passed out of the photo, it would still look a mess. And there would still be nothing to tell you that this was Egypt, not Algeria or Mauritania or any other country with desert.

So we ignored the landscape and chattered our way through five hours. It was no-man's-land chatter, the sort which strangers have when they meet, briefly, in strange settings, and then only if they like one another; every now and then somebody exposing a little and very personal bit of their past or present, like a careless poker player exposing his hand, but, unlike the poker player, knowing that he or she would move on before the hand was played out. Sometimes you just caught sight of an ace and you guessed at the rest; occasionally you'd glimpse a royal flush. Then the hairs on the back of your neck would quiver and you'd nudge yourself a little closer to the edge, exposing the Achilles heel, just for the hell of it, knowing that the only rule in this particular game was not to shoot. But most of all it was nice to be in the company of women again (it is that, much more than home, that most travelling men crave) but I was not alone in thinking so, even here on the lonely beaches of the Red Sea. The sun was already falling behind us –I suppose it was about 3.30 – when a car pulled up a hundred yards away from where we were. Out of it came three men, early middle-aged, slightly obese, and wearing Western clothes of such nondescript design that one might have mistaken them for government-supplied uniforms. Their shirts were off-grey and open-necked, their sandals were sand brown and plastic, and their ill-fitting trousers, when viewed from the rear, gave the occupants the dry, folded appearance which lends a certain charm to the backside of an elephant but none to that of a man.

They left the car and strolled down to the sea's edge, coming to within fifty yards of us before sitting down. One of them waved to us.

Assunta shuddered. *'Ils sont laids, les mecs d'ici.'* (They are ugly, the men here.) Anna agreed, though she said that she'd found the men of upper Egypt, of Aswan and Luxor, very fine.

The men stood up after five minutes or so and walked towards us, rearranging themselves on the sand again less than twenty yards away. Each lay with his head propped on an elbow. A white rose behind the ear, and a cat at the feet, and they could have been modelling for Manet's 'Olympia'. They were absolutely guileless. They never took their eyes off the girls and whenever we looked in their direction they smiled and waved back in the most cheery manner. One of them even took a short tour in order to inspect the girls better. As he passed a few feet in front of us his eyes flickered unrestrainedly from one bit of female anatomy to another. The girls reacted by shrouding themselves in towels. It was obvious that the men had no intention of leaving as long as we remained. They watched us gather together our stuff. Anna attempted to remove her bikini and get dressed without revealing too much of herself. Alan and I offered to do what rugby players do when one of their number is forced to change his shorts on the field – that is, to make a circle and protect the changer from the eyes of the crowd – but she declined, preferring to put on a tee-shirt and trousers over her wet swimwear. The three men waved as the peepshow left.

When we reached the Sheraton Hotel Anna went in ahead to ask if we could go in for tea. The rest of us – sunburnt, scruffy and ragged from a day in the open – hid behind some bushes. She returned to say we could. We dumped our bikes, went through reception and sat on some plastic garden furniture by a small fountain.

Alan announced that it wasn't his sort of place and a waitress made it very obvious that we weren't her sort of people. She observed Alan's prodigiously tattooed arms with an expression of horror and she evidently felt little attraction for Mirjam, whose hair style was rather more punk than she could have been used to, and whose single tattoo winked provocatively at the scattering of wealthy tourists.

The Sheraton was a monstrously ugly six-storey building, round and hollow, like a futuristic sea squirt set in concrete. We sat in its atrium – appropriately, as it is in the atrium that the sea squirt digests its food – and after a quarter of an hour the waitress deigned to serve us. Assunta ordered an ice-cream and the rest of us tea. It took a long time coming. The waitress set the ice-cream, a multi-coloured affair about five inches high, in front of Assunta with no more delicacy than a farmer placing a bucket of swill before a pig. There was a brown hair, no bigger than a flee, attached to a strawberry-flavoured ball. Before Assunta had time to lift a spoon, Anna summoned the waitress. She pointed at the hair. After a while the waitress found it. The manager was called.

'Hair in the ice-cream,' announced Anna.

The manager's lips twitched. 'I'll get you another one,' he said reluctantly.

'Don't bother,' said Anna curtly. 'We wouldn't dream of eating here.' Malevolent stares followed us out of the hotel and into the sunlight. We had to search for our bikes, which had been hidden away behind some dustbins, presumably because the management thought they lowered the tone of the hotel.

Back in Hurghada we found a shabby café full of jellaba-ed men and loud music. A great favourite of the Egyptians (and of mine), Oum Koulsoum, was singing what sounded like a tortured love song. We drank two cups of tea.

'What's the damage, John?' said Alan to the waiter before we left.

The damage was 10 piastres a cup. (At the Hurghada Sheraton, £E4 a pot.)

It was dark when we reached our bungalow, and the water was off, so Anna and I went next door for a shower. Alan's landlord was incensed when he found out. He asked us to pay him £E2 each, which was double what we were paying for a night. He explained that all Hurghada's water had to be pumped a hundred miles across the desert from Qena in the Nile Valley. The taps from Qena were only turned on twice a week or so, he claimed. He stuck out his hand to receive our money. We didn't intend to give him any, and our resolve was hardened when Mirjam recounted how he had burst into her room without knocking when she was half-naked. He hadn't bothered to retreat. 'He just stood gawping,' she said. We didn't give him any money.

That evening Anna, Assunta, Alan and Mirjam arranged to take a boat the next day to the coral reef. I couldn't accompany them as I had agreed to meet Eric back at the Venus in Luxor. Our landlord offered to take Anna to buy a bus ticket to Cairo, where she was going to in a couple of days. She was away two hours and she returned in a rage. His overtures had not been welcome.

The following morning Anna and I went round to fetch Alan and Mirjam for breakfast. I waited outside the bungalow. Anna sauntered in, then shot out with all the urgency of a rabbit flushed from its burrow by a ferret. The landlord had shoved her against a wall and tried to kiss her. We returned together.

'Get out!' shouted the landlord. 'You're in the way here.'

After I had breakfasted and said goodbye to the others, I went to catch the morning bus back to Luxor. Alan's landlord was waiting too. When the bus arrived he pounced on six young tourists. I joined them and suggested they found somewhere else to stay.

They asked me why, and I told them how he treated female visitors. They left me and the landlord staring at one another. He spat on the ground, shrugged his shoulders and wandered home to his wife and three children.

I climbed on to the bus. It headed south, away from the spaghetti town, past the oil rigs, past the Sheraton, and on to Safaga, where we picked up a couple of passengers before veering away from the sea and into the desert. Six months later, on a cool and drizzly afternoon, I met Anna in London. She said the coral reef was lovely.

The great thing about deserts is that they encourage cerebral activity. Here, where nature celebrates dreadful monotony, there is little else to do but lead the life of contemplation. St Anthony, marooned in the sands of the Eastern Desert, was perfectly placed to consider God, the Devil and eternity, three subjects upon which I didn't dwell during the long, hot and tedious crossing from the Red Sea to Qena. Instead I thought about women.

My reaction to the lounging lechers on the beach at Hurghada was one of disgust. But if I put myself in their sandals, would I have behaved much differently? I hoped so, but I couldn't be absolutely sure. The social mores governing sexual relations in Egypt are of such strictness that many single people suffer from frustration. I was frequently told as much. For young Egyptian men who see little more of their women than the face or a tantalizing calf, the sight of a scantily clad European girl is one which can only excite lust.

I was often accosted by teenagers who pestered me with questions about girlfriends. They invariably assumed that all European girls were harlots; that they were fruit ripe for picking if they happened along. When I arrived back in Luxor I went to sit by the river. I hadn't been there long when three boys in their mid-teens came to sit with me. I was reading Trollope and I was much too engrossed by the goings-on in an English vicarage to want a prurient conversation about sex. But that was what I got. Realizing I was to get no peace, I decided, having parried half a dozen crude questions, to go on the offensive. I asked them some questions about sex. Their knowledge was pitiful and their bravado soon vanished.

They stood up sheepishly and left. It was nice to get back to *Barchester Towers* and the very unpromiscuous Miss Eleanor Bold.

However, if there is any worrying to be done about the female condition, we should be directing it towards the indigenous population rather than to those few foreigners who are subject to harassment. 'In Egypt,' says a government publication, 'female emancipation is no longer an issue.' This is nonsense. I am well aware that spending a couple of months in the country does not make me an expert on the subject. I only encountered one Egyptian woman who talked frankly about female emancipation, or the lack of it, and that was after I had left. And most men, when asked about the status of women, were evasive. There were, however, the odd exceptions, the most illuminating being a Nubian man who lived in Aswan and who had travelled widely in other Arab countries and in the West. I asked him about 'honour killings', the practice whereby adulterers are punished by husbands or brothers.

'Of course, they still happen,' he replied. 'If a man finds that he's married a woman who isn't a virgin, or if she sleeps with another man after their marriage, he will kill her. And he won't be locked away for doing so. He'll go to the police and say: "She was a wicked woman." Maybe he'll get a £E20 fine.' Such killings, he claimed, occur frequently in Upper Egypt, particularly among the peasantry. He added that adulteresses bring shame upon the whole family, and after the event their close relatives often feel forced to move from the village where they are known to another far away.

On the positive side, Egyptian women have fared slightly better, particularly since the 1952 revolution, than those of many other Arab countries. During the two decades after the revolution the number of women at university rose from 8 per cent of the total to 28 per cent, which compared with 19 per cent for Syria and 8 per cent for Saudi Arabia. However, 80 per cent of Egyptian women, compared to 60 per cent of men, are still illiterate; and the few emancipated women there are belong to a small urban élite. Once you get outside Cairo and Alexandria you seldom see women sitting in cafés; most are confined to the home or taken up with chores like fetching water, bearing children, or working the fields (four fifths of Africa's agricultural labour force are women). And the state does not take kindly to those who champion women's rights. One woman who gained fame in Europe and notoriety at home was Nawal El Saadawi, an Egyptian doctor and writer. In 1974 she met a prostitute awaiting execution in Qanitar prison. One of her novels, *Women at Point Zero*, explored the fate of this prostitute, whose crime had been to kill a pimp. In 1981 Sadat had Sadaawi imprisoned as a subversive, and the book is still banned in Egypt.

In the year or so which I have spent in Africa I have not once heard the subject of female circumcision mentioned by Africans. Yet it is practised in over twenty countries, and nearly all the women in northern Sudan and southern Egypt are circumcised. It is difficult to think of a more barbaric custom. Three main types of mutilation are carried out: the one properly referred to as circumcision, where the hood of the clitoris is removed; excision, which involves the cutting out of the clitoris and all or some of the labia minora; and infibulation, the removal of the clitoris, the labia minora and most or all of the labia majora. Infibulation is the method most widely practised in Egypt and Sudan, and the operation is carried out on girls up to the age of seven. After the mutilation the vagina is sewn up, leaving a small fissure for menstruation and urination. Needless to say, the scar tissue must be broken before the girl can have sex. The reasons given for mutilation are many. Some Muslims see it as a religious custom sanctioned by the Koran, although others have told me that there is nothing in the Koran advocating or condoning it. But it is also practised by Copts, Catholics, Protestants and pagans, and the custom of infibulation may well have originated among the ancient Egyptians. The practice is also sanctioned on grounds of beauty and cleanliness, and in Egypt uncircumcised girls are referred to as *nigsa*, which means unclean. And, of course, infibulation acts as an inbuilt chastity belt: in countries like Egypt and Sudan premarital virginity is of enormous importance. It is said that many members of the educated classes wish to see the practice of mutilation brought to an end. But it is also pointed out that as it is a practice carried out by women on women, its eradication will not be easily accomplished. I raised the topic with one man, a government civil servant, who told me curtly, 'If it is a problem, it is our problem, not yours. You should mind your own business.' I don't see why. In the West we make a tremendous fuss about torture – and quite rightly – but we remain almost silent about the mutilation of women in Africa. One organization which has devoted time to the issue is the Minority Rights Group, whose sensitive study highlights the difficulty of getting people to jettison customs and traditions to which they have adhered for centuries. It quotes a *daya* (a birth attendant) from the Delta.

Once I learned I was going to be circumcised [she was seven at the time] I was filled with fear and ran as fast as my legs could carry me. Soon the assistant of the operator caught up with me . . . The assistant caught hold of me, stretched my legs apart and the operator sterilized the area with oven ashes and alcohol, and cut off the pieces with a razor. She cut off the tip of the clitoris and the two leaves. Of course I screamed from the pain, but soon the pain disappeared . . . We can't afford being different. We found our mothers circumcised; we learnt that our grandmothers and great-grandmothers had been circumcised, and we have to carry the tradition to our children and grandchildren. We can't think of anyone who is not circumcised. Once a man divorced his wife as soon as he discovered that, out of negligence, one of her two leaves was not cut off. This man told his wife: 'What have I married? A man or a woman?' News of the incident was propagated, and the woman did not know where to hide because of the scandal.

I had hoped to write something intelligent, or at least sensible, about the condition under which women must live in Egypt. I find I can't, and though the reasons for this may be several, the main one is ignorance. One gets a glimmer of what is happening – old women, gnarled and bent, slowly returning to their homes with huge jars of water balanced on their heads; the canal banks lined with women (never men) laboriously scrubbing their washing; women, still in their twenties, already haggard and weary with childbirth – but virtually everything I know about how women are treated in their homes, about circumcision and so on, is derivative.

CHAPTER NINE
THE NILE BESTIARY

You can sail the winding stretch of river between Luxor and Aswan in three or four days. Or you can take a taxi, which covers the distance in three or four hours. You can even take the train, but it is slightly slower than a taxi, considerably less interesting and only marginally cheaper if you travel second class. I visited Isna, Idfu, Kom Ombo and Daraw, the main towns along the river here, several times and always by collective taxi. Having failed to get a story about perfumes, I resolved to write a piece about camels, and I began my investigations at Isna. The State Information Bureau at Luxor had suggested that I would find camel markets both there and at Daraw, and I set off from Luxor at five o'clock one morning. It took an hour to get to Isna, where I sat by the river and ate some breakfast.

The air was cool, and every few minutes a puff of wind would ruffle the Nile, which creased for a few seconds like a slept-in sheet before the stillness ironed it out again. The Nile is always loveliest at dawn, the sun risen but hidden still behind the barren and shadowed hills, her waters glass, reflections of palms soft green and beige. On the far bank there were feluccas at half-mast and men on donkeys twisting along a path at the water's edge. It was very quiet over there: even the hoopoes and hooded crow were discreet. I sat by the river till the sun broke clear of the hills in front of me and the somnolence of dawn evaporated. I drifted into town, drank a coffee in a small café and smoked a *shisha* with a turbaned teacher. The back streets were unpaved, narrow and lined with mud houses. Behind Isna temple seven long-horned cattle chewed *berseem* in a small shack, and square-eyed, long-haired goats prowled the alleys in search of food. A couple of small boys followed me everywhere, whining for baksheesh and biros (which struck me as an odd demand), and I passed a small workshop where men and boys sat crosslegged constructing fruit boxes out of the ribs of palm leaves. I asked around for the camel market, but I couldn't make myself understood, and the only camels I saw all morning were two beasts which swayed by a café where I was sharing lunch – goat, I think – with three men who had invited me to join them. The camels were impressively decorated. One had its whole flank striped vertically with red lines and horizontally with green ones, as though marked out for a giant game of noughts and crosses. The other had a neat crucifix branded on its neck. Perhaps it was a Coptic camel. (As it happened, these two creatures were working camels. They were not for eating. I never discovered whether modern Copts eat camel, but if they do, it is a recent addition to their diet. 'Camel's flesh they consider unlawful,' wrote the drole Edward Lane, 'probably for no better reason than that of its being eaten by the Muslims.')

After lunch I crossed Isna barrage, and I very nearly caught a fish. A young boy had half a dozen lines trailing in the white water which streamed through the barrage. He was using Coca-Cola tins as reels, and as I passed him he was busy pulling in a small fish. Another reel began to twitch and he signalled to me to pull the fish in. I lost it. Once across the river I went into the station and inquired after the camels. The stationmaster invited me into his office and sent a boy out to fetch some tea. He couldn't understand why I was interested in camels, and instead he explained to me the pleasures of travelling third class. For one thing it was cheap: a ticket from Aswan to Cairo, a distance of over five hundred miles, cost only £E1.80. And for another, 'you'll never run out of people to talk to'.

We returned, after our appraisal of third class, to the subject of camels. If I hung around for a while, said the stationmaster, I would see the camel train. I left the station and walked south, past a police roadblock towards a bridge which crossed a small canal. There were twenty camels there. Most were sitting chewing the cud and looking, as camels always do, very haughty. Five Sudani camel-herders squatted beside them. I tried to talk to them but all I understood was that they were from Darfur, the Sudanese province a thousand miles to the south-west, bordering on Chad. A little later a herd of a hundred or more camels came charging across the barrage towards the station. Three Sudani herders, magnificent in their white robes, led at a fast trot. At the rear three others followed on foot. They carried long leather whips with which they mercilessly beat the stragglers. Then in their wake came a cloud of dust and a queue of cars, whose drivers honked their horns and revved their motors, almost drowning the clatter of camels' hooves on the tarmac. The beasts' long necks swayed back and forth, like inter-twining elvers pushing against a current, and the solid mass of their flanks quivered above a mirage of shimmering legs. They shot across the main road and into a loading bay. A train pulled up and the animals were goaded on to it. They were bound for Cairo and the slaughterhouse.

There is good money in the camel business, though the men who do best are not the camel-herders who drive the animals for forty or more days from Sudan up to Isna and Daraw, but the middle-men, the camel-brokers who operate out of the business quarters of Cairo and Khartoum. Once the camel reaches the Imbaba market in the western suburbs of Cairo, it fetches anywhere between $500 and $1,000. However, it has a one in ten chance of dying of thirst or exhaustion on its way through the Nubian desert. Intriguingly, the boom in the Sudanese camel trade coincided with the oil boom in the Arabian peninsula, where the bedouin have forsaken their traditional life of nomadic pastoralism and cashed in on the more lucrative oil business. With the decline of the Arabian and Middle Eastern camel trade, the Sudanese have taken over, and Egypt now imports over 100,000 camels every year from the south. Not that the Sudani camel-herders have reaped great profit from the burgeoning trade. Few earn more for the forty-day trip than $300.

I returned to Isna again after my little jaunt on the Red Sea coast. This time I was accompanied by Eric, who had arrived back in Luxor after failing to get a Sudanese visa in Cairo. We took a collective taxi of quite remarkable unroadworthiness, and a couple of miles before Isna station there was a loud explosion under the bonnet, followed by a vigorous hissing. The driver got out, fiddled with the engine and set off again. Three of the passengers got off at the station, leaving me and Eric in the back seat, two men in the middle, and the driver alone in the front. We had gone no further than ten yards along the road to the barrage when black smoke rose from under the bonnet. The driver switched off the engine, swore, and jumped out. We clambered out and stationed ourselves at a safe distance from the car. The driver opened the bonnet and shied away from the flames which licked round the engine. He shovelled up some sand from beside the road and threw it over the flames; then he produced a fire-extinguisher from under his seat and gave it a good hosing. We were ordered back into the taxi and we drove into town, as though nothing had happened.

We sat by the river for a while and watched a pied kingfisher diving for fish. It dived six times but caught nothing, and when it sped across to the far bank, a black-and-white blur like a flying domino, we headed for the temple, which was sunk far below the level of the surrounding dwellings in the town centre. While Eric sketched the outside, I sat at the foot of a massive column and studied the hieroglyphs. Many were of animals and plants. Nile perch, vultures, kites, buffaloes, geese, duck, snakes, lotus flowers, crocodiles, papyrus, sacred ibis, fox – these denizens of the river made up the alphabet of the ancient Egyptians. A few letters from the alphabet are no longer to be found in the surrounding country-side – the crocodile has been pushed further south into the Sudan; and the sacred ibis and ostrich no longer breed in Egypt. But vultures still scavenge in the desert, kites seem as plentiful as pigeons, and buffaloes still pull the plough and turn the waterwheel. I had no idea what the script around the walls said. Not that it mattered much. Nature, divinity, community – they were written here in symbols so durable and on a material so indestructible that the sacred history of the river will be remembered for all time. No need to hire a guide. Though had one been handy, there was one question I should like to have asked. Why no camels?

It came as something of a surprise to learn later that the camel was a recent addition to the Egyptian fauna. There had been a sort of wild camel here in Quaternary times, but it became extinct, and the camel which we see today is descended from the beasts intro-duced by the Persians in the sixth century BC or thereabouts. Once the camel arrived it had a dramatic impact on desert life all across

north Africa. It was not only a first-class beast of burden, but the ideal creature with which to fight wars. It was also edible (though I suppose that goes for all herbivores). The importance of the camel was well-described in E. W. Bovill's classic study, *The Golden Trade of the Moors*:

When we look back through the centuries at the Roman period there clearly stands out an event which transcends all others in importance . . . This was the introduction of the camel, an event of such far-reaching consequences that it marked the dawn of a new era for the northern half of the continent. It widened the field for human endeavour and affected the economic life of the whole community. The camel gave man a freedom of movement he had never known before and brought within his reach the remotest pastures. The caravan routes lost half their terrors and new roads were opened for the flow of trade and culture.

With all these changes came a man new to Africa, the camel-owning nomad, turbulent, predatory, elusive, and unassailable. Thus was civilization faced with a menace from which it has never been wholly free and one which the legionaries of Rome never knew.

The market at Daraw, a small village a little way upstream of Kom Ombo, had a much finer stock market than Isna. I arrived one mid-morning, and a young boy was kind enough to attach himself to me as soon as I entered the market. He said he would protect me from bad men, whom he alleged to be here in considerable numbers, and who would undoubtedly strip me of all possessions were I to abjure his protection (he was about four foot six high), and he offered to translate for me. There were about two thousand peasants in the market, and a handful of camel-herders, small, handsome men, black as jet and decked out in beautiful white robes. There were less than a dozen of them and they stuck together in a small enclosure with fifty or sixty camels. Some of the animals had their right forelegs fettered, the limb bent double and tied with a short length of rope, but most stood patiently while prospective buyers inspected them. But the camels were far outnumbered by other animals. There were some *gamoose*, fine grey buffaloes, and many *bogara*, the yellow variety of cattle. There were also flocks of sheep and some goats and donkeys for sale. However, I had great difficulty in establishing how the animals were being sold. There was no formal auction, yet my guide claimed that all the time animals were changing hands. He led me around, asking the stockmen how much they were selling their beasts for, and the prices were much higher than I would have imagined. Camels were going for over £E300, *bogara* for £E400, and *gamoose* for £E600 or more. Even the sheep were said to be fetching £E60 or £E70 each.

We were staring at the camels when a peasant came rushing across and shook me warmly by the hand. I didn't recognize him at first as he was decked out in jellaba and *emma*. He had been wearing Western clothes when I met him before, which was in a collective taxi between Qena and Luxor. He had just sold two camels and we went to celebrate with a glass of tea. We sat beneath a makeshift roof of palm leaves and chatted. He offered me a smoke from a *shisha* made from an insecticide can, but I declined. I noticed that among the other *shishas* going the rounds was one made from a Gillette shaving-foam aerosol.

My acquaintance was delighted that I was interested in farm stock, and with the help of my young interpreter he explained at great length how one could tell a good camel from a bad, how one knew when a camel was feeling off colour, and how much I should pay for a camel if I bought one. He added, in a very roundabout way, that if I did need a camel, he knew of one that would be absolutely ideal – the right age, pleasant temperament (by camel standards), good teeth and so forth. I asked him who it belonged to, and he replied that by remarkable coincidence, and great good fortune, this magnificent beast belonged to none other than himself. We were about to go off and inspect it at close quarters when he was suddenly distracted by two white girls. Both wore shorts, tee-shirts and no bras. They strolled past where we sat, clicking their cameras at men and beasts without bothering to ask whether anyone objected to being photographed. 'If our women dressed like that,' said the man, 'we would kill them.' I took this as an extravagant metaphor for his disapproval. 'It happens,' said the young boy.

CHAPTER TEN

A VERY MODERN OLD PLACE

We of the Western world are so very,
very young, mere babes compared to the Hindus,
the Chinese, the Egyptians, to mention only a few
peoples. And, with our youth goes our ignorance,
stupidity and arrogance. Worse, our intolerance,
our failure to even try to understand
other peoples' ways.
Henry Miller (1977)

In his guide to Alexandria, E. M. Forster included a map titled 'The World According to Eratosthenes, 250 BC'. At the centre of the three ragged petals of Europe, Asia and Africa lay Alexandria, scattering the pollen of her knowledge and discoveries out over her less civilized neighbours. Eratosthenes drew two rivers on his map, the Nile and the Ganges, and two latitudes, one which passed through Alexandria, where he worked, and another through Aswan, where I now was. Forster explains:

> He knew that the earth is round, and he was told that the midsummer sun at Assouan in Upper Egypt cast no shadow at midday. At Alexandria, at the same moment, it did cast a shadow, Alexandria being further to the north on the same longitude. On measuring the Alexandria shadow he found that it was $7\frac{1}{5}$ degrees – i.e. $\frac{1}{50}$th of a complete circle – so that the distance from Alexandria to Assouan must be $\frac{1}{50}$th the circumference of the Earth. He estimated the distance at 500 miles, and consequently arrived at 25,000 miles for the complete circumference, and 7,850 for the diameter; in the latter calculation he is only 50 miles out.

So at a time when our own country was in a state of secluded barbarism, and the scientific and artistic achievements of Alexandria and its Mouseion were unimagined and unimaginable there, Aswan was already occupying a prominent position on the world stage. It lay within the sphere of Mediterranean knowledge, if not influence (the Ptolemies made no attempt to hellenize Upper Egypt and the temples they built here continued the architectural traditions of the Pharaohs), and it was seen as the last 'civilized' outpost before the vast desert wastes of Nubia. Casting one's mind over the last two thousand years, one is struck by how the scientists and the religious leaders of Europe ignored the simple assumption behind Eratosthenes' assertion, that the earth was spherical. It was strange, as Forster noted, that 'mankind should ever have slipped back again into fairy tales and barbarism'. It is therefore with a sense of *déjà vu* that one recalls Aswan's intrusion on the British conscience shortly after Egypt had gained its independence. For it was the West's refusal to finance the building of the Aswan Dam which encouraged Nasser to nationalize the British-controlled Suez Canal, an event which prompted Anthony Eden's famous remark, 'The Egyptian has his thumb on our windpipe', and which led to the futile and barbaric attack on the canal zone by British, Israeli and French soldiers. The Suez crisis was a squalid and shameful little affair, a final reminder to the British, who still administered over half of Africa, that their imperialistic world was destined to crumble. We lost control of the canal immediately and the rest of our colonies soon after. From a military point of view the invasion of Egypt was a success for the aggressors (the British lost twenty-two men compared to Egypt's 3,000), but diplomatically it was a triumph for Nasser. Whatever else can be said against the Aswan Dam, it has become a symbol of immense importance, not just for Egypt, but for all those countries striving to assert their independence against the economic hegemony of the super- and not-so-superpowers.

Eric and I passed our first evening in Aswan contemplating this most beautiful stretch of the Nile from the balcony of the Cataract Hotel. We had checked in at the Aswan Palace at midday, and we'd slept through the heat of the afternoon. It had been 104 degrees in the shade; so hot, in fact, that a cheap thermometer I had with me, having climbed to this stupendous peak, never descended again. From that day on it was only reliable for reading temperatures over 104, which meant it was OK for the Sudan, but not much good for anywhere else. By the time we reached the Cataract there was a slight breeze and the temperature, though not my thermometer, was back in double figures. We sat in wicker chairs by a wicker table and ordered a beer, which cost rather more than our nightly bed in the deceptively named Aswan Palace. Rich maroon and orange tapestries hung from the balcony's awnings and swayed gently. The atmosphere was peaceful and very *fin de siècle*. Cicadas scratched away among the oleander and bougan-villea in the garden below, and an ibis tiptoed through a reed bed where Elephantine Island fell from a jungle of palms into the rocky river. A kite, the river's aerial leitmotiv, floated effortlessly over a small temple, and on a granite boulder which jutted through the water sat a seagull. It was eight hundred miles from the Mediterranean. 'Think of all those dreams,' said Eric in oblique appreciation of the scene as the sun disappeared – 'those dreams carried back from here to the East End.'

The hotel was a building of eccentric beauty, a mishmash of colonial, Ottoman and classical styles. Apart from the keystones above the Queen Anne windows, which were white, it was painted a pleasant burnt sienna, a colour which blended harmoniously with the river rocks and the hills behind. This was in stark contrast to some of the other buildings in Aswan. The view to the south was ruined by the New Cataract Hotel, a tall, neo-Corbusier affair, painted white and sprouting two black flues like ship's funnels. But for sheer ugliness and bad taste this was outclassed by the Oberoi, a five-star monstrosity which had risen on Elephantine Island some time since my last visit. The Oberoi's guests were carried back and forth from the mainland in ludicrous mock-funerary boats. The pharaohs' mummies would decompose in their tombs if they could see them. And the late Aga Khan would turn in his mausoleum, which stood on the west bank of the Nile. He had chosen the spot as he thought it would afford his spirit the finest view in the world. That was before the Oberoi.

There are, as far as I am concerned, only two types of hotel worth staying in in Egypt. The cheap and the colonial. Despite their great differences, they have one outstanding merit in common, and one which distinguishes them from the Hilton, the Oberoi, the Sheraton and all the other purpose-built egg-boxes with gaudy boutiques, beauty salons and indoor swimming-pools: they are untainted by the deadening and synthetic stamp of Americanism. Better to live with Egyptian bedbugs than American piped music. Better still, if you can afford it, to sleep between the crisp linen sheets of one of the old imperial watering holes. To the diplomats of half a century ago, returning from the empty wilderness of north Sudan or the swamps of further south, the Cataract and the other colonial hotels strung out along the Nile must have evinced the same feeling of joy and relief as the desert water-holes still do for the camel-herders of today. The Grand in Khartoum, the Cataract in Aswan, the Winter Palace in Luxor, Shephard's in Cairo, the Cecil in Alexandria – each was a step nearer home; each a micro-cosm of the sophisticated world which was to be found at the end of the journey, in the clubs on the Mall or in the drawing-rooms of country houses (though not, I suspect, down in the East End). There must have been an interesting mix of guests in those pre-Suez, pre-Nasser days: rich old ladies escaping the European winter (Agatha Christie wrote one of her books while staying at the Cataract); archaeologists, returning each evening to the comforts of the bar after sweltering days scraping away at some ruin or un-earthing a mummy which had avoided the depredations of Egyptian Rail and I. Augustus Stanwood, paper-maker; and explorers and hunters having a last taste of Western civilization before heading into the wilds to take on bedouin, beasts, and drought. And among this menagerie of oddballs would come and go the diplomats and soldiers, staying just long enough to sink a few gins or oil a rifle, and perhaps to spend an evening dancing or watching the women gliding through the immense corridors, their delicate hands obscured by lace gloves, their pink and modest cheeks hidden behind oriental fans. Well, it isn't like this now; and perhaps it never was. At the table next to us were two elderly couples from Barnsley. They were on a package tour and having a wonderful time.

'Aswan's just like Nice beside the Nile,' someone had told me when I was in Luxor; and before I got here I heard five more people independently offer the same judgement of the city. It said little for either their originality of thought or for their powers of observation. Aswan is not remotely like Nice, though it is the cleanest and most conspicuously prosperous city in Egypt, and perhaps, if you allowed your imagination an exceptional degree of latitude, you might perceive some similarity between Nice's seafront and Aswan's Corniche. Both are punctuated by trees – palms in Nice and flame trees in Aswan – and the souvenir shops along both are pricey and plush. But they have nothing else in common.

On my first morning I drank a coffee in a small café beside the Aswan Palace, which was situated a hundred yards back from the river on the edge of the souk, and watched the pigeon-seller perform mouth-to-mouth feeding. It seemed the most laborious operation. These pigeons dearly loved to eat, and no sooner had one been fed than it wanted more. At the same small stall there were a couple of dozen rabbits (which sat on top of their crates rather than in them), a goat, a turkey, two ducks, and a population of cats. After breakfast I made my way along the Corniche to the State Information Bureau, where I was presented with various forms to fill in. The office was run by Mr Adam, a handsome man with sharp features – very tall, very thin and very black. He spoke in a soft silky voice, and he inquired what he could do for me. I asked, among other things, if I could see the chairman of the Nile Valley River Transportation Company. Much to my astonishment, he suggested we go immediately. No question of *bokkra*.

A couple of minutes later we were sitting with the delightful Mr Abbas, a large man who was stationed in a comfortable armchair beneath portraits of the two great men whose countries presided over the Aswan Dam, Presidents Mubarek and Nimeiri. Now I was here I couldn't remember why I wanted to see Mr Abbas, and within a couple of minutes I had asked him what few questions occurred to me about his company and the boats which connected Aswan to Wadi Halfa. He informed me that there were no longer two boats a week, as his Cairo office had supposed; and indeed there hadn't been since 25 May 1983, when one of the boats caught fire, and three hundred passengers, nearly all Sudanese, were burnt to death, drowned, eaten by crocodiles or killed by poisonous snakes. The Cairo office had also been out of date about the class arrangements. There were no longer three classes, just first and tourist class. 'We call it tourist class,' said Mr Abbas, 'because it's not as good as second class and not as bad as third.'

We drank *karkadee*, a delicious cold drink made from purple hibiscus flowers, and Mr Adam and Mr Abbas, who evidently had not met before, turned to one of the Nubian's favourite topics of conversation: What is a Nubian? Mr Abbas proceeded to explain his genealogy, going back five generations or so. It was not easy to follow. One generation had lived near Wadi Halfa, but shifted south to Dongola after the British invasion. Then when the Mahdist uprising overthrew the British and put paid to General Gordon in 1885, some of the family came north to Aswan, while a few stayed behind. When Kitchener re-invaded the Sudan in 1896 there was more movement and dispersal. Mr Adam, greatly excited by this short history, advanced that of his own family, which seemed even more complex. 'So you see,' he said when he had finished, 'I have a Sudanese passport, but men like me and Mr Abbas are just people of the Nile Valley. We are Nubians.'

Wherever you go in this part of the country, the inhabitants are keen to assert their separate identity from the Egyptians of further north. They are darker in complexion, they speak Nubian as well as Arabic, and they see the border which divides Sudan from Egypt as no more than an artificial line drawn through their huge territory. They are proud of their culture and their history. A European parallel might be the Welsh in Britain or the Catalans in Spain.

The history of Aswan and Nubia has been one of trade and turbulence. For thousands of years Aswan was a meeting place for pilgrims making the trek east to Mecca, and the river provided the link between black Africa and the Mediterranean. Through Aswan would come gold, slaves, ivory, perfumes and animal products. In the marketplaces young girls from Abyssinia, from the Upper Nile and from Nubia itself (Nubian women were highly prized as their skin was said to remain cool to the touch in the hottest weather) were bought from the slavers and despatched to the harems of Cairo and the Middle East. The same merchants might buy the ostrich plumes which were used in Turkey to decorate the helmets of the janissaries and spahis, and the skins of leopard, lion and cheetah. Aswan must have been used to marauders too. It was the southerly outpost of the Roman Empire, and there have been few centuries since when some military operation was not pushing north or south through this part of the Nile Valley.

The Nubians gained a reputation for hostility. In *The Blue Nile* Alan Moorehead recalls the aggression which the artist Vivant Denon encountered when he visited the temple of Philae, a little way upstream of Aswan:

> His every effort to land by boat was met by howls, threats, and eventually the spears of the natives living in the ruins. The Nubians, it seemed, were people of extreme barbarity ... the Philae islanders were determined to defend their families against the French [who were busy driving the Mameluk leaders from the country], and it was not until the place was taken by assault that they fled. Denon, who had come to admire and sketch the temples, was horrified to see mothers drowning their children in the river rather than allow them to be taken ...

Both Flaubert and Amelia Edwards commented on the wildness of Aswan. Flaubert thought it 'negro, African, savage', and Edwards – one can imagine her clomping through the markets in sensible shoes – found for sale such 'objects as speak only of a barbarous present'. Aswan today is almost unrecognizable from their descriptions. For the first time on the way south you are aware of black sub-Saharan Africa; and the Mediterranean seems very far away. But it is skin colour, not displays of a 'barbarous present' that tell you you are approaching the Sudan. In many ways it is a thoroughly sophisticated city.

I had spent over six weeks now without eating an Egyptian dish worth writing home about. But I found a small café in the souk at Aswan which served a vegetable stew, *targin*, which even Egon Ronay would have approved of. And how fitting that it should have been here that I found it: by far the most intriguing explanation of Aswan's etymology is gastronomic in origin. 'The meaning of the name Uswan,' claimed Abu Salih, the Armenian chronicler of Egyptian monkish life, 'is "swallow", for it was built by the king for a body of Abyssinians whom he made a guard for himself, and since they were voracious in eating, he said to them "swallow"!'

Eric and I ate in this café on each of the few days that remained to me in Egypt, and the café owner would sit with us and chat about politics and economics. He tried, though with little success, to explain some of the more outstanding eccentricities of the Egyptian economy. But I still failed to understand why any country should need four different exchange rates. Tourists could change money at £E1.12 to a dollar. This compared with the 'central rate' of £E0.84 to a dollar, the £E0.70 rate for oil company dealings and for internal book-keeping, and the £E0.40 rate for repaying the large debts which Egypt had incurred with East European nations in the early seventies. I suggested that this sounded suspiciously like cheating (especially if you came from Eastern Europe), and the café owner, who had a degree in economics, said: 'Well, perhaps, but maybe not quite.' I was also at a loss to understand why land prices in the Nile Valley should have been so astronomically high. A hectare of good land in the Faiyum cost £E40,000, which is about seven times as much as the best land in England (assuming you convert at the tourist rate). And even the desert outside Aswan was worth double our best land. The café owner was more illuminating, and intelligible, on the subject of domestic politics. Elections were due to be held in six weeks' time, and he said it was the first time during his thirty years of life that people could be critical of the government without fear of imprisonment and possibly torture. Egypt was about to make a tentative first step in the direction of democracy, and he, like most people I spoke to, considered Mubarek a big improvement on his predecessors. Paradoxically, it was among that sector of the population which since the revolution has flourished most, the middle classes, that Nasser, who was responsible more than any other for giving Egypt back to the Egyptians, was most reviled. I seldom heard a good word said about him. He was described variously as cruel, tyrannical, vain, arrogant and dishonest. The same cathartic vilification was now being heaped on Sadat, who had had that special blend of charisma and corruption which so appealed to the leaders of the West. I do not recall seeing any publicly displayed picture of Nasser, although icons of Sadat were still to be seen occasionally, the most curious being a framed photograph tacked on to a concrete pillar beneath a pedestrian flyover in Cairo's Tahrir Square. Mubarek you simply couldn't escape from. He stared gloomily from the walls of cafés, offices, shops and, for all I know, private houses.

A brief footnote is in order here, an addendum to my ignorance, so to speak. Several months after I returned from Africa, I became friendly with an Egyptian woman who had been forced to flee her country. We talked a lot about Egypt, and I learnt more about Egyptian politics from her than I did during the whole time I spent in the country. I was particularly interested in her views about Nasser. Although she'd been briefly imprisoned while he was in power, she had much respect for him. 'I don't think he really knew quite what terrible things were happening,' she suggested, referring to the persecutions and purges. 'It was those underneath him who were really responsible.' She thought him sensitive, intelligent and honourable. 'Quite a soft man, really,' she added intriguingly. I told her that I was surprised by how vehemently so many people seemed to hate him. She replied that he was still enormously loved, but as the fashion, officially sanctioned, was to denigrate him, most people were too scared to speak up on his behalf. 'You must understand,' she said, 'the Egyptian people are frightened of saying what they think if it goes against government policy.' I asked her if she would like to go back. 'Of course,' she replied, 'there's nothing I'd like more. But I'd say what I thought – about the poverty, about the corruption of the middle classes – and I'd be in trouble again. Maybe when I'm a hundred and fifty years old I'll be able to go back and they'll leave me alone – an ancient eccentric, no longer worth worrying about.'

Whether you are sitting in Aswan souk eating *targin*, or in the Cairo Hilton partaking of some fancy delicacy, or in a mud hovel eating boiled rice, your debt is to the river. And the river is no less important now for the country's survival than it was in pharaonic times. To the ancient Egyptians it was the god Osiris who flooded the valley every year. 'Thou art the Nile,' said the pharaoh Ramses IV in his hymn to Osiris, 'gods and men live from thy outflow.' And they still do. The early Egyptians believed that the Nile broke forth from the cataracts and rapids a little way upstream from Aswan, though one suspects that they must have understood not only the cyclical nature of its annual floods, but how water was recycled in the atmosphere. (No geographer ever put it better than the preacher in Ecclesiastes: 'All the rivers run into the sea, yet the sea is not full; unto the place whither the rivers go, thither they go again.')

Viewed from a space satellite the Nile appears as a fork of lightning, striking south from the Mediterranean and forking where Khartoum stands today. The westerly fork, the White Nile, strikes towards the region of Lake Victoria; the easterly, the Blue Nile, has its source near the ancient Ethiopian capital of Gondar. From source to sea the Nile is over 4,000 miles long. It dominates Sudan and Egypt (which would be 100 per cent, rather than 96 per cent, desert without it), and it leaches parts of Ethiopia, Uganda, Kenya, Tanzania, Zaïre, Burundi and Rwanda. The annual floods owe their origin to the clouds which gather in the south Atlantic ocean, and which are driven across Africa to fall as rain on the Ethiopian Highlands. The Blue Nile begins to swell with the rains in March and April and it peaks around the end of August. The level falls progressively through to the following April, when the river's flow may be as little as a fortieth of its summer flood level. The White Nile also fluctuates, but much less ostentatiously, its lowest level never being more than four tenths of its maximum. And even this span can be attributed to the Sobat River, which drops from the Ethiopian Highlands and provides the river with half its flood waters.

The annual cycle is always the same, but, as so many sub-Saharan countries know too well today, the amount of rain which falls can vary greatly. For the ancient Egyptians drought in Ethiopia meant famine for them, and the history of the country has been dominated by attempts to regulate the flow of water. The earliest river people must have behaved much as the pastoralists of southern Sudan – the Nuer and Dinka, for example – do today; moving on to higher ground during the floods and back on to the revived pastures with the waters' recession. This was not a satisfactory state of affairs. King Menes, who reigned around 3400 BC, is thought to have been the first ruler to build banks along the Nile, thus protecting some settlements from floods; and since that time the Egyptians have been continually refining their irrigation system. The Aswan High Dam is the latest and most spectacular attempt to tame the Nile. Its purpose is very simple: to store water in the season of plenty, and to discharge it in times of want. For the first time in history, the Egyptian farmer is protected from the vagaries of climatic change further south.

So on either side of the equation which dominates life in Egypt we have two variable factors, water and food. The more water there is available, the greater the amount of food which can be produced, and the greater the amount of desert land which can be reclaimed and brought into cultivation. The big problem, however, is the country's expanding population. At the beginning of this century there was a half a *feddan* (a *feddan* is about an acre) of cultivated land for each Egyptian; now there is less than a sixth of a *feddan*, despite the massive sums of money poured into reclamation projects since the dam's completion in 1960.

When Nasser commissioned the High Dam many Egyptians were starving, life expectancy was thirty-five years and annual per capita income was £25. Today nobody in Egypt is starving, though some are malnourished, but the government faces a seemingly impossible task. Agricultural production must grow at 4 per cent a year to keep pace with the rising population (by the year 2000 there will be another twenty-five million mouths to feed), yet the World Bank believes that production will rise at most by 2 per cent a year. When I saw Dr Kholi in Cairo he said he believed that within five years the country would be self-sufficient in everything except wheat. Perhaps, as chief advisor to the Minister of Agriculture, he felt he had to paint an optimistic picture. But I don't know how he did his sums.

In 1964 Egypt imported 2 million tonnes of wheat. In 1976, it was 4 million. Since then it has risen each year. In 1970 the cost of imported food was £E6 a head. Ten years later it was £E45. Food imports are the biggest burden on the country's balance of payments, and food subsidies, whose purpose is to keep prices low enough for the poor to afford to eat, consume more than £2,000 million a year. Thus it is not surprising that the government's main goal is food self-sufficiency. Desert reclamation will continue, but it is slow and costly, and it is impossible to know how, in the foreseeable future, the Egyptians will produce enough food even to keep imports down to the level they are at today. 'Just to keep the ratio of land per person to a sixth of a *feddan*,' Minister Samaha had told me, 'we must double the area of cultivated land by the year 2000.'

The Aswan Dam has undoubtedly brought some benefits to the country. It has enabled over one million *feddan*s of desert to be reclaimed, and it has enabled approximately the same amount of land already in cultivation to be switched from the old-fashioned system of basin irrigation to the more efficient perennial system. This land now grows two crops a year rather than one. The expansion of rice cultivation from 0.4 to 1.2 million *feddan*s can also be attributed to the dam.

However, the dam is more famous – in the Western press, at least – for its ecological impact. Osiris not only delivered the flood water to moisten the land, but the silt to fertilize it. The dam has put an end to the god's – or nature's – way of sustaining soil fertility as it traps the silt. The pile of fertilizer bags in the home of Abla Azim, where Richard and I had lunched after our trip to St Anthony's, was today's substitute for Nile silt. The era of technochemical farming has begun in Egypt, and the traditional ways of farming, at first glance little different than one imagines they must have been in the times of the Pharaohs, are now subject to the insidious influence of chemical farming. Coupled to the use of chemicals, incidentally, has been the trend of replacing animal power with machines. A little under half the population still work on the land, but with the introduction of the new technologies, it is difficult to see the number of peasants doing anything other than falling. Today you can still see the whole range of irrigation devices in use, from the simple shadoof (a pole and bucket device), to the Archimedean screw and the *saqia*, both of which were introduced by the Ptolomies. The *saqia* is one of the most beautiful machines invented by man, combining aesthetic grace with bestial energy, and one can never go far along the Nile without seeing these buffalo- or camel-driven waterwheels slowly lifting water and slopping it into irrigation ditches. However, I expect the *saqia*, having lasted two thousand years, will soon be obsolete. In twenty or thirty years' time electricity and oil will power most of the machines in the Egyptian countryside, and the children of today's peasants will have been forced to leave the land and settle in the slums of the cities. 'Don't worry about the peasants,' one official had told me, 'they can always go and work for the Saudis or one of the other oil-producing countries.' However, to plan the economy on the premise of exporting labour seems to me quite obscene.

I spent my last day in Egypt with the Fisheries Department, whose offices were situated in the desert on the north-west shore of the dam. I heard about the reproductive habits of catfish and Nile perch. I was told about the various studies of fish biology instigated by the Japanese, who had built the offices and provided the Egyptians with a research vessel. And I learnt about the efforts which the Fisheries Department was making to help the dam's three thousand fishermen, known as *arraqa*, those who sweat. I promised Engineer Safwat Ghattas, the general manager who gave me so much of his time, that when I returned to England I would write an article about the excellent work he and his staff were doing. And I did manage to fit a couple of paragraphs about the fisheries into an article I wrote about the Egyptian food problem. I was even paid for the article, but the magazine which had solicited it went bust before it was published. So, belated apologies to Engineer Safwat and his scientists.

It was latish afternoon when the fisheries office locked its doors and I headed back towards Aswan with the workers. Road repairs delayed our journey, so I sat on the dam wall, listening to the nagging vibration of automatic picks as I waited for the traffic jam to clear. I had the pleasant illusion that here I was at last far enough above the Nile to see Africa's fluted catheter unfurling into the Mediterranean, and I suddenly realized how much I was going to miss Egypt. I tried to put my finger on why I felt such an intense affection for the country. There were many reasons, but I think it was the country's remarkable diversity that appealed to me most. In England and the other nations which are pleased to call themselves 'developed', our knowledge of how our forefathers behaved a hundred or two hundred years ago must be gleaned from books or paintings or museums. It is not there, out in the open, for all of us to see. But in Egypt the ancient ways of life have coalesced with the modern; they have not been obliterated by them – yet. If you want to know how the peasants worked their fields at the time of the Roman conquest, forget about history books, just go to the Faiyum, or for that matter almost anywhere up the Nile Valley. And even in cities like Cairo, where the motor car has had such a profound and wrecking influence, you still come across shepherds driving their flocks along six-lane highways. It is almost as though they are deliberately holding out against the pervasive uniform of modern life.

I could never think of Egypt without smiling, for among the debris of the modern cities, in the poorest of villages, in conditions where people were subjected to hardship beyond any I had known, there were always people laughing, haggling, shouting and making the best of what little they had. Many visitors to the country complain about how the Egyptians haggle. But why shouldn't they? How else can the poor survive except by taking from the rich?

CHAPTER ELEVEN
THROUGH NUBIA

Eric and I arrived at the dam at mid-morning. A couple of hundred people jostled around the jetty gates like expectant – if somewhat desiccated – salmon queuing at a fish ladder. We drank some sweet and tepid tea in a shanty café and watched a train pull on to the crest of desert near by. More people staggered over to the gates, weighed down with luggage. Every now and then a taxi would arrive, its roof piled high with cardboard boxes, bulging suitcases and carelessly wrapped parcels. One Sudanese family – there was hardly an Egyptian in sight – had a Kenwood mixer and six giant packs of disposable nappies.

We talked about what Eric might sketch in the two weeks which remained to him in Egypt, and I made him a rough street plan of Alexandria, marking down the Athineos tea-rooms ('There was this funny old bloke with a twitching jaw,' he told me when I saw him again in the summer, 'so I drew him'), Sofianopolos's coffee shop, the Leroy, Cavafy's house, and some churches and mosques. I said I didn't see how he could do any sketches of the Sudan if he wasn't coming. 'I don't see why not,' he replied. 'I'll do an "Impressions of Sudan".' For almost as long as I had known Eric, which was ten years or so, he had been urging me to read Raymond Roussel's *Impressions of Africa*. I had never done so, yet he had mentioned it frequently enough for me to develop a picture of the bizarre Roussel, if not of his imaginary and surreal work on Africa. I had imagined an eccentric Frenchman arriving in Tangier in the early years of the century. Once there, I saw him taking a room in some small hotel, never to venture out until he had finished his great opus. His task completed, he would screw the top back on the ink bottle, file his pens away with his underwear and toothpaste, brave the streets down to the harbour, and catch a boat back to the safety of Europe. It seemed, as we sat waiting for the gates to open, a perfectly sensible way to write about this vast and confusing continent.

A little after midday the gates were thrown back and the crowd began to push through to the passport shed. I shook hands with Eric and left him in his Tangier. Whites, I'm sad to report, still get preferential treatment – *carte blanche*, so to speak – over much of Africa, and officials waved the five Europeans and single oriental through to the front of the queue. We were the first through the customs shed and the first to walk down the long concrete slipway to the boat. It looked little different from the *Ibis*, the one I had taken nine years earlier. (One of my letters home had claimed that the *Ibis* was a paddle steamer, though I doubt it was.) The boat consisted of three vessels; the one in the middle housing the engine, the crew's quarters, the first-class cabins and the restaurant; the two steel barges on either side, the 'tourist class' accommodation – knobbly wooden floorboards. The port barge was two-storeyed, if you counted the hold; the starboard, three-storeyed. I climbed on to the latter and laid a sleeping-bag out at the foot of a rusty pillar which supported a rudimentary roof of corrugated iron sheeting. It was rather like bedding down in a scrapyard. It was 105 degrees, which brought my thermometer back to life. I drowsed. The other Europeans spread themselves out near by, and over the afternoon the rest of the barge filled up. No one seemed to know when we would sail. The Frenchman next to me was reading Mishima's *Confessions d'un masque*. He was thirtyish, and smartly dressed in pressed khaki trousers and a khaki shirt. He had a small and ill-executed tattoo on his chest, the sort which makes one think instantly of prison. Also beside me was a stocky and bearded German, who sat crosslegged reading Carlos Castenada's *The Second Ring of Power*. He saw me watching him and asked me if I liked Castenada. I said I didn't. He shook his head sadly and carried on reading. There was an English couple, too; the man, blond and spectacled, was reading something by Anthony Burgess; his dark-haired girl-friend was trying, simultaneously, to read *War and Peace* and make a cucumber sandwich. Most of the Sudanese were sprawled across their luggage and sleeping, though a few were playing cards.

I had nothing to read (Eric had taken *Barchester Towers*) so I wandered over to the side of the boat and watched the catfish messing around beside the barge's hull. There were four of them, about three foot long and eight inches deep. Their bulldog faces trailed long streaming whiskers which undulated as the fish moved in sinuous circles just below the water's surface. I counted six different species of dragonfly. The largest had black and white stripes, like an insect version of the pied kingfisher. Another was small and azure. The most numerous looked like wax matchsticks with pink heads.

Most of the forty-four-man crew were in the standard uniform of jellabas and white skullcaps. A few had an *emma* swathed over the skullcap. From where I lay I had an excellent view of the wheelhouse. The captain sat on a table, slouching against the back wall. He was turning the spoked ship's wheel with his bare feet; his hands were reserved for drinking tea and smoking. Six of the crew sheltered from the setting sun in the shade of the wheelhouse, and Sheban stood out from the rest like a lone poppy in a cornfield. He was a fine-looking Nubian, black but not coal-black, and sheeny-skinned. His eyes were almost oriental, sloping down to high cheekbones; his chin was sharp; his mouth was wide and there was a small gap between his two front teeth. He was in his early thirties. He sauntered down the side of the boat and crossed over to our barge. He was wearing a pale green jacket with wide white lapels and gold buttons. It was beautifully cut, full at the shoulder, narrow at the waist. The trousers were of the same green, beautifully cut too, and tapered like plusfours to stop on the calves. Toes which looked as though they had been through a clothes mangle pushed out from green plastic sandals. His frizzy hair was restrained by a yellow and white peaked cap.

He sat down and introduced himself. I asked where his suit came from. 'I used to be a merchant seaman,' he replied. 'I worked on an Italian ship.' Thus the fancy clothes.

He didn't like the dam. 'It is a disaster,' he said. 'It was a beautiful Nubian valley before they built the dam. Before they began work they had to throw everyone out of their villages. Everyone was crying. They were beautiful villages; I knew them all. And now the fish are sick, and we must eat terrible food in Egypt because the peasants use too much fertilizer.' A hundred and twenty thousand people were displaced when the dam was built. Approximately half were moved north into Egypt to live in desolate mud villages on the desert slopes near the head of the dam and round Kom Ombo. The rest were repatriated in Sudan. Many ended up on the banks of the Blue Nile at Khashm el-Quirba, a thousand-odd miles to the south.

Sheban took me to see the engine-room with Jol, the English girl. It looked exactly as an engine-room should: hell to work in. Two German engines dripped oil and made such a noise that it was impossible to talk. Sheban regarded them with affection. I don't think he spent much time down there: he had five assistant engineers.

He invited us into his cabin for a coffee. The cabin throbbed above the engine-room. It was little bigger than a dog kennel, hotter than a sauna, and whatever grease had left the engine-room had passed by here on its way elsewhere. A fan whirred ineffectually from the ceiling. There were two pairs of wooden bunks, and a man in an oily jellaba was asleep on one. Sheban woke him up to tell him a joke. He laughed and went back to sleep again.

'You can't get hot drinks in the restaurant,' explained Sheban, 'because it's a fire risk to make coffee.' He fished out an electric kettle from under a bunk, inspected the bare wires at the end of the flex and wedged them into a socket with a couple of matches. Two more engineers came in. One was tall, skinny and shy. The other was small and round with a fine hooked nose, like an Ottoman version of Punch. Sheban handed round the coffee and perched on a bunk. I offered him a cigarette. He took one.

'Do you know this woman?' he asked, pointing to the picture on the cigarette packet.

'Yes,' I replied. 'It's Cleopatra.'

'Do you know where she was from?'

'Alexandria,' I said.

'No,' said Sheban with a big gap-toothed grin. 'No, she was a Nubian woman.'

'Which Cleopatra are we talking about?' I asked.

'The one who loves Antonius from Italy. She loves him too much.'

Sheban asked for a piece of paper and a pen. He wrote, in capital letters, KILU BABA TARATI. 'Read it,' he ordered. Jol read it aloud.

'There, you see!' he said excitedly. 'Cleopatra is how the Egyptians say *kilu baba tarati*. The Egyptians claimed her as an Egyptian. They did the same with Ramses.' *Kilu baba tarati*, explained Sheban, was Nubian for 'beautiful woman'. He said she was born near Wadi Halfa.

Someone came to fetch Sheban.

'We're stopping for the night now,' he said as he left. 'I have to go. But friend, if you want to stay here you can.'

Jol and I said we'd go back to the barge to sleep. On the way we met one of the crew. He was smoking and he asked us to join him. We squatted in a corridor, drew deep on the neat grass and watched cockroaches scuttle furtively along the broken skirting like private detectives on a tail job. You could almost see them squinting over their upturned lapels.

We returned to the barge. There was a warm breeze blowing off the crags which lay to the west. A full moon rose behind them and the shining and placid surface of the lake stretched as far as the eye could see to the east. The engines were switched off and I lay down to sleep. Some frogs were making as much musical sense as a Schoenberg opera; some of the sleepers were snoring. I was thinking about a Nubian Cleopatra when I fell asleep.

Once during the night I made the tortuous journey to the WC, which was situated at the opposite end of the barge on the deck below. Crumpled heaps of bodies carpeted the floor like a rock fall below a mountain scree. The moon hung above a scarp and shone feebly through the fencing round the deck to cast blurred striations across the sleepers. A young girl of perhaps twelve or thirteen sat propped against a pillar. The man who accompanied her – I'd noticed him the day before: he was a handsome south Sudanese with tribal scars across sharp cheekbones – lay asleep beside her, a shawl wrapped across his face, his legs bent into a question-mark. The girl was very thin and her legs were bowed, the result possibly of childhood rickets. She was heavily pregnant and she was weeping. She hid her face as I passed. There was just enough light downstairs to see a rat disappear into one of the two showers when I reached the WC.

I returned to my sleeping-bag and slept till dawn. We had cast off and the boat was moving swiftly south. The dam was so wide here that I couldn't see the eastern shore. Turquoise waters faded into a wedgwood-blue sky. The boat woke slowly. Gerrald, the Frenchman, disappeared into the first-class lounge, where he was to spend most of the day. Wolfgang, the German, produced some wool from a plastic bag. He spent the morning knitting (with five needles simultaneously) a pair of multicoloured socks, an activity which fascinated the Sudanese. The oriental traveller – he was Japanese, I think – sat crosslegged and indulged in what was presumably meditation. The bundles of rags and blankets gradually shook themselves awake and the card-games began again. At ten o'clock I fell asleep and didn't wake till early afternoon, when Sheban appeared with the ship's purser, a young man from Port Sudan called Yahia, who produced from the pocket of his blue jellaba a piece of paper with a list of seventeen names in Arabic. He read them to me. The first was Aswan, the last Wadi Halfa; the intervening fifteen were the names of villages which had been drowned by the dam. We talked about the villages for a while, then I asked them about the fire which had destroyed the *Ramadan 10* a little under a year ago.

'Yes, I was on it,' announced Yahia to my surprise. 'We'd stopped for the night just south of Abu Simbel, near where we'll stop tonight. We tied the boat to the shore and everyone went to sleep.'

'The crew shouldn't have been sleeping,' suggested Sheban.

'That's true,' agreed Yahia. 'Some time in the early morning the cook wanted to make some tea. He turned on the gas but he didn't have any matches, so he went in search of some. He was away a long time. When he returned to the stove he lit a match. The gas was still on and it blew up.'

The fire soon spread through the boat. 'You know how the Sudanese travel,' said Sheban, motioning to the piles of luggage all around us. 'So much stuff! Lots of them were taking cans of kerosene and benzene back to Sudan and these began exploding all over the boat.'

'I was very lucky,' continued Yahia. 'I swam from the ship to a rock offshore and I waited to be rescued by a police boat.' He said that the next day they found one of the burnt-out barges on the opposite side of the dam. Many people had tried to swim ashore. Some were killed by crocodiles before they got there. And some were killed by snakes and scorpions when they did. Sheban thought 333 people had died, and a slightly smaller number had survived.

'Now I have one great ambition in my life,' said Yahia inconsequentially. 'I want to come to Britain and see Mrs Thatcher.' Sheban roared with laughter.

'Do you like Charles Dickens?' asked Yahia.

I said I'd never read him. 'I love *Oliver Twist*,' he said on parting. Sheban left soon after, and I went to lean on a rail which had a handwritten notice attached to it: 'In Case of Fire. 1. Reach quitely the shore. 2. Ask For Help From whoever Can Use the nearest Fire Extinguisher.' Some very old and porous-looking life belts were strung on the railings, but I couldn't see the nearest fire extinguisher. It was probably in Wadi Halfa.

There was the slightest of breezes coming off the water, but not enough to dry the sweat which trickled itchily down my neck and chest. A chubby man with the tribal gashes of the Shaqiya tribe on his cheeks came over to join me. He was dressed in Western clothes and he was carrying a copy of the Koran in Arabic and Aquiano's *Travels* in French. 'I think you people in England are going to be surprised in the coming years,' he announced gravely, 'for today you are living in a paradise.' He left before I could ask him what he meant. But I think I knew anyway.

After dusk I went over to Sheban's cabin with Jol and her boyfriend. We ate *fasoulia*, a delicious green bean stew bathed in a thick russet-coloured sauce. Once we'd eaten we went up on deck. Ahead of us beads of lights were strung across the desert, picking out the township of Abu Simbel. A little further south, a vast rock shaped like the reclining body of a woman lay beside the water. We could just make out the huge statues which guarded her temple. Half an hour later we stopped for the night. At nine o'clock the next day we pulled into the shore near Wadi Halfa.

Our vessel was slewed sideways against an ancient barge which served as a customs and passport control shed. There was no point in hurrying. I sat down and watched the passengers trickle through the barge and climb down a wooden ramp on to Sudanese sand. It took three hours to clear the boat of its passengers. On shore there were a couple of wooden shacks selling tea and a dozen or so Landrovers and Toyota trucks waiting to take passengers the three miles to the train station. Nine years earlier, loath to waste precious pennies, I had walked it. This time I paid £S2 for a ride to the station. (There were approximately 2.5 Sudanese pounds to one pound sterling.)

Wadi Halfa lay some way back from the dam: cadaverous, desolate and unwelcoming. Her ribs, stripped bare and bleached by the desert sun, poked through the drifting sands. It was midday when the Toyotas dropped us outside the station.

Wadi Halfa may not have courted fame but Flaubert and the weather have endowed the town with a certain mystique. Du Camp alleged that Flaubert, much preoccupied with a future novel, declared from the summit of Gebel Abusir, a hill near Halfa, 'I have found it! Eureka! Eureka! I will call her Emma Bovary!', thus settling on the title for his next novel and the name of the principal character. It is a nice story, and most probably nonsense.

I don't suppose people give much thought to Flaubert in Halfa. It is the heat that preoccupies the visitor. The old town, now below the Aswan Dam, holds the world record: 125.2° F. Once it gets above 100 degrees it seems to make little difference whether it is 105, 115 or 125 degrees. It is simply hell on a sliding scale. It was 110 when we arrived.

The train was waiting silent and engineless in the desert. I dumped my bag in a third-class carriage and Sheban led me towards the souk. It was a painfully hot walk. There were no roads and we had to dodge trucks and cars which drove through the wide swathes of sand between the low mud buildings. We sat outside a small café and drank sweet sickly tea with a dozen other men. Sheban greeted them enthusiastically. 'These people,' he said, encompassing the Nubians with a broad sweep of the arm, 'these people, I love them too much.'

Waxy black flies crawled all over us as we drank our tea. It was useless trying to drive them off. They waded through the sweat which dripped from our temples and crawled round our eyes and lips.

Jol and I went off to buy some food for the train journey. The market was a pathetic sight, bereft of any fresh food apart from three wrinkled water-melons, which looked like mummified scrotums, and a few purple-skinned onions. Everything else was tinned and very expensive. A small jar of pilchards cost £S2; and a pint jar of powder for making orange drinks cost £S12. Beans, figs and dates were outrageously priced. Everything had been brought north from Khartoum. We didn't buy anything.

'Come,' said Sheban, 'I'll take you to another shop.' Again it sold nothing but tinned food. Sheban introduced us to the shopkeeper. 'If you need anything next time you're here,' he said, 'just ask for Hassan and say you're from me. I have an account here. If you need money, food, anything . . . have it on my account.'

Sheban walked back to the station with us, where we shook hands and said goodbye. I was sad to leave him.

I bought a ticket for the train journey (£S13 for the eight-hundred-mile trip to Khartoum) and changed a little money on the black market (there were no banks here). I returned to the carriage and remained there throughout the afternoon. Time passed, but slowly. A little after four o'clock a diesel engine was attached to the train, and soon after four camel-herders climbed on. They shoved their tents beneath our feet and filled the WC – a doorless alcove with nothing but a hole in the floorboards; but a WC all the same – with hide bags full of luggage. What luggage wouldn't fit into the WC or beneath the seats was piled along the corridor.

They were magnificent-looking men. Each wore a white smock with baggy arms and white trousers which stopped tight round the calf. Long leather black whips were slung diagonally across their shoulders and from their upper arms hung short knives and leather amulets the shape and colour of seaweed air-bladders. I had never seen a man as handsome as the graphite-black herder who placed himself on the luggage at my feet. Like the others he was small – no more than five feet six – but his body was wonderfully athletic. He had a large hooked nose, sharp features and a small crescent-shaped moustache cut to a point. On the second finger of his left hand he wore a large pink stone set in a lustreless silver ring, and on his right wrist he sported a very smart Rolex watch. His eyes were the darkest brown, almost coffee-bean coloured, and the

whites around them were stained a dirty nicotine: he was obviously sick and he wheezed frequently.

There was seating space for sixty-four people on the hard wooden benches in our carriage, but by the time we pulled out of the station, a little after five o'clock, there were two hundred or more people in the carriage. Those without seats squatted in the corridor or lay beneath our feet.

I had happy memories of my first journey through the Nubian desert. It took the steam train forty-eight hours and many break-downs to reach Khartoum, but the overwhelming strangeness of the desert, and the excitement of riding the whole way south on the roof, outweighed the discomfort of intense heat and aching bones. I remembered the night best, lying on the domed roof (tied on for safety by a piece of rope) and gazing at the cloudless sky. For the first time I could see the North Star and the Southern Cross, the two best-known denizens of their respective hemispheres, sharing the same sky; each affirming its opposition to the other, one signalling where the Nile began, the other where it ended. I felt none of the excitement now. I was tired, dispirited and filled with a sense of foreboding.

We were an hour south of Halfa when the sun fell from the sky in a blaze of magenta and pink. There were no lights in the carriage and we were soon enveloped by darkness. The windows had neither glass nor shutters, and dust swirled in from the desert to clog our eyes and noses. The wood carriages creaked like ancient and over-worked beds as we ambled along the tracks.

I slept for a while but woke when somebody turned on a radio. 'Railways in India are a great source of prosperity,' said the commentator in impeccable Queen's English. Wolfgang was still knitting. Jol and her friend slept. Gerrald, the Frenchman, was arguing with a couple of young Sudanese students, one of whom was praising Hitler's treatment of the Jews. 'The Jews are bad people,' he suggested. 'Hitler was right.' Wolfgang brought the argument to an abrupt halt by explaining the joys of yoga cleansing.

At eleven o'clock we pulled into Station No 6. It consisted of half a dozen mud houses with conical roofs and a water tank. There were eight tables on the sand beside the tracks. A paraffin lamp on each illuminated urns of beans, and travellers flooded out of the doors and windows to eat. Young boys rushed up and down selling glasses of iced water and tea. The camel-herder with the crescent moustache bought me a glass of tea, and when we left he called a young Sudanese over and said something to him in Arabic. The youth turned to me.

'He wants to know about the weather where you come from.'

I told him about it. The youth translated. The herder nodded thoughtfully, keeping his eyes on me while he listened. 'The rain!' he exclaimed after some deliberation. 'Yes, that's it! That's the big difference between our countries.'

The herders were from Darfur, way out in the west of Sudan. It had taken them forty-two days to drive 103 camels up to Egypt. I expressed such an interest in the camel trade that the herder offered to take me along on their next trip for £S100. I said, no thank you. Jol asked me why I didn't do it. I explained that I didn't have the nerve.

At two o'clock in the morning we stopped again. It was impossible to get to the door of the carriage so I slid out of the window into the sand. I had violent diarrhoea and I felt foul. I was so weak by the time the train pulled off again that I had to be hauled up the six feet through the window. The rest of the night passed in a nightmarish haze of sickness and exhaustion. I had dysentery.

At 3.30 we stopped at Abu Hamed. I lay down for a while in the sand.

At 6.40 we pulled into the small mud village of Shereik, Dum palms grew by the Nile, the village was sprinkled with date palms, and acacia bushes were dotted across the sand to the east.

Slow as the trains are in Sudan, the journey through the Nubian Desert – the most easterly lobe of the Sahara – is quickly accomplished, or so it seems when one reads the travelogues of the adventurers and soldiers who passed this way in the eighteenth and nineteenth centuries. James Bruce, returning from Ethiopia to Europe in 1772, took seventeen days to journey from Berber to Aswan with a small caravan of camels and baggage-bearers. Many of the camels died, and his band was harried by bedouin. One man went mad, so they abandoned him in the desert. Some forty years later John Burkhardt, alias Sheikh Ibrahim Ibn Abdullah, became the first white man to cross the desert going south. His letters to the Association for Promoting the Discovery of the Interior Parts of Africa described the awful journey across the desert in the company of robbers, rogues and thieves. The sick and weak were abandoned on the way.

It took us less than a day to cover a distance which took Burkhardt three weeks. At Berber his caravan was greeted by hordes of Abyssinian slave girls who delightedly led the men away to their squalid hovels. Burkhardt was shocked by the drunkenness and debauchery. We were greeted by the ubiquitous tea-sellers; and slim girls with wonderful lithe bodies and marvellous pharaonic eyes dashed from window to window selling peanuts and bitter tamarind seeds.

At midday we reached Atbara and stayed for an hour. Wolfgang, who had just begun another pair of socks, left the train here to get a connection to Port Sudan. My insides were still in turmoil but I managed to stagger into the small market and drink some *karkadee*.

At five o'clock we arrived at Shendi. 'Invasions, slave-raiders, traders' caravans and the Mecca pilgrimage – Shendi has known them all for a thousand years,' wrote Alan Moorehead. Its market, he wrote, 'was a microcosm of the river, and what happened at Shendi was, very largely, the fate of all the other inhabitants on the Nile from Lake Tana to the sea'.

I looked at Shendi, I'm afraid, through dysenteric eyes. I recalled wistfully the verdant banks of the Nile in Egypt and the rich colourfulness of the villages. Here I saw a dreadful and oppressive monotony: the low mud dwellings cowering in the sand like frightened partridges on a stubble field; the market drab and ugly; the desert stretching brown and uniform as far as one could see; the spiny branches of the sparse acacia scrub scorched and contorted.

We left soon after nightfall and evening prayers. Another eight hours to Khartoum. Aching bones, gummed eyes, heaving stomach.

Khartoum, two o'clock in the morning. Three of us spent an hour looking for a hotel. Everywhere cheap was full, everywhere expensive was expensive. Packs of yapping dogs roamed the otherwise deserted and dimly-lit streets. Every ten minutes I had to squat. Not that I was a threat to public hygiene: the sewers stank, the drains stank, and the walls of houses exuded the sweet odour of hot piss. Eventually we returned to the station. There were about two hundred people lying on the ground outside. I lay down beside them and fell into a deep sleep.

CHAPTER TWELVE
REFUGEES AND RUMOURS

*President Nimeiri's Sudan is continuing
its descent into pseudo-Islamic fanaticism
in the north, civil war in the south,
and near-bankruptcy everywhere. With the heat
in Khartoum reaching 120° F, the latest
presidential gesture, of the purely worldly kind,
is the confiscation of air conditioners to save electricity.*
The Economist, June 1984

I suspect that the principal task of history is to gather the disparate events of one time, weave them together to fuse with those which preceded them, and prepare them for those which will follow. In other words, to construct some sense out of chaos. Throughout the years before I left for Africa I collected clippings from the Western press about the Sudan. I ended up with a file on diseases, another on agriculture, and others on transport, war and politics. The largest was the one on politics. The reports' analyses of the growing turmoil and unrest in Khartoum and the south were predicated on the assumption that whatever happens can be logically explained. Such-and-such happened, therefore . . . I'm not convinced that the affairs of men can be so simply interpreted, but for what it's worth I shall give a brief sketch of what I had learned about the country before I arrived.

This vast country – 1,200 miles long and 1,000 miles wide – was split into a predominantly Arab and Islamic north and a negro south which was Christian and animist. There is a long history of the north suppressing and exploiting the poorer and less-developed south. Shortly after independence the country endured seventeen

years of civil war, with the Anyanya guerrillas fighting for seces-
sion. The war ended in 1972 when President Jaafar Nimeiri signed
the Addis Ababa Agreement with the guerrillas. The agreement
gave the south regional autonomy. Soon after the fighting ceased
the government began to exploit the natural resources in the south.
Chevron and other international companies struck oil and started
to extract it. And a French company, CCI, began the enormous
task of digging the 225-mile Jonglei Canal, whose purpose, when
completed, will be to reduce evaporation of water in the Sudd
Swamp and to increase the Nile's flow downstream by 5 per cent.
But the northern government paid little attention to southern
aspirations – economic or otherwise – and by the early 1980s it
was clear that it had no intention of sharing the spoils. For
example, instead of building a refinery in the south, Nimeiri
decided to ship oil north along a pipeline to Port Sudan and the
Red Sea.

The president had sown the seeds for renewed discontent, and he
proceeded to water them by tearing up the Addis Ababa Agreement.
The regional government in Juba was abolished and the south
divided into three regions, with presidential stooges appointed to
administer them. The final insult to the southern negroes came
with Nimeiri's declaration of Islamic law in September 1983.

By the time I'd arrived, civil war had begun again. Many soldiers
had defected from the army and joined up with the Sudanese
People's Liberation Army, which had mounted an offensive against
the government under the leadership of Colonel Garang. Foreign
workers had been kidnapped and killed, and Chevron, CCI and
other Western companies had been compelled to pull their workers
out of the south. Meanwhile, the president's harsh repression of all
his opponents in the north – there were over two thousand political
prisoners in May 1984 – had further diminished his popularity. The
country was massively in debt, there was famine in some areas,
and refugees continued to pour in from neighbouring countries,
further straining Sudan's ability to feed herself.

I woke a little before daybreak, drank a cup of tea in the station
and set off with Jol, her friend and Gerrald to look for a hotel.

We found one down an unpaved back street not far from the station. I slept through the day.

The hotel consisted of five rooms which opened on to a courtyard. Each room had between five and seven iron beds and the walls were painted a pale green-blue. Two rooms were occupied by Ugandans and two had a mixture of Eritreans and Ethiopians. I was in the other room. I woke at five o'clock in the afternoon, and from my bed I could see most of what was going on in the hotel. Outside our room a man was ironing a pile of laundry, using a simple iron which he heated on a charcoal stove. Beyond him, and under a wide awning in the courtyard, there were twelve beds in two rows of six. A sick and emaciated Ethiopian woman lay on one. She had a large crucifix tattooed on her forehead. Underneath her bed there was a charcoal stove and a bundle of rags. A stocky man with a moustache was sitting on the end of her bed and talking to her. She didn't seem to have much to say. Beyond them was the hotel entrance, where three men sat round a table. One of them was Mohammed. He had fought with the Eritrean Liberation Front; now he managed the hotel. He was beating another Eritrean at chess. Girma, an Ethiopian, was watching the game, but not with much interest. When the game was over he set up forty beds in the courtyard. It took him half an hour. He spaced the beds about eighteen inches apart. It took him another ten minutes to put mattresses on them. At six o'clock the laundryman packed away his stuff and left. At about the same time, fifty or so refugees, mostly Eritreans and Ethiopians, drifted into the hotel. Some lay on their beds and drowsed. A few joined Mohammed near the door to watch television. The Muslims laid out their prayer mats and prayed.

Girma came over to sit on the laundryman's table, which at night became his bed. He was thirtyish and round-faced, with strong brown eyes and a boyish smile. He asked me for a cigarette and I went out to sit with him. He told me the story of how he had escaped to the Sudan. Stories like this are two a penny in Khartoum.

'We made such a stupid mistake,' he began. 'We thought we could start a revolution in the cities. We should have begun in the countryside – slowly, slowly – with the peasants. We made it too easy for Mengistu's people. We were wiped out so soon.'

Girma was captured and taken to prison. He never saw any of his friends from outside, nor did he know what had become of his parents or his brothers.

'It was so hard for us. Some of those who were caught with me were tortured until they died. They tortured me too. They used to come every week during my first year, always on the same day of the week at the same time. You spent all week thinking about the next time: that was almost as bad as the torture itself. Sometimes they'd beat me. And sometimes they'd strip me and make me stand with a bottle of water suspended from my penis.'

After three years in prison, Girma broke out with eleven others. Ten of them decided to stay in Ethiopia and continue the fight against Mengistu's regime. Girma and one other resolved to flee the country. 'I was too tired. I'd had enough. All I wanted was to get out.'

He contacted his mother, who told him that his father had been taken away. 'I'm not sure what he'd done,' said Girma. 'He wasn't part of our movement.' His mother hid him for a few weeks, then he went to stay with an old girlfriend in the country south of Addis. She hid him and fed him. After a couple of months Girma and the other prison escapee who wanted to leave Ethiopia joined up with three more men. Together they raised enough money to buy a Toyota and three rifles. It took them two weeks to drive from Addis to Gambela, about 500 kilometres west of the capital and not far from the Sudanese border.

'We had to travel very slowly. We knew we would be killed if we were caught. We'd only drive at night. Before dawn we used to drive the car into thick woods and hide up for the day. Sometimes we came across army road blocks. Two of us had army uniforms and forged papers. We were lucky. We always got through.

'At Gambela we sold the car and walked north into the mountains. I knew the country well because I used to go hunting there with my father when I was a boy. We were careful to avoid the peasants, though we had to hunt to keep ourselves alive. We were there nearly three months, waiting for the right time to cross to Sudan.'

It took them thirty-two days to reach a small village just over the Sudanese border.

'On the thirtieth day,' continued Girma, 'two of my friends died of thirst. We were too weak to bury them, so we left them where they died, out in the sun. My tongue was so swollen that I could no longer talk. I thought I too was going to die. We had no food with us: just our guns. When we arrived in the village the people stole our guns and the few possessions we had. We asked them to help us but they wouldn't; although they did feed us. We were frightened that sooner or later they'd kill us. After a week we felt stronger. One night, the village asleep, we got our guns back and walked all the way back to Ethiopia.

'When we got to the border we headed south till we reached the Sobat River. We crossed into Sudan again. This time the villagers didn't rob us. We made our way to Malakal and the police locked us up. We were brought to Khartoum, where I spent six weeks in a camp. There was hardly any food and few medical facilities. People were dying there.'

When we'd arrived in the morning only one of the five beds in our room was occupied – by a Rwandan who was rubbing oil through his hair. Mohammed chucked him out, much to the Rwandan's disgust, and for reasons which we didn't understand. I suppose it was because we had a girl with us. The Rwandan transferred himself, though not his possessions, to a bed outside the door. Above his now vacated bed was a crumpled and torn poster of President Nimeiri in full military regalia, a flag which I assumed to be Rwandan, and some prayer beads. A couple of jellabas and a black coat hung from a hook beside the bed, beneath which were two cardboard boxes full of papers and newspaper cuttings. He had some more papers and books in a plastic bag on the window sill. Though banished from the room he frequently came in to rifle through them.

The Rwandan had been staying in this hotel for the past seven years. He was a most impressive-looking man – fine-boned, and very tall and slender with a loose gait. He was always muttering and droning to himself and laughing at his private jokes. Initially, and not surprisingly, he resented our presence, but after a few days he became quite affable. He had no real friends among the other

157

refugees, though he often talked – generally unintelligibly – to whoever was standing near him. One morning I heard him swearing most fluently in French, so I addressed him in that language. His reply was most interesting. Half the words were recognizably French. The remainder weren't, though they were full of Frenchness. The Ugandans in the room next to ours told me that he spoke a similar genre of half-intelligible Swahili. One day he presented a long letter to Jol, written in his crazy French. It was a very crude love letter, but it was impossible to grasp the full meaning of what he was saying.

Some days the Rwandan never stirred from his bed, remaining from dawn to dusk hidden beneath a sheet. Other days he would disappear at daybreak and return after dark. 'I've been terribly busy today,' he announced after one such day. Nobody seemed to know where he went or what he did during the daytime. Many of the refugees had work in the city, but I don't think the Rwandan was one of them.

He was the most assiduous washer and prayer. He would spend hours combing his frizzy hair and applying sweet-scented oil to his body, and – so one of the other Muslims told me – his prayers were most unorthodox. One can normally count on about five minutes for the evening prayer, yet the Rwandan could drag this out to an hour. Once he fell asleep with his head pressed to the ground and keeled over. We called him the Mad Rwandan; but, on reflection, I think he was one of the most contented human beings I have ever met – uncomplaining, self-assured and cheerfully resigned to his fate.

For two nights the Rwandan's bed remained vacant, then John, a Ugandan refugee, moved in from next door. He was a shy and delightful man. Every day he went down to the offices of the United Nations High Commission for Refugees, and after the fifth day I asked him how he was getting on. 'I haven't got through the office door yet,' he sighed.

He would lie on the bed for hours listening to his radio. Mostly he tuned into English-language programmes, but sometimes he would just play with the dial, stopping briefly to listen to a programme in Swahili or Arabic. One evening he stopped on a French station. The reception was poor but we caught snatches. '. . . *deux cents personnes tuées en Rwanda hier* . . .'

'Funny,' said Gerrald, who had been contemplating going that way, 'I thought Rwanda was a nice quiet place.' I offer this snippet of conversation not because it has any intrinsic interest, but because it typified the desultory, *waiting-for-Godot*ish atmosphere in which we spent our days at the hotel.

For the first few days I didn't stir much from the hotel. It took a while to shake off the dysentery. I slept a lot, sweated a lot and lost a stone or so.

The day would begin around seven o'clock with Girma turning off the huge fan which hung from our ceiling. He'd sweep the tiled floor of dust, cigarette ends and the accumulated detritus of the previous day. I'd fetch a cup of tea from the tea-seller who operated from a small charcoal stove in the street outside. If you got to him early enough you could get it with milk – *chai laban*. Sometimes it was spiced with ginger.

By eight o'clock most of the refugees had disappeared, the court-yard beds were cleared away, and the laundryman had taken over one of the three WC-cum-showers to pump dirt from the linen. Among the refugees who stayed was the sick Ethiopian woman. She looked close to death. And the Ugandans next door ventured out little. There was a young couple with a child of their own, a six-year-old orphan girl, and another woman with a baby and no man. Some days I would sit and chat with these refugees from West Nile province. They had fled Obote's soldiers. Conversations about politics were held in whispers. 'Please be careful,' pleaded one of the women when she overheard her husband telling me of massacres near his village. 'Even here I think there are spies.'

Most of the time I lay on my bed, and between long bouts of sweaty sleep I read a soiled and much-fingered copy of Patrick Marnham's *Dispatches from Africa* – 'A wonderful book,' said an Ethiopian. 'One of the few great books about what is happening in Africa by a European.' Occasionally I would play chess against Mohammed and lose. The days seemed very long, and I looked forward to the evenings, when I'd hear news from the outside world.

Around dusk Gerrald would return. I hadn't taken to him at first: he had seemed aloof and I was suspicious of the stories he told – but he grew on me. He was incapable of venturing out of the hotel without getting into some sort of scrape.

One evening he returned in a state of great agitation. His black eyebrows were bouncing up and down his forehead and he was rolling his eyes. I asked him what he had been doing.

He whistled through his teeth and shook his head from side to side. 'Been to a bordel,' he announced. 'Crazy! Crazy! Crazy! I met this guy – nice guy, really nice guy, Sudanese – in the souk at Omdurman. He took me to this bordel. You wouldn't have believed it! There were twenty-five men waiting in a queue. I stood in the queue for a while. Then I thought: I don't like the look of these people! So I left. But I want to go back. You know how it is? If you can't get any mango, then you carry on looking for mango till you get it.' He sank back on his bed and closed his eyes. 'You should have seen those men! *Oh là là!*'

'When are you going back?' I asked.

'Can't,' he replied absent-mindedly. *'Je voudrais bien retourner la nuit. Mais je peux pas. On pouvait être tué là-bas!* Yeah, it's true. You could get killed there.' He fell asleep.

A few days later he disappeared for the night with an American traveller. He returned while Girma was sweeping our room the next morning. Together they'd spent the evening scouring the big hotels in search of entertainment. They had been to the Grand, the Meridien, the Oasis and the Hilton.

'Dead,' reported Gerrald disgustedly. 'No music, no dancing, no girls, no drink.'

After midnight they had decided to try a nightclub next to the station, from the outside a most sleazy-looking place. They picked up two girls who asked them to go home with them. 'These girls,' said Gerrald, 'they were nice girls.' By which I think he meant they were nice looking.

'We got into a taxi,' continued Gerrald, 'and we drove and drove and drove. Eventually the driver dropped us at the end of a street – he refused to come down it – and we had to pay. Twenty pounds! Imagine, twenty pounds!'

I lost track of his story here. He painted a picture of unlit streets, shabby slums, a violent atmosphere. They ended up, as far as I could tell, in a pimp's apartment.

'They asked us if we wanted a jug of *marissa* – you know, Sudanese beer – and we said yes. We drank it and they asked for fifty pounds. We said we weren't going to pay. Then we started bargaining with the girls. They wanted fifty pounds each. Then things turned nasty. We gave them ten pounds for the beer and left. The girls were screaming at us as we set off down the street. We hadn't gone far when we looked round and saw them talking to a man with a truck. He revved up and came slowly towards us. When he got close he accelerated and tried to run us down. We split up then and I ran for an hour, never knowing where I was going, scared all the time that the truck would find me and try and kill me again.'

Somehow the two of them had made it back to the hotel.

'I'm going to a wedding tomorrow,' said Gerrald before he fell asleep. He was always going to weddings. He was obsessed by the idea of going to a wedding. It was his Holy Grail. I don't think he ever got to one.

In 1975 I passed through Khartoum twice, once before heading into Ethiopia, once on my way back north from south Sudan. I liked it. Architecturally it had little of interest, but it wasn't marred, as so many African cities were, by the juxtaposition of Western affluence and native squalor. There was none of the outright poverty one saw in, say, Nairobi or Mombasa or Addis or Cairo. People were fed. Nor did one see the African élites cruising round the city centre in Rolls-Royces and Mercedes. A town of little contrast: a bit too hot, but peaceful and friendly.

I was shocked by Khartoum this time. It used to be remarkably clean, but now the streets were left unswept, and the drains were open and blocked. Even in the city centre there was the permanent stench of sewage. People shat and pissed on the pavements, and sand, blown in from the desert, lay in drifts across the main roads. The roads hadn't been repaired for years and traffic had to negotiate gaping potholes and crumbling kerbs.

At the heart of Khartoum lay Athenae Square. It fascinated me, such was its appalling atmosphere of desolation. It was about sixty yards square, and surrounded on all sides by four- or five-storey concrete buildings of great ugliness. Their facades faced outwards, and their backs towered over the square. The windows at the back, of which there weren't many, were blocked up with huge air-conditioning boxes. The square itself was dominated by a bleak entrance to an underground car park and by rows of concrete piles. Apparently there had been an intention to build a hotel in the square. The piles were erected but work never progressed any further.

There were a couple of small pyramids of building sand between the redundant piles, and at night these served as communal beds for the dozens of beggar boys and street urchins who lived rough. The shops and cafés which were hewn into the bleak backsides of the larger commercial buildings were scruffy, dirty and miserable. There was one for the tourists – the few there were – selling ivory, ebony, reptile skins and silver. And there were a couple of juice bars and a café selling camelburgers and lurid pink ice-cream. Some evenings I wandered down here and sat on one of the rickety blue metal seats to eat. The square was so poorly lit that you had to peer hard at your plate to see what you were eating. Much of the time was spent fobbing off the beggar boys who'd pinch you till you gave them something.

In 1975 there was scarcely a beggar in Khartoum. The few there were seemed to come from neighbouring countries. Now the town was hotching with them, and most were Sudanese. The beggar boys had no families. Either they had been deserted or they had done the deserting. Irritating as they could be, it was impossible not to admire them. They wandered round in gangs, begging what money they could and scavenging for food. There was great camaraderie between them and they were fearless. Much more distressing were the destitute and diseased adults who lined the streets around the business centre. Some had leprosy; some were blind; others were grossly deformed by accident or disease.

The shops outside Athenae Square were somewhat smarter than those within. There was a bookshop run by a Greek family and some moderately respectable clothes shops in a small precinct, the sort they were building in towns like Bolton or Dewsbury in the early 1960s. Then there was the Casa Blanca, an upmarket ice-cream parlour where the rich, both local and expatriate, would

gather in the evening. A bowl of 'Chocolate Mud' cost £S4 and a banana split the same. The banana split contained every imaginable fruit with the significant exception of banana. I went there one evening with an English teacher who had just returned to the capital after nine months in the bush. He was so fascinated by the ingredients of the banana split that he returned every night and ordered one, on the offchance that he might one day get banana with it.

'I'd like a banana split without the banana,' he said to the waiter.

'Certainly,' replied the waiter. And that was what he got.

There was another small and smartish café between the Casa Blanca and the British Embassy. The food was good and it was here, after five days in Khartoum, that I ate my first decent meal. A ghetto-blaster played Sudanese music (for which I never acquired a taste), but just before I left the waiter put on Bob Marley's *Rastaman Vibration*. 'Does this make you feel at home?' he inquired.

I was amused by him asking me if the music of a man from Trenchtown, Jamaica, made me feel 'at home'. But it did. For me, Marley had become a leitmotiv for home. When Richard North left me in Egypt he gave me a cassette with Marley's 'Kaya' on one side and 'Rastaman Vibration' on the other. I carried it round with me and sometimes I would get it played in cafés. I felt enormously reassured whenever I heard him. His was the only 'Western' music one heard in the cafés in Sudan – no Peter Tosh, no Yellowman, no Aswad, no Eddie Grant, no other reggae but Marley.

I remember going back late one night from Athenae Square to the hotel, which was about a mile away. Once off the main streets I walked in darkness. The side streets were unlit and deserted except for a few sleeping beggars. I passed a small juice stall off Souk Arabi, where a man stood alone behind the bar. He was playing Marley at full volume through a crackling set of speakers which faced on to the street. The music followed me home:

> Excuse me while I light my spliff
> good God I got ta take a lift
> from reality I just can't drift
> that's why I am staying with this riff.

Ten minutes later, far away from Souk Arabi, I stood for a while outside the hotel. I could still make the music out, very faint, above the barking of the city's dogs. Thank God for Marley, I thought. (Intriguingly, it was Michael Jackson, not Marley, who was most popular in Egypt. And that seemed fitting. Tricky soul stuff for the Arabs; earthbound reggae for the Africans.)

'How are you, sir?' asked a smartly dressed gentleman. 'Fine,' I replied. 'And how are you?'

'Marvellously well,' he said. 'Do you like the *tej?*'

I said I did. I was half way through my second pint and feeling mildly tipsy. I had drunk a lot of the honey wine in 1975 when I was in Ethiopia. It was always yellow but varied in its degree of cloudiness, and it came both with and without dead flies. I had tasted, as far as I could remember, none better than that which I was drinking now, which was an opaque amber and fly-less.

'This is very poor *tej*,' announced the Ethiopian. 'On account of the bad bees. They get their honey here from valley bees. The valley bees are bad bees. They produce a yellow honey. The best bees are the mountain bees. They produce a wonderful white honey which makes the best *tej*.'

The Ethiopian swilled some *tej* round his mouth, swallowed it, denounced it again as poor stuff and ordered another pint.

I came to this small, illegal drinking joint half a dozen times. Fortunately I only coincided once with the man who conversed with me now. He was an outrageous snob and unbearably smug. He was in his fifties, balding, festooned with gold jewellery and accompanied by two younger men. They listened to every word he said – I think they understood English – and smiled whenever he cracked what he took to be a joke.

'I live in Poona,' he said. 'India is a wonderful country for people like me and you.' He spoke perfect, clipped English, like that of an upper-class Indian. 'Next door to my house lives an Englishman. He is a doctor. He lives like a king. You would love it.'

I said I didn't think I would.

'Of course you would!' he said imperiously. 'You could have

six servants like he has. Marvellous country for the white man.'

I asked him how he came to be in India. He claimed to have been a crony of President Mengistu, whose purportedly Marxist regime has ruled Ethiopia since the 1974 revolution. (This bit was in whispers, which was just as well as three Eritrean Liberation Front fighters sat at the table behind us.) Mengistu, he said, had sent him to India a few years after the revolution to act as the country's ambassador. For reasons which I didn't fathom, he sought asylum there. He now ran a business in Poona and another in Khartoum. He didn't have much time for the Sudanese; but he thought very highly of the English upper class. As a representative of the English middle class, I am pretty sure that an upper-class Englishman would have been as appalled by him as I was.

The drinking parlour was run by Ethiopians for Ethiopians and Eritreans; but whites were welcome too. From the outside it was a nondescript building on an unpaved back street, no different from the houses on either side. To get in you tapped gently on a door and waited. Twice I was refused entry – there was no *tej* left, apparently – but the other times I was led through a small courtyard with half a dozen beds beneath a flame tree, down a corridor with doors to more bedrooms, and then into a large kitchen. Off the kitchen was a small room with a still where the *tej* was prepared. Once through the kitchen another corridor led to a large room which was clean, colourful and brightly lit. There were five small tables there, each surrounded by comfortable armchairs of the sort one associates with smart English conservatories: wrought iron, painted white, with soft cushions in William-Morris-style covers. Several paintings were hung on the light blue walls. They were African 'Rousseaus' depicting giraffes, baboons and other animals in luxuriant foliage. And very pleasant it was to be in a room without a picture of Nimeiri.

The *tej* was served by a bony-featured, narrow-waisted, tight-breasted Ethiopian woman whose neck was embroidered with a lattice of abstract tattooes. A pint mug cost £S2.50, and one was enough to put you in high spirits.

I find it sad that my happiest memories of this visit to Khartoum come from this drinking parlour and the hotel. Sad because both places were refuges from Sudanese life. No Sudanese ever came into the drinking room while I was there, and few stayed in the hotel. They were unwelcome.

When I came on my own I was invariably invited to sit with refugees already there. Most were very frank. They would tell me why they had fled Ethiopia or Eritrea, and how they had made their way to Khartoum. They were not searching for sympathy nor for help of any kind. They simply had stories to tell, mostly unpleasant. There was never a hint of self-pity; just anger, or more often, resignation.

Most of the Eritreans I met here had been born when the Eritrean province was already up in arms against Selassie's Ethiopia – the civil war began in 1962 – and had known nothing but war ever since.

One, in his mid-twenties, had fought for eight years with the ELF. He had left for Sudan after he had been shot. One of his hands was a mangled ruin. 'I haven't seen or heard from my family in Asmara for ten years now,' he said. 'I don't even know whether they are alive or dead, nor can they know what has become of me.'

Like all the other Eritreans I talked to, he could see no end to the fighting. 'We may not win independence, but we'll never stop fighting either.'

In 1952 the United Nations decided that Eritrea should be an 'autonomous unit' federated with Ethiopia. However, ten years later Selassie abolished its parliament and annexed Eritrea. The civil war began. Selassie received the support of the West, while the Eastern bloc and some Arab countries gave ideological and a little military support to the Eritreans. When Selassie was toppled the new regime, backed now by Moscow, stepped up the campaigns against the Eritreans. The partisans will tell you this. They smile wryly. Neither West nor East, as far as they are concerned, is to be trusted. Over two thirds of Mengistu's 300,000-strong army is stationed in Eritrea, and the weapons used against the Eritreans are now Russian rather than American.

There were other refugees there who had fled simply out of fear. One young man came from a rich family in Gondar, a large town in a province adjacent to Sudan. 'Under Mengistu things got worse and worse for us,' he said. 'My father's property was confiscated. Then I realized that we were likely to be killed.'

I remembered Gondar from 1975. It was a large, shabby town dominated by an old fort. The poverty there was worse than any I had seen before. The streets were full of lepers and beggars and many were hungry.

'It was a lovely town in those days,' continued the Ethiopian, 'but it changed so fast. There was so much killing. Before I left you couldn't walk down the main street without seeing bodies hanging from the branches of trees.' He claimed that 200,000 people had been killed during the recent purges in Gondar province. I am sure this figure was vastly exaggerated, but his descriptions of the purges fitted with those of Girma.

One of the best accounts of what had been happening in Ethiopia comes from Ryszard Kapuscinski's commentary of the conditions under which he carried out research into the final days of the court of Selassie, and is to be found in his book *The Emperor*. Girma had told me about *fetasha* and the Red Terror. He described the endless searches which everyone had to endure and the everyday killings in the streets of Addis. I would have liked to have quoted his descriptions in full. Unfortunately I lost my notes and it would be unfair to reconstruct them from memory. So here is Kapuscinski:

We all fell victim to [*fetasha*] – everyone, without regard to colour, age, sex, or social status. *Fetasha* is the Amharic word for search. Suddenly everyone started searching everyone else. From dawn to dusk, and around the clock, unceasingly, and not stopping for breath. The revolution had divided people into camps, and the fighting began. There were no trenches or barricades, no clear lines of demarcation, and therefore anyone could be an enemy. The threatening atmosphere fed on the Amharas' pathological suspicion. To them, no man could be trusted, not even another Amhara. No one's word can be trusted, no one can be relied upon, because people's intentions are wicked and perverse; people are conspirators . . .

All of them have weapons; they are in love with them. The wealthy had whole arsenals in their courts, and maintained private armies . . . A couple of years ago, you could buy guns in the stores like any other merchandise. It sufficed to pay for them; nobody asked any questions . . .

A man's life – what is that worth? Another man exists only to the degree that he stands in your way. Life doesn't mean much, but it's better to take it from the enemy before he has time to deliver a blow. All night (and also during the day) there is the sound of shooting, and later the dead lying in the streets . . .

To get things under control, to disarm the opposition, the authorities order a complete *fetasha*, covering everyone. We are searched incessantly . . . Anyone can search us, because we don't know who has the right and who hasn't, and asking only makes things worse . . . They frisk us: back, stomach, legs, shoes. And then what? Nothing, we can go on, until the next spreading of arms, until the next *fetasha*. The next one might be only a few steps on, and the whole thing starts all over again . . .

So from the Ethiopians and the Eritreans came stories of *fetasha*, of street killing, of torture. Most hated Sudan, or at least they said they did, yet they appreciated living in relative safety. 'At least I can walk on the streets here without fear,' said the young man from Gondar.

I found the refugees' disenchantment with the Sudan sad, even if understandable. To many, whether from Ethiopia, Eritrea or Uganda, its climate and culture were as alien as they were to me. As far as I could gather the ones who had reached Khartoum were lucky. The vast majority lived in camps near the borders of the countries from which they had fled. There were about 700,000 refugees in the Sudan at the beginning of 1984. The numbers continued to swell as the year progressed. I never visited any of the camps though I spoke to many who had moved from the camps to the capital.

'When I arrived in Sudan,' said one Ugandan who had fled the chaos in the West Nile province, 'I was given a room and a small plot of land to grow vegetables. But it takes time to prepare a garden. Once we went three weeks without getting any food.' Others complained that their camps were sometimes without any fresh water as well as food.

But however bad conditions were for the refugees, at least they had found a temporary sanctuary, whether from civil war in Eritrea, from forced labour and military conscription in Ethiopia, or from famine in both; whether from the looting remnants of Idi Amin's army, or the purges of Obote's. They were fortunate in their misfortune.

I met not one who said he or she would like to stay. Most nurtured a pathetic dream that they would one day escape to the West to begin a new and more permanent life. A few – very few – have got out: that has been enough to provide the many who wait with hope. There was scarcely a refugee in my hotel who didn't speak English and most spoke it fluently. Many were well qualified – there were doctors, lawyers, social workers even – and they believed that in America, or Britain, or Canada, the three countries most wished to end up in, they would find work. They believed that their adopted countries would welcome them with open arms. I tried to explain to one Ethiopian the problems of unemployment in Britain, among both whites and blacks. He couldn't even see it as a problem. And why should he? Compared to what was happening in his country, the existence of three million people without work in Britain was nothing. Good heavens, these three million even had food and shelter!

A few refugees like Girma were going to get out of Sudan. Many more believed they would – it was just a matter of time. Some would even give you the date by which they expected to leave. It was normally about three months ahead of when you were talking to them. And it will remain three months ahead, this year, next year, the year after, until the day arrives when they realize that they will never leave – unless, of course, they are among the lucky few.

I listened to the stories of the Ethiopians, the Eritreans and the Ugandans, but I learnt nothing more about the political and economic conditions which prevailed in their countries than I would have done had I stayed at home and read the *Economist* or the *Financial Times*. However, they gave me a glimmer, albeit faint – for those I spoke to were removed from the immediate threat of hunger and destitution – of the calamities which have befallen this part of Africa. I saw the tragedies no longer in terms of a vast collective trauma embracing hundreds of thousands of people, but as an agglomeration of hundreds of thousands of very personal misfortunes – each individual carrying around his individual tragedy like a tortoise its shell; and each shell different from every other shell.

In Sudan alcohol consumption was punished by lashing – eighty lashes for a Muslim, forty lashes for the likes of me. I always felt reasonably safe once inside the *tej* joint – going in and out one had to make sure the street was deserted – though there was a scare one night while I was there. Apparently three Sudanese had walked through the main door. The woman who served us rushed into the room where a dozen of us were drinking. The door was closed and we sat in heavy-breathing silence for ten minutes or so. The lady who ran the place – a huge woman with a podgy face and tight-plaited hair, the archetypal brothel-keeper – eventually got the Sudanese to leave. Drinking continued as normal.

At the end of September 1983 President Nimeiri imposed *sharia* (Islamic) law on the country. His reasons for doing so were twofold. He wanted to impress Saudi Arabia and the Gulf Emirates, from whom he needed financial aid and free oil. And he wanted to appease the Muslim Brotherhood, a powerful group of funda-mentalists who wished to see the creation of an Islamic state in Sudan.

Western systems of law take no account of God. They regulate man's behaviour towards man. *Sharia*, however, represents divine law. It regulates man's conduct with other men, but more im-portantly with God. God, so to speak, is the attorney-general, and the courts make decisions on His behalf. There are two distinct groups of penalties: those as punishment for crimes against religious and military discipline; and those which involve private vengeance. Because the former are crimes against God, there is no chance of pardon. Nor are there any courts of appeal.

Nimeiri's first step, once *sharia* was declared, was to release 13,000 common criminals. They were told that the next time they transgressed they would be punished under the code of *sharia*. Punishments are severe. Unlawful intercourse carries the death penalty by stoning. Theft is dealt with by chopping off the right hand, and the left foot for a second offence. Murderers are beheaded. The prisoners freed under Nimeiri's amnesty were given £S100 each and promised employment. It was difficult to find out what had happened to them. One Western diplomat said he thought that most were behind bars again. 'I heard of one,' he said, 'who had about a quarter of an hour's freedom. A bunch of them were given £S100 and loaded into the back of a lorry. Before they set off, one of the prisoners realized his hundred pounds was gone. They searched the rest and the one with £S200 was carted back into prison.'

Many others just hung around outside the prison, committed minor offences and were stuck back in again.

By summer 1984 an estimated fifty-eight amputation sentences had been carried out, many publicly in Kober prison. On 9 December 1983, three thousand people witnessed the hand amputation of two thieves, Mohammed Salih Hamid and Mohammed Yahia el-Fadil. Here is the description of the event, supplied by the government's SUNA news agency:

They had their right hands covered at the wrist with cotton and two prison clinic male nurses tied a band on the convicts' right arms and fixed a string of some medical instrument which is supposed to hold back blood when the hand is amputated.

After the male nurses had checked the blood pressure, the convicts had their legs tied with strong leather rope and their eyes [blind]folded.

The convicts . . . were talking to the guards and nurses before and after they were seated on the chairs, and would from time to time feel their right hands, which were anaesthetized and dressed with cotton and band . . .

At ten o'clock two soldiers of the prison force, dressed in surgical theatre aprons and holding tall sharp sterilized knives [entered] and each approached his assigned convict.

Each convict was held . . . by strong prison guards and each amputator, using the sharp end of the knife, simultaneously held the hand to be amputated by the fingers and cut it swiftly and skilfully from the wrist.

The cutting operation took about one minute and none of the convicts uttered a word, moved or made any sound.

As they were given local anaesthesia and high doses of sedatives they obviously did not feel any pain, or at least did not show that they did.

The amputators did their job amid cheers of approval from the spectators, towards whom each amputator held the removed part of the hand.

The chopped-off parts of the hands were first raised up high for the public to watch and then were displayed on the podium for a while before prison warders carried them away.

The handout ends by saying that the prisoners were examined by doctors before the amputation 'to see how fit they were for the operation'. The following year the *Observer* reported that Dr Kamal Zaki Mustapha, a Fellow of the Royal College of Surgeons in Edinburgh, had supervised *sharia* amputations in Khartoum.

Back in the 1930s, one of my favourite travel writers witnessed a hand amputation in Ethiopia. I first came across Henri de Monfreid when I was rummaging through a rubbish skip in the French Midi. Among the building rubble and broken furniture was an old copy of his *Aventures de mer*. It was a large paperback with a cover photo showing two turbaned Arabs – pirates, presumably – shooting from their dhow at a smart yacht. The flavour of the book can be gleaned from the chapter titles: The Blockade, The Eunuch, The Capture, Adji the Spy, I Work for the Admiralty, Death of the Ship, The Mystery of Aden . . .

De Monfreid's literary output was considerable, but he was, first and foremost, an adventurer. He wrote, one feels, simply to pass the time between running whatever merchandise came his way up and down the Red Sea; or between his journeys into the Ethiopian interior and his battles with British naval police off Djibouti. In his *Aventures de mer* (published in 1932 and still in print) he described his arrival in Addis Ababa shortly after Haile Selassie's enthronement. Corpses hung from the great fig trees in St George Square; and he noted that the bodies had been there for two days and had to remain for one more: *'Il faut que la justice se montre au peuple et que le condamné serve d'exemple avec le maximum de rendement.'* Justice must be seen to be done, etc.

The day after his arrival he witnessed a hand amputation.

The operation took place with great simplicity. On the signal of the *zabanias*, who led the condemned, a butcher left his block. His clients waited patiently.

The butcher sharpened his knife on a stone in a professional manner. Then, as though he was cutting a shoulder of lamb, he chopped off the wrist . . .

If the patient has parents, they will have prepared a bowl of boiling butter, into which they plunge the bleeding stump. The victim gathers up his hand as it must be buried with him when he dies. He can go; he is free; justice has been done . . .

If he doesn't have any parents he bleeds to death where he is . . . When the corpse begins to smell, a fatigue party of prisoners drags him with ropes across the town and buries him in the fields.

Our European sensibilities are disgusted; but, with the mentality of the people of this country, justice as we conceive it would be inoperable and absurd.

I'm quite sure that de Monfreid wouldn't endorse the application of *sharia* in Sudan today. Indeed many Muslims – including Sadiq el-Madhi, the leader of the Ansar sect – have opposed it. They point out that during the times of the Prophet Mohammed amputations were very rare, and then were only carried out on hardened criminals.

With the declaration of *sharia* Sudan officially went dry. Nimeiri poured into the Nile a symbolic bottle of whisky (or beer, depending on who you talk to and what you read) and an estimated £S3 million pounds' worth of alcohol was thrown in after it. Nine tenths was said to have been recovered by soldiers downstream and fed back into the black market.

All the bars and liquor factories in the province had been closed down and their merchandise confiscated, but the Ethiopians continued brewing *tej* as usual, and it needed little initiative and not much money to acquire *marissa*, a local beer, or *aragi*, a powerful spirit, from the many illegal traders who operated down the back streets. Foreigners were not exempted from *sharia* punishment, and I heard of an Italian and an Englishman who had received the forty lashes. The Englishman had apparently claimed that his hangover was so bad he hardly felt the whip.

The price of both alcohol and marijuana had risen since prohibition. Sudanese grass was on sale down a sandy alley near our hotel. The dealers had some sort of agreement with the local soldiers. Once the buyer had paid for his grass he was likely to be stopped by a soldier. The soldier would threaten the buyer with exposure to the law. (Marijuana is illegal.) If the buyer had any sense (most had) he bribed the soldier – the going rate was £S5 – and continued on his way with his grass. If he didn't produce a bribe he was likely to have his grass confiscated. It would make its way back to the dealers to be resold. I never saw any of the refugees smoking in the hotel but most of the travellers did.

My original plan had been to take the steamer from Kosti, a short distance south of Khartoum, up to Juba, eight hundred miles away near the border of Uganda, but the steamer was no longer running. On 14 February it had been attacked by guerrillas using small arms. Some passengers died in an explosion and the fire which followed, and others died in the water. There were about a thousand people on the steamer and estimates of the death toll varied from a couple of hundred to six hundred. Since then all river transport south had ceased, and south Sudan was closed to travellers.

I had suspected, long before I arrived in Khartoum, that I would be unable to get to Juba overland (it was still possible to fly in if you booked five weeks ahead) so I had entertained the idea of going into Ethiopia and making my way to Lake Tana and the source of the Blue Nile. However, the border with Sudan had closed shortly after I crossed it in the mid-seventies, and I now discovered that it had never reopened. I could fly to Addis, at great expense, but I was warned that it would be impossible to travel freely within Ethiopia. Some Eritreans offered to get me taken into Eritrea to report on the war. I said no thank you, I wasn't a war correspondent and trusted that I never would be. So Ethiopia and the Blue Nile were out.

Reading over my notes from the days I spent in Khartoum I find frequent entries giving vent to my frustration. I was hardly halfway up the Nile and it didn't look as though I was going to get much further.

One night I went for an early post-dusk drink in the *tej* joint. There were a couple of English teachers there, just in from their nine-month stint in Nyala, a five-day train ride west of Khartoum. I explained how my plans had been thwarted.

'You could still get to Lake Victoria,' said one.

'Not overland,' I replied.

The teacher explained how I could do it. I would have to take a train or bus to Nyala, and from there a lorry to Bangui in the Central African Republic. That would take around three weeks. From Bangui I could make my way into Zaïre, and from there cross into Rwanda, a small country to the west of Lake Victoria.

I ordered a second mug of *tej*. The idea of reaching Lake Victoria via Central Africa and Zaïre became increasingly attractive as the level of the *tej* dropped. By the time I hit the street, around eight o'clock, I had determined to do it. I returned in jaunty mood to the hotel and wandered into the fug of my room. There were six people there. Gerrald was talking, predictably, about women. 'These European women with their short pants and tight tee-shirts, hitching on their own through Arab countries – they may be alright 90 per cent of the time; but what about the other third?'

He and Jol had been over to Omdurman to watch the whirling dervishes – a regular spectacle on Fridays, the Muslim holiday. They had been befriended by some wealthy Sudanese and taken back to their home for drinks (whisky and gin). They had returned – inevitably – with the latest rumours.

'There's going to be a military coup this week,' announced Gerrald. Everybody laughed. 'Sure,' he said indignantly. 'These guys were very reliable. They said there was going to be a coup.'

Two men were playing chess on the Rwandan's bed. One was a cantankerous little Scotsman with steel-rimmed spectacles. He was famous among the English teachers, largely because of his dourness and hatred of things Sudanese.

'He hates Sudan,' said another teacher. 'He hates the people; he hates the climate; he hates the job. But every year he comes back for more. The first year he was somewhere nice – Barbanusa, I think. He didn't like it. The next year he asked to go somewhere else. He didn't like that either. This year he ended up in Gedaref. Nobody could like it there, and naturally he didn't. There's no running water there, the town's full of refugees, and the people are unfriendly. But he's coming back again next year.'

The man who sat across the portable chess set from the Scotsman was a large, languorous Londoner, very good-looking and easy going. He had been travelling round Africa for eighteen months and didn't plan to return to England till the end of the year. All I knew about him, apart from the fact that he had travelled through the countries I now intended to visit on my way to Lake Victoria, was that he had played fifty-eight games on his small chess set and won every one; and that he had been arrested in Bangui for kissing a girl on the street.

It took him half an hour to win his fifty-ninth game; and it took

14. Loading the ferry at Aswan High Dam

15. The ferry from Aswan to Wadi Halfa takes two days.
It is a serene and pleasant journey

16. The train which goes from Wadi Halfa to Khartoum. The journey
is unbearably long, especially if you're in third class and have dysentery

17. The conical building to the right of the minaret is the Mahdi's
tomb in Omdurman. The Mahdi's troops defeated General Gordon in 1885

18. Only the mosques save Khartoum from total drabness

19. President Nimeiri looks down on the Mad Rwandan's bed.
The Rwandan, ejected from his bed on our arrival, had spent
seven years in this refugee hotel

20. Drinking and chatting

21. Slaughtering a camel. A crude death, perhaps;
but arguably more humane than the beast would have met with
in a conventional abattoir

22. Back-street Khartoum

23. Village gathering in the Nuba Mountains.
Westerners have been barred from visiting the area – to protect
the Nuba, according to the government; to enable the government to persecute
the Nuba, say some of its critics

24. Nuba Mountains: one man and his cattle

25. Baskets of dried fruit
in a Sudanese market

26. The ubiquitous tea-seller

27. The steamer from Juba to Kosti. By the time I reached Sudan
in 1984 guerrillas had blown up one of the Nile steamers,
and all public transport connecting north and south had ceased

him just a few minutes to make me abandon the plan to reach Rwanda. He thought I'd be lucky to do the journey in less than three months. 'If you were on the move every day you could do it faster. But you won't be. You'll find yourself getting stuck for days or maybe weeks in some pissy little village in the jungle. Specially as the rainy season begins soon.'

So I abandoned the idea and slept.

I'd been in Khartoum a week before I felt fit enough to spend a whole day away from the hotel. One morning I rose early, just before sunrise. Some of the refugees were already up and out. Others were just waking and queuing for the showers and toilets. Girma was folding away the vacated beds. Mohammed was praying. The Mad Rwandan was lying with his head propped on his elbow and reading a book by René Fallut. A fat Ugandan doctor with a gleaming bald head and a limp was smoking a huge cigar near the hotel door. He was beautifully dressed in pressed trousers and starched shirt. Outside the hotel two turbaned lorry drivers were inspecting the engines of their Bedford trucks. It was already hot, over eighty degrees and rising.

The tea-seller was emptying a jug of milk into a large kettle of tea. I paid him 12 piastres and he poured me a glass. I sat on the kerb and smoked. After a second cup of tea I walked to the end of the street and headed down El Jami Avenue to Souk Arabi. There was a huddle of men, black-faced and white-robed, praying together outside a small ironmonger's. Souk Arabi was already busy. People were piling into country buses – Bedford trucks with rows of benches behind the cab – and into 'boxes', small pick-ups which cram a dozen passengers into the back. A chorus of *kawadga!* – white man! – followed me through the square.

The sun was rising by the time I reached El Kabir mosque. I tramped across the oil-slicked sand of United Nations Square, and headed for my favourite street in Khartoum. It was tucked away behind a Bata shoe shop. The street must have had a name but none was displayed. It was about a hundred yards long, unpaved and lined on either side by avenues of old trees whose crowns were dense and impenetrable, the result of frequent pollarding and pruning. At the southern end of the street was a large café with rusty blue tables covered with a veneer of dirt and seams of rotting food. I sat down and ordered *addis* – lentils – and salad. Breakfast cost 25 piastres. The café was only half full. Two men I'd never seen came across and shook hands with me. They asked me how I liked Sudan.

Breakfast over, I bought a bowl of fruit from the fruit-seller who operated from dawn to dusk under one of the trees. He had an enormous aluminium bowl which took about ten gallons of figs, guava, banana, orange and ice. A bowl of fruit cost 33 piastres. I ate one standing up, then strolled down to the other end of the street where you could buy the best coffee in Khartoum. It was the scruffiest of establishments but always busy. A man sat at a blue table under a tree. In return for 15 piastres, he gave me a brass token and a small cup, half-full of unrefined sugar. I took my token into a small shop – it looked more like a back-street car-repair shed than a coffee shop – and exchanged it for a small aluminium flask of coffee.

Once you had got your coffee you could either drink it standing up in the street or you could find somewhere to squat. In the evenings that was easy enough, for there was plenty of sitting space under the trees on the opposite side of the street. But this morning, as every morning, the far side of the street was taken up by plasterers, carpenters, masons, electricians, painters and plumbers waiting for work. Each sat crosslegged, quiet and expectant, beside his tools.

The carpenters had the most elaborate piles before them, their tools turned into jagged pieces of sculpture topped by saws and chisels. They had more than a hint of Braque about them. The plumbers, too, must have spent care and time constructing small monuments to their trade, but the curvacious nature of their tools – curling pipes, U-bends, S-bends – made their sculptures less amenable to the Cubist style favoured by the carpenters. The painters and brickies were less ostentatious, the former sitting beside brushes and sandpaper, the latter next to heavy chisels, plumb-lines and trowels.

During the time I spent watching them none moved. Perhaps those seeking their services would come later in the day, although I couldn't imagine how they chose between one plumber and the next, between one mason and the others. Had I been doing the choosing I think I would have plumped for the man who had created the most satisfying piece of sculpture, just as the slave dealers must have picked out the fittest and firmest girls at the markets last century.

It was after seven o'clock when I left. In the fruit market near by peasants on donkeys were selling boxes of fruit to the marketeers and the marketeers were laying out great piles of water-melon, grapefruit, orange and mango. I spent five minutes bartering for half a dozen limes and then walked down to the Nile.

Nile Avenue is the finest street in Khartoum, and it is the only one which is regularly swept. It is lined by tall trees and government ministries, and it runs past the People's Palace to where the two Niles meet. Within the palace grounds is the Anglican Cathedral, now permanently closed. If you look carefully you can see bullet damage round the belfry. It was from here that rebels attempting to overthrow Nimeiri fired on to the palace. The palace guards – they are magnificently dressed in white uniforms with plenty of gold braid and plumed headgear – overcame the rebels. The incident gave Nimeiri a good excuse to close the cathedral. It must have been galling for him to have Christians singing in his back garden.

It was a lovely walk west from the palace towards Omdurman. Buzzards and kites flapped over the river and pied kingfishers dived from the hull of an upturned boat which rose like a hippo's back from the murky water. In the trees beside the Grand Hotel ibis were copulating, and uniformed waiters were serving lemon juices to early-morning risers on the terrace.

By the time I had reached the bridge which crossed the White Nile to Omdurman I was sweating profusely. It was eight o'clock and over 100 degrees. Every guidebook tells you that from here you can see the different-coloured waters of the two rivers, the White and the Blue, running side by side. I couldn't. A herd of cattle grazed on the river bank and women were standing in the water washing clothes. Some men were washing themselves.

I had picked the wrong day to visit Omdurman. The Sudanese were on holiday, celebrating the ascension of the prophet Mohammed, so the souk was almost deserted; and the British were celebrating the Queen's birthday, which meant that the British

Council office was closed. A pity, as I was hoping to see the exhibition of Hogarth prints. More than that, I wanted to see what sort of people worked there. The longer I spent in the Sudan the more intrigued I became by the small expatriate community.

Once every year, when I was very young, a small, dapper man with a bald head would arrive at my parents' home in Huddersfield. He would stay a couple of weeks, disappear for another year, then return again, sometimes in an old Rover, always with a mahogany suntan, invariably with a pipe between his teeth. It was my Uncle Percy. In the early 1950s he came from Sudan, later from Ethiopia, Nigeria and the Lebanon. His stories, which were many, were liberally interspersed with snatches of Arabic, in which he was fluent; and once he demonstrated – in that high quivering wail familiar to anyone who has travelled in the Muslim world – the muezzin's call to prayer. One year he sent me an Arabic newspaper with instructions to read from right to left, and once a red and white chequered headscarf, of the sort which became popular in Islington when Islington first learnt of Mr Yasser Arafat and the Palestinian Liberation Organization. Occasionally he produced on his annual visits black and white photographs of the Sudan. The one I remember best showed him having dinner in the bush. He was sitting at a table outside his tent. Surrounding him was a small army of black servants – cooks, baggage-bearers and so forth. He was of the 'old school', a benign paternalist. Uncle Percy left the Sudan when I was still in short trousers, but I read whatever I could lay my hands on about the country. It fascinated me; that it was known as 'The Sudan' rather than plain 'Sudan' endowed it with particular importance, though quite why, I'm not sure. I read about the Mahdist uprising and the death of Gordon (who I saw as a military version of Dr Livingstone) and I read about the Battle of Omdurman where the British (whose forces were led by the unsavoury Kitchener) slaughtered large numbers of Sudanese.

In 1975 I came to the Sudan with a letter of introduction from Uncle Percy to a government minister and a vague intention of finding work. I found neither.

During my two stays in Sudan in 1975 I met not one expatriate. This time I was hoping to meet some of the British in Khartoum, not through want of white company, but simply to see how they lived.

My appetite for this little exercise in sociological research had been whetted partly by Uncle Percy – I wondered if any of his kind still remained – and by an eighteen-page British Council document which fell into my hands just before I left England, titled 'Record of Living Conditions – Sudan', and stamped 'In Confidence'. It had been prepared by the Council in 1978 for staff going to the Sudan. 'It should *not* be taken to the country it concerns', said the document, and I could see why once I had read it. It advised staff what bed-linen and clothes to take, how to hire pots and pans from the British Women's Association, how to dress for cocktail parties and where to hire furniture. It exhorted staff to take with them a selection of tap washers and cotton nappies (which, like sugar, were often in short supply in Sudan), and warned about the problems of obtaining regular supplies of Tampax and electricity. It contained advice on everything from health and shopping to buying a car or disposing of one. And it provided valuable guidance on hiring servants; to wit:

Servants' wages have continued to rise, although probably more slowly than inflation. Most cooks would now be paid around £S100, *suffragis* £S70–90, cook-*suffragis* £S100-150 and *ghaffirs* (watchmen) £S50–60. It is becoming common for *ghaffirs* to double as gardeners, although most specialize in the slash-and-burn school of gardening. Many *ghaffirs* feel that their job requires them only to sleep prominently in the middle of the garden during hours of darkness. If you wish your *ghaffir* to remain awake while on duty it is as well to establish this early on. With large numbers of Eritrean refugees in Khartoum more and more servants these days are Eritreans. Many of them are well-educated men who have left Ethiopia for political reasons, and night watchmen with university degrees are not unknown. Those with degrees, on the whole, sleep as soundly on duty as those without, but will be able to give more coherent reasons for not having noticed the men who were burgling your house.

I had gathered together, before leaving England, a handful of contacts in the Sudan. Four were attached to the University of Khartoum, which had closed down shortly before my arrival, because of 'student unrest', so I didn't manage to contact any of them. I also had an introduction to the British Council representative in Juba. I never saw him as I never got to Juba this time. I was particularly sad not to meet him as I wished to verify some of the stories I had heard about the Council's office there. Apparently this man's predecessor went mad and failed to contact the head office in London for three months. He was replaced by the present incumbent, who, on his arrival, found himself in need of a typewriter. He calculated, or so it was alleged by one expatriate I met in Khartoum, that the cheapest way to acquire this vital piece of office equipment was to fly back to Britain and buy one, which he did. I hope he hasn't run short of ribbon.

The only person to whom I had an introduction and whom I did meet was a senior official in the British Embassy. I dropped in to see him three times and the short chats I had with him proved an excellent corrective to all the rubbish I read in the papers and heard on the streets.

I asked him about the Omdurman bombing. The Sudanese authorities will be glad to learn that he concurred with their view (which the BBC didn't) that the Omdurman bombing was not a lunatic act on the part of an increasingly unpopular president, but a lunatic act on the part of Libya's Colonel Gadafi. 'Go and see the bomb craters, if you wish,' said the man at the Embassy.

I decided, on this day out to Omdurman, that a bomb crater was almost as good as a Hogarth. I spent an hour searching for the bombed houses. I stood staring at the ruins once I found them.

'What are you looking at?' asked a Sudanese in Western dress.

'The bomb damage,' I replied.

'Oh, that!' he said. He scratched his head and gazed upwards into the sky. I thought he was going to tell me about the aeroplane and describe the bombing. Some urchins swarmed across to stand beside us. I began to feel very foolish.

'Are you interested in Libya?' asked the man.

'Not really,' I said.

'Good,' he replied. 'Gadafi's a very bad man.' I agreed with him, more or less.

We stood in silence for another minute. One of the urchins demanded baksheesh but he was repulsed by some sharp words from my companion. We were both dripping sweat.

'I must go now,' he said at length. He offered his hand and I shook it. 'Incidentally, Nimeiri's a very bad man as well.'

He disappeared. I drifted back to the market and slowly made my way through the sprawling and dusty suburbs and over the river to Khartoum.

The diplomat's views on the Omdurman bombing would have pleased Nimeiri, but his views on Nimeiri would not. 'I can't understand these people,' he said one morning. 'Every week they get poorer and poorer, yet they do nothing about it. In any other country in the world Nimeiri would have been overthrown years ago.'

The more I heard of the president, the more he reminded me of the ruler in Gabriel Garcia Marquez's *Autumn of a Patriarch*, a man increasingly out of touch with his people, hidden away behind his palace doors with a small coterie of sycophants and fanatics. His chief adviser was a green-robed and henna-haired Sufi dervish, a lawyer and sometime missionary in Nigeria; Nimeiri's court was now peopled, according to the *Economist*, 'by mystics, lawyers and students claiming Islamic authority'. The secular state, under Nimeiri's guidance, had been floundering. So the president called on Allah's support. Which was bad luck on the 30 per cent of Sudan's twenty million people who weren't Muslim.

President Nimeiri, incidentally, served in the same army corps as Uncle Percy. The British considered him 'very uppity – someone to be watched'.

I must profess disappointment with the British Embassy. It didn't live up to my grandiose expectations. I had imagined some fine neoclassical building overlooking the Nile, with a long sweeping drive leading up to a portico of imposing columns, and a garden full of brilliantly coloured flowers and extravagant displays of tropical shrubs. I found, instead, a very ordinary office in a drab block behind Athenae Square. I expected to find the Embassy full of suave, silver-moustached gentlemen like Polk-Mowbray, the British ambassador to Vulgaria in Lawrence Durrell's short stories about the Diplomatic Corps, the sort of gentlemen who would wear monogrammed pyjamas, drink large quantities of port, and reminisce about the old days. At the very least I expected a few Uncle Percys. I found, instead, men and women who would have looked not the slightest bit out of place in a firm of City chartered accountants, casually dressed and not remotely anachronistic. They were, it must be said, most helpful.

More entertaining, from a sociological point of view, were the English teachers, many of whom had descended recently on the capital and were waiting to fly, Allah and Sudan Airways willing (which they often weren't), back to England. Most had applied for teaching jobs in the Sudan after reading advertisements in either *The Times Educational Supplement* or the *Guardian*. No teaching qualifications were necessary, and the only training they received was brief: one hour's instruction in Arabic and three hours on how to teach. They arrived *en masse* in the autumn, spent a few days in Khartoum, and then departed to various points round the country. They mixed little with the rest of the expatriate community and many led lives of extreme isolation. About a third of the teachers returned after their first year for more. Nearly all those I met loved Sudan.

'I've been here two years now,' said one who taught in El Fasher, a four-day ride west of Khartoum. 'I've spent every day with Sudanese. I speak Arabic. But I still haven't worked out how Sudanese society ticks. When I look at a Sudanese I can't imagine what goes on in his head, what thoughts he has, how he sees the world.

'And I've seen such weird things. One day I was sitting in a café in a tiny mud village out west, watching some wild rats strolling around the street. The building opposite the café had a soldier on guard. All of a sudden he dropped his gun, disappeared inside the building and came out with a small cage. He walked over to some rats and put the cage down on the ground. A big rat climbed into the cage, ran round in circles for a few minutes, then jumped out again. The soldier picked up the cage, returned it to the building and took up his guard duties.

'I turned to some men sitting in the café. "What was all that about?" I asked.

' "What?" they replied.

' "The business with the rat."

' "What rat?" they said, and went on drinking tea.'

Sharia law appeared to have bothered the teachers little. Most had continued to drink *marissa* and *aragi*, unperturbed by the illegality. And young men who looked as though, not long ago, they might have supported Moral Re-armament, had become experts on the quality of Sudanese marijuana and where to buy it.

One of the teachers staying at my hotel was a delightful, elfish character who taught in a village on the Blue Nile. I asked him what he did for women.

'Aha!' he grinned. 'That's an interesting question.' He thought about it for a while. 'Nothing,' he said eventually. 'And I can't say it bothers me. I think the women teachers miss sex more than the men, and they seem more inclined to do something about it. But I don't mind being celibate.'

The teachers were great gossips. There were about three hundred in the country, and though most had met only a few of the others, the grapevine kept them well informed. 'Now, there's so-and-so in Barbanusa,' they might say, 'and he went out with so-and-so for a while. And Liz in Port Sudan, now she's been out with one of the Sudanese teachers at her school . . .'

The grapevine was of the highest quality. 'I had a friend,' said the teacher from El Fasher, 'who woke up one morning with maggots in his eyes. Two days later we left on a fortnight's trip walking through Jebel Marra. After ten days we bumped into an English teacher from Port Sudan. He asked us if we'd heard of the English teacher who'd had maggots in his eyes. The story had crossed the country – over 1,000 miles – by lorry, train and bus, and returned again in under two weeks. No need for telephones out here.'

The teachers had become fine judges of a good story, which would be treated with reverence, like a piece of fine pottery, and handed round the country for each to inspect and admire. I told one of them about an English acquaintance of mine who had travelled through the Sudan in the late seventies. He was arrested for smoking marijuana and failed to bribe his way out of trouble. He was locked up for two days and then brought before the local judge. A crowd of Sudanese cheered him and wished him luck as he entered the courtroom. The judge found him guilty and sentenced him to two days' imprisonment, which he had already served. The judge then apologized profusely and invited the Englishman to stay at his family home. For the next four days he was wined and dined by this delightful dispenser of justice. The teacher to whom I recounted this story said he liked it very much. I could see him repeating it behind glazed eyes, getting the feel of it and memorizing whatever nuances he liked most. I was not surprised, ten days later, to bump into this same story, slightly elaborated and better polished than it had been in my telling.

And, of course, the teachers had much to say on the subject of disease. Some had had malaria, some hepatitis, most dysentery and giardia. 'I've had giardia on and off all year,' said one. 'But you get used to it. The first time you have it you are really sick. After that it's not so bad.' He lifted up his tee-shirt to reveal a domed stomach, the outer manifestation of the stomach parasite.

'The water in El Fasher was like a biology experiment,' he said. Once he found red worms in it. 'But they were very small,' he added, as if they didn't matter much.

I soon became resigned to the impossibility of travelling further up the White Nile or heading into Ethiopia. So after two weeks in Khartoum I decided to make my way as far up the Blue Nile as possible and then return slowly to Egypt, this time following the great loop in the Nile through the Nubian Desert.

I spent most of the morning on the day I intended to depart queuing for a ticket. The first hour I passed standing in the wrong queue – it was for passengers booking to go west – and then I waited another hour and a half in the right queue. It wasn't particularly long, but in Sudan even the simplest operation can take a ridiculous amount of time. The man serving us disappeared for forty minutes without giving any explanation. There would have been a riot in Egypt, but here everyone waited patiently. I asked for a first-class ticket to Ed Damazin, but they'd been taken up weeks ago, so I booked a second-class ticket for a train scheduled to leave at five o'clock that afternoon. I rushed down to the Aliens' Office by the Nile and acquired a travel permit and dropped into the post office to see if any mail awaited me.

The post office could be a frustrating place to do business, though this day I was served quickly enough. Similarly, the first day I went to pick up mail at the poste-restante counter I encountered no problems. A rather morose character handed me the piles from the boxes marked P and S. There were two letters for me and a fair number for people whose names began with neither P nor S. The second time I went, early one evening a few days later, I waited half an hour before the same man appeared and installed himself on the stool beside the poste-restante shelves.

'Can I see under P and S?' I asked.

'No,' he replied. He produced a wooden afro-comb from his beige safari jacket and proceeded, unsuccessfully, to comb hair over a small bald patch on the crown of his head.

'Why not?' I asked.

'The poste-restante service is only in the mornings,' he replied.

'But I came this time the other day,' I remonstrated.

'Impossible,' he replied.

'You served me,' I reminded him.

'You are mistaken,' he said. 'There is never anyone serving here in the evenings.'

'Why are you here now?' I asked, smiling what was intended to be a smile of pacification. He pretended not to hear me. I waited across the counter for another five minutes, hoping my silent presence would wear him into submission. Eventually, he gave up the battle with the bald patch.

'Come tomorrow,' he said, disappearing into the room behind.

The postal service in the Sudan is not renowned for its reliability. Nor was the solitary notice pinned to a board outside designed to give one confidence. It was brown and furled at the edges. It gave the last dates by which packages had to be posted from Europe to reach Khartoum in time for Christmas 1977.

Letters to Europe probably travelled quicker than those sent from one Sudanese town to another. A correspondent in the government's English-language magazine, *Sudanow*, complained that he had sent six letters from Juba to a town in north Sudan. Five never arrived and the one that did took over a month. An Irish teacher said he once sent a telegram from the village of Korti, where he worked, to Dongola, about a hundred miles down river. It took three weeks to get there, which made even the rail system seem efficient.

CHAPTER THIRTEEN
SUDAN'S LAST STEAM TRAIN

An ancient and toothless gentleman slipped a large ball of snuff into his mouth. He handed some to me and I wedged it behind my lower lip. Sudanese snuff, which in looks and texture differs little from brown soil, is a wonderful drug.

'Thirty piastres an ounce,' he said. 'I get through an ounce a day. That's why I've lost my teeth.'

'Very cheap,' I replied. My head was already buzzing.

'Not really,' he replied. 'I once bought a horse for four pounds.'

We were sitting in a second-class carriage waiting for the Ed Damazin train to leave. The lights in the carriage didn't work, nor did the fan; the windows had no glass, the shutters were broken, and from the black leather seats stuffing erupted like fungus from dead bark. But at least there was stuffing in the seats, which there wasn't in third class, and at least we had space. By the time we set off (which, astonishingly, was at five o'clock, when we were scheduled to depart) there were a mere twelve of us sharing the eight places.

The old man was a delightful character. His skin was the colour of teak and his hair grey. He wore a toothbrush moustache above an impish mouth, and he reminded me of an elderly dormouse. He spoke excellent English (my Arabic was disgracefully poor, though adequate for the purposes of getting what I wanted in the markets) and by the time we left he had given me a short history of his life. 'I have fourteen children,' he said in a squeaky voice, 'and I don't know how many grandchildren.' He worked as an accountant in the irrigation department at Damazin.

The train pulled slowly through the suburbs of Khartoum. Before we left the city, we passed a large piece of waste ground where the skeletons of old cars, stripped of engines, seats, wheels and all their innards, had been stood side by side to form a rusty corral. Inside was a small herd of long-horned and hump-backed cattle. Outside were clusters of shanty tents, built with bending wooden struts, like those of the desert nomads, but covered with cardboard rather than hide. Ragged children scuttered among the flocks of goat which nibbled at scraps of food and rubbish. A small building-site with half a dozen uncompleted houses marked the end of Khartoum.

'There's a good sign for the economy!' suggested the old man. 'There's so much construction going on today in Khartoum.'

Of the other ten passengers in our carriage only one understood English. He gave me a surreptitious smile, which meant, I suppose, that he didn't share the accountant's optimism for the economy. He was a handsome man, very tall and very black. Across his forehead he carried ten cicatrized growths which stretched in a semicircle from one ear up and across to the other. I think he was a Shilluk. He seldom spoke in English, and not often in Arabic.

Less than an hour out of Khartoum the sun set. We settled into our seats and darkness and I fell into an uncomfortable sleep. Occasionally I awoke for a few seconds and stared blearily at the bleak and featureless landscape which absorbed the weak light from a sliver of moon.

At ten o'clock the turbaned man next to me shook me awake. '*Enta kweiss?*' he demanded. 'Are you well?'

'*Anna kweiss,*' I replied. 'I'm fine.' I had been building myself up, a consequence of Mohammed's Arabic tuition at the hotel, to give that wonderful reply, which one frequently heard delivered with religious zeal, '*al hamdu lilla, anna kweiss!*' Praise be to God, I'm well! I failed yet again.

We were somewhere near Wad Medani, a hundred-odd miles south-east of Khartoum. It would have made more sense to have stopped at Wad Medani itself rather than in the middle of nowhere, where there was no chance of getting a tea or water, or buying fruit or beans. 'Now we eat,' said the old accountant. I produced from my bag all I had in the way of food – three kilos of oranges – and between us we rustled together a very reasonable meal.

189

Someone had brought bread – flat brown discs that made up in nutrition what they lacked in flavour and chewability; and others produced halva, jam and some very sharp cheese. Hospitality in the Sudan, once you are out of Khartoum, is overbearingly generous. A train ride is invariably a feast even if it isn't always movable. I was slightly ashamed that all I could offer was oranges. The old man ate three. He thanked me profusely before declaring that they were rather poor, which they were. Once we'd finished our meal I fell asleep again. It was 3.50 a.m. when we arrived at Old Sennar. We were greeted by an albino beggar.

What struck me most about Alan Moorehead's two fine biographies of this great river was the eclectic mix of races which, at one time and another, had come up the rivers in search of slaves, gold, ivory, a scrap with the natives or the solution to a geographical problem. There were the European explorers, mostly English, occasionally from France, Switzerland or elsewhere. There were the Arabs of Egypt, who for centuries before the Europeans appeared had plundered the negro tribes south of Khartoum. And there was Dr Poncet, who in 1699 visited Sennar, which was then the capital of the Fungs, whose vast kingdom stretched from the Red Sea east to the White Nile, and from near the present Egyptian border south to the Ethiopian Highlands.

'In the markets,' wrote Moorehead,

one could buy in addition to slaves, camels and horses, such things as ivory, tamarind fruit, civet for fixing scent, gold dust and tobacco. There were large forests outside the town with wild animals roaming about in them ... the king, according to Poncet, kept up considerable state. Once every week he would ride out to one of his country houses, accompanied by three or four hundred horsemen and footmen, who sang his praises and played the tabor while they marched. They were followed by hundreds of women who carried on their heads baskets of fruit for the royal *fête champêtre*.

Seventy years after Poncet's visit, James Bruce arrived in Sennar. The Fungs' magnificent capital was already in a state of decline and the surrounding forests were vanishing.

In 1820 Mohammed Ali, the ruler of Egypt, dispatched his son Ismail to the Sudan. Ismail took with him four thousand soldiers, over half of whom were either Turks or Albanians. They were mercenaries and Mohammed promised them 50 piastres for every human ear they took in battle. The purpose of the expedition was to provide Egypt with slaves. Sennar no longer had a hint of its former glory and its king surrendered on Ismail's arrival. Ismail, who thus far had sent few slaves back to Egypt, was joined by his brother Ibrahim. Together they meted out the most appalling treatment on the native populations along the Blue Nile. They followed the river south towards Roseires, where I was heading, rounding up every negro in sight; they captured about thirty thousand men, women and children, only about half of whom survived the journey back to Egypt. The expedition was not a success. Mohammed Ali called Ismail home in 1822 and he left Sennar immediately. He was killed at Shendi. His father made sure that the son's death was fully avenged. 'The town of Metemma was first sacked and burnt,' wrote Moorehead, 'and then it was the turn of Damer and all the other settlements along the Nile from Berber to Sennar.' Male prisoners were emasculated and women had their breasts cut off. Mohammed's cruel retribution led to the death of fifty thousand Sudanese.

Recent visitors to Sennar and the Blue Nile include the British army, which, under the leadership of Orde Wingate, led Haile Selassie back to Ethiopia in 1941. The Italians, who had occupied the Emperor's country, were repulsed, and by the end of the year Selassie was back in Addis Ababa.

The albino – oblivious, I suspect, to the men both great and monstrous who had passed this way (I myself was giving them no thought either) – begged a few piastres off me and my awakening companions. He was a horrible mess. He wore not one jellaba but three or four. They were no more than rags full of holes, but between them they covered his body. His head was swathed in bits of cloth and his face, negroid in features but pigmentless, was covered with open sores. He was almost blind, and he was soon overwhelmed by the hawkers who swarmed on to the train with hard-boiled eggs, guavas, tamarind seeds and plastic toys.

The old accountant bought an aeroplane for 90 piastres. 'How much would this cost in London?' he asked. About the same, I suggested.

'No!' he said. 'Much less.' He slipped a ball of snuff into his mouth and chuckled over his new possession. I asked him who the toy was for.

'A grandchild,' he replied. 'One of them is bound to have a birthday soon.'

I got off the train and bought some tea, which I drank beside the track. A young man came over to sit beside me. 'Are you Kitchener's grandson?' he asked. I said I wasn't.

The diesel was detached from our train and shunted into a siding. I lay down and drowsed. The night was pleasantly cool, no more than seventy degrees. A young man sat in an empty carriage on another track and strummed slowly at a guitar. Dawn broke quickly. There was still no sign of the steam train which was to be hitched on to ours, so I went for a walk round the station. Half a dozen steam engines in various states of disrepair were lined up outside a shed. They were all British models and about the same age as me, early 1950s. At seven o'clock I returned to the carriage.

'Perhaps we'll stay here all day,' said the accountant. He was looking pained. 'It isn't easy for an old man like me to sleep on these trains.' I fervently hoped I shouldn't still be doing this sort of thing when I was seventy. My spine ached, my backside was numb and my skin was coated with a thin mortar of grime and sweat. I had also developed, in the space of just a few hours, a stinking cold.

At eight o'clock the sound of one of the old trains letting off steam gave us fresh hope and an engine pulled past us and backed on to the carriages. I went to inspect it. The albino beggar was still shuffling along the side of the train asking for money. The oval plaque on the flank of the engine read:

NORTH BRITISH LOCOMOTIVE COMPANY LTD
Hyde Park Works
Glasgow
1952.

'We're discussing the cost of living,' announced the accountant when I returned. 'When I was in the south, thirty years ago, I used to pay a third of a piastre for three kilos of fish. That was when I bought a horse for £S4.'

The Shilluk smiled.

'I was working with the Dinka,' continued the old man. 'Then they hardly wore any clothes. Now they dress very well; better than us in fact.' This amused him enormously.

We were four hours late out of Sennar. This surprised no one. Although Sudan's rail network stretches over 1,200 miles from west to east, and nearly as far from north to south (although guerrilla sabotage had stopped trains running from Barbanusa to Wau), the national timetable fits on to a single sheet of paper, such is the infrequency of trains. However, the timetable is no more than a statement of intent and drivers appear to take even less notice of it than passengers. If a two-day journey takes three days, if the engine breaks down eleven times between sunrise and set, if the driver decides to stop for three hours at prayer-time rather than one, the explanation is always the same: *'Inshallah'* – 'It is God's will.' The deity has a lot to answer for in the Sudan.

When I first came to Sudan, the railways relied entirely on steam trains. They have all been replaced, with the exception of the one I was now taking, by German diesels. This has nothing to do with nostalgia on the part of Sudan Railways – the silty soil between Sennar and Damazin is too soft to take the heavy diesels. It was a curious entourage which set off at 8.30: a Scottish train leading one Hungarian first-class carriage, two Belgian second-class carriages and three Egyptian third-class carriages. Soon after we departed I was plied with a breakfast of halva, sardines, jam and guavas. Outside, the slick of oily smoke which rose from the engine fell like a black eel across the stark and monotonous landscape of fallow cotton prairie. The empty sardine tins ('Not for sale – Norwegian aid', read one) glinted like flashing fish as they sailed through the window. Breakfast over, the carriage fell into a sweaty slumber.

By midday, sleep was out of the question, so intense was the heat. Two students from third class invited me for lunch. One was a squat, ugly character. The other was slim and very beautiful, olive-skinned with eyelashes a London debutante would have been proud of. We clambered over the bodies on the floor and found a space where we could sit by an open door. We ate sardines, halva and jam, this time mixed into a thick paste. The student with the eyelashes, Mohammed, produced a bottle of *aragi*, from which we took surreptitious sips. Meanwhile he explained the dangers of *sharia* law.

We left the cotton fields and the train chugged and puffed through sparse scrubland. The distant vegetation looked like white mist. Gradually the trees became more substantial. The acacia trunks gleamed orange and we passed villages of round huts, the old ones dove grey, the new sandy brown. Around the villages grew pastures of *gesh*, the grass used to make huts and fencing. We stopped frequently at tiny villages where goats scavenged round the habitations, and once, for no apparent reason, by a small water-hole. A dozen maribou storks stood round the water's edge. They looked rheumatic and disapproving, like elderly judges about to pass a death sentence. We were coming into the tropical zone of Africa and the birds celebrated the cessation of the desert by dressing in the brightest of colours. I saw beautiful bee-eaters and rollers and green parrots.

The desert in Sudan has been steadily moving south for the last century. Pastures have been overgrazed: in Kordofan Province the numbers of livestock increased sixfold between 1958 and 1975. At the same time more and more forests have been felled for firewood. Most people in Sudan cook with charcoal, and so severe have the shortages been in recent years that there have been armed battles between forest rangers and wood cutters. In Poncet's day Sennar was surrounded by magnificent forests. Now it is not until you get 150 miles further south that one finds such forests. Women swaying home with bundles of wood on their heads were as familiar a sight from the trains in north Sudan as cattle egrets were in the fields of Egypt. Every now and then we passed neat piles of wood awaiting carriage to the charcoal manufacturers and the cities.

At three o'clock we rounded a small clump of rocky hills. I left the students and returned to my carriage. The old accountant was staring at the cover of Graham Greene's *Honorary Consul*, which I had bought in Khartoum. He opened it and read the first paragraph aloud. 'This is very easy English,' he announced before passing the book to me.

He asked me where I was going to stay in Ed Damazin. I said I didn't know. He suggested I stay in the Irrigation Department's rest house. 'There was a thief there last week,' he added, 'but he won't be any trouble now.'

I asked why not. 'They chopped his hand off,' he chuckled.

Just before dusk I climbed up on to the roof. Forty or so young men, their white jellabas streaming into the wind, turned their black faces to the sun, which fell like a lump of molten copper and scarred the sky, for a few magic moments, with vivid weals of crimson and purple. At sunset we stopped for evening prayer. I climbed down and sat beneath a flame tree. I listened to the familiar murmurs of Muslim prayer. My bones ached, my hair was matted with dust, and sweat pricked my eyes. I could almost feel the salt crusting my eyelashes. But those first few minutes of the evening darkness soon washed away the weariness of the day's travel.

We pulled into Ed Damazin just after midnight. It had taken us thirty hours to cover a little over 300 miles.

I had an accommodation problem. Mohammed invited me to stay at his parents' house at Roseires, across the Blue Nile from Damazin. (Though the train ran the whole way from Khartoum to Damazin near the Blue Nile, we never once caught a glimpse of the river.) Another man I had never met offered me a bed in his house. And the old accountant said his son would drive me to the rest house. It was many weeks since I'd slept in a room on my own and I plumped for the rest house. The accountant's son arrived, a big burly man who seemed none to pleased to see me, and I climbed into the back of his pick-up. We set off from the station into town, but we stopped before we got there. 'Do you work for the Irrigation Department?' asked the old man's son. I said I didn't. He conferred with his father. In that case, said the old man, I wouldn't be able to stay there. 'We'll take you to the best hotel in town,' he added.

A few minutes later I was dropped outside a dilapidated building which had a sign over its door in Arabic, but none in English. I shook hands with the accountant and took my bag. There were fifty-odd beds outside the hotel, sprawling into a lorry park. A single light blazed from above the door and cast a mesh of shadows over the bare ground. I found the hotel manager.

'Sorry,' he said. 'We're full.' He waved airily at the beds and their sleeping incumbents, and pointed across the lorry park to a dim light which shone far away on the other side, towards which I now walked, stumbling as I went over ruts and rubbish. Once I tripped over a body, which woke up and shouted at me. It was an eerie walk. I was wishing I had taken up Mohammed's offer. The light belonged to Damazin's other hotel. It was the foulest of establishments. The beds were covered with stained and stinking mattresses. The water which came from a rusted tap was brown and undrinkable, and it cascaded through a broken sink to run in gulleys between the courtyard beds. The WC consisted of a simple hole in the concrete, and from the hole, when they caught a whiff of human flesh, crept forth enormous cockroaches like mice in armour plating. The clientele were none too pleasant either, and some of the looks I received on entering suggested criminal tendencies of the sort which even *sharia* law might fail to eradicate. However I slept soundly enough and left early in the morning.

Ed Damazin was a scruffy and unprepossessing place. At its centre lay a large sprawling market enclosed by one-storey concrete buildings. I ate half a chicken for breakfast and a bowl of raw chillis.

Mohammed had given me the name of an aunt who ran a fruit stall at Roseires. We'd arranged to meet at ten o'clock. I took a box from the market. It was a lovely half-hour drive. The road wound its way round *gesh* villages and through rich forests down to the Blue Nile, which ran in torrents and eddies across a granite cataract. Cattle and goats grazed on the river banks and tropical birds dashed between the trees. We crossed the bridge and drove over rolling downland. Great baobab trees, their huge misshapen trunks like elephantiasis legs, sprouted tiny crowns of green leaves.

The box came to a halt under a large leguminous tree festooned with long pods which swayed in the breeze. Near by there was a small shed in which two whirring liquidizers were macerating grapefruit. Outside the shed were two benches. I bought a glass of grapefruit and sat down. There were twelve men there, noticeably blacker than the people of Khartoum. I shook hands with all of them. None spoke English but they directed me to Mohammed's aunt's store. Roseires was indescribably beautiful, and never had I seen a village more perfectly blended into the landscape. It had been designed, or so it seemed, that the houses and huts should fit into nature's mosaic of trees, rather than the other way round. The whole village lay in dappled shade; and the trees were full of nesting ibises.

Mohammed's aunt was away and he didn't turn up. I spent the morning in the village, then took a box back to Damazin. We stopped for minor repairs to the engine by the Blue Nile. To my right the river rushed east. To my left rose the towering wall of Roseires Dam. I reflected, wearily, that this was as far as I was going to get up the Nile this time. This great concrete construction, plugging the undulating landscape with the brutal lines of the civil engineer, struck me as a fitting symbol for the barriers which have, over a short period of years, sprung up across the continent to thwart the traveller.

'I rejoice,' wrote Evelyn Waugh 'that I went when the going was good.' He travelled between the two world wars. In 1975, travelling round this part of Africa was tricky. The barriers were already beginning to rise. But at least it was possible. Today it isn't.

CHAPTER FOURTEEN
THE BLUE NILE, WHEN THE GOING WAS BETTER

Most travellers allay their feelings of insecurity by moving around in company. All across Africa strange and sad alliances are struck up by people who on their home ground wouldn't dream of spending more than five minutes in one another's company. These odd, ill-assorted bands shuffle thousands of miles together across the continent, their only bonds their colour (white), their itchy feet and their desire to travel cheap. Such a band arrived, in dribs and drabs, at the Ethiopian border town of Gallabat in late April 1975.

The only written record I have of my journey through Ethiopia is in the letters I wrote home. I do not consider them reliable. My first letter, written from Gondar, was a remarkable concoction of lies. The reasons for my dishonesty were twofold: first, letters were said to be subject to vetting – the Revolution which overthrew Selassie was little over a year old; second, I didn't wish to scare my parents. Some of those who accompanied me on parts of the journey I recollect only in the most hazy way. Through the prism of time their light has been all but extinguished. Others I remember well. There was Luc, a thin, spindly Frenchman who had spent three days with me at the Ethiopian Embassy in Khartoum, where the official had persistently refused to give us visas, claiming that the country was too dangerous for travellers. Eventually he'd relented and given us what we wanted.

There was Jacques, whom I had first met in Luxor, accompanied by his lecherous acolyte from the Paris slums. The disenchanted and unenchanting New Zealander with $7,000 and no place to go was also at Gallabat when I arrived with Luc. And there was a curious and very quiet Japanese couple who never slept together. There may have been one or two others. I no longer remember them if there were.

Luc and I arrived in Gallabat one mid-afternoon. It was very hot and very dry. The man who stamped our passports led us down a side street to the local black-marketeer, an obnoxious character, obese and dressed in scruffy Western clothes. He sat behind an archaic metal desk in a small mud shack. I converted some English pounds into Ethiopian money. I asked him what he did with his foreign currency. 'Send it to Israel,' he replied. 'When I'm rich I'm going to get out of this place.'

He pointed down the street. 'That way to Ethiopia.' We walked towards the border. Goats and children were rummaging around in the dirt outside mud shacks, and big black flies fed around the children's eyes. A ditch, ten feet across and waterless, marked the border. Beyond, at the top of a dust road which fell through a smoky village, was a small army hut surrounded by coils of barbed wire. Inside were three soldiers. We spent three nights waiting here for the bus to Gondar, sleeping on the ground outside the hut. One of the soldiers spoke a little English and a little French, always in a whisper. He said he hated Gallabat. He told us we should turn back to Sudan, claiming that the last white traveller to cross here was killed by bandits on the way to Gondar.

After dusk one night a soldier took Luc and me to a drinking hovel. It consisted of two rooms. A family lived in one. The other was dimly lit with an oil lamp and full of smoke from a charcoal burner. Four men sat silently against one wall. They stared unsmilingly at us as we drank warm home-made beer. Their heads were partly hidden by white shawls and each held an old rifle. The silence unnerved us and we left once we had finished our drinks. There were no lights in the street and we stumbled back to the army hut in pitch darkness, impaling ourselves on the barbed wire when we arrived. We were greeted by a shout and the sound of a rifle bolt being pulled back. The soldiers guided us in once they realized who we were. I slept badly. Tiny adolescent scorpions, white and waxy, swarmed round my sleeping-bag and in the middle of the night I was awoken by the sound of shooting at the east end of the town.

The next two days passed slowly.

At four o'clock on the third morning we were given an armed escort to an ancient bus which was waiting on the outskirts of town. The driver said this was the first bus for over a week. The last had been ambushed by the *shifta*, the mountain bandits. Long before dawn the bus was full. When light broke over the distant hills we saw the other passengers. There were fifteen men, each carrying a rifle. The rest were women and children. At seven o'clock two soldiers appeared. Each carried an automatic rifle. One stationed himself at the front door, the other near me at the rear. We set off.

It was a long tortuous climb up from the desert scrub into the mountains. We climbed all morning. The road was rough, in places strewn with the debris of rock falls; and sometimes scarred by landslides. As the sun pushed higher in the sky the mists rose to reveal wonderful hanging valleys and sheer cliffs, dried-up river-beds and trees with maroon and white blossom bunched in clusters on silver branches. The passengers were in good and garrulous mood till mid-morning, when the soldier at the back of the bus loosed off a rapid stutter of bullets into the woods. Some passengers responded by poking their rifles through windows and firing randomly in the same direction. The man in front of me shouted *shifta* and motioned to me to duck. The soldier shouted to the others to stop shooting. He was just testing his weapon, he explained. Chatter and banter ceased and a stony-faced silence took us the next four or five miles.

Then all of a sudden we rounded a corner and before us a tree trunk lay across the road. The driver, with commendable speed of decision, accelerated, and the bus took off as we hit the trunk. It wasn't quite large enough to stop us. Some shots were fired down on us from a cliff, but nobody was hit. The soldiers returned fire. The women and children had dived beneath seats. Luc and I, paralysed by fear rather than heroism, never budged. I noticed, once we were free of danger, that both of us had our hands clutching our balls. The Japanese girl was whimpering like a wounded dog.

At noon we pulled into a small village set in a landscape of stunning beauty. We had climbed three thousand feet and the air was fresh. Jagged tree-covered hills stretched to the north and to the south lay a deep gorge. We sat in a low-ceilinged mud building at wooden tables. A large aluminium platter, almost two feet across, was placed at each table. Great rounds of sour bread – *injera* – lay beneath small piles of spicy vegetables. I tore off clumps of *injera* with my fingers and scooped up the fiery *wat*. A dozen armed peasants sat on a bench outside. They were handsome, morose characters, not given to any great shows of warmth towards the bus passengers. Their rifles were so old that if one had been fired it might well have blown off its owner's hand.

'Come,' said the driver, wagging his finger at me. He took me round to the back of the bus and jammed his finger into a hole beneath the rear window. '*Shifta* kill white man,' he announced. He roared with laughter and his moon face split to reveal a mouthful of broken and rotting teeth. He took my arm and conducted me through the back door of the bus. He pointed to where the bullet had come through the leather seat. It was just the right height to catch the heart.

We drove through more valleys, some like great sweeping Scottish glens, others hemmed in by steep rock precipices. The landscape widened out and the forest disappeared. In mid-afternoon a group of thirty or more horsemen rode down from the north and stopped on the road ahead of us. Their chests were crisscrossed by bullet belts. As far as we could gather, they were bandits, but much to our relief they wished us no harm. One of their number had been shot in the shoulder and they asked us to take him to the next town, where he could receive treatment. The wounded man was helped into the bus. He sat on the floor. Nobody said a word to him, now or later. The horsemen parted to let the bus through.

We stopped before nightfall in a small village. Jacques and his friend – they had left Gallabat before us on a cotton lorry – were staying in a brothel. Luc and I ate some more *injera* and *wat* and drank two bottles of *tej*. We slept in the bus. It was a cold night.

Mid-morning the next day we arrived in Gondar, a large, decaying town wrapped round a fine castle and a beautiful stone monastery. I stayed two days. I had never seen so much disease. It was impossible to find a café where there wasn't at least one man suffering from elephantiasis, and lepers were too numerous to count. The only food I could get was beans. One morning I rose very early and found a dead child on the pavement outside the hotel. I left Gondar as soon as I could.

I was to spend three more weeks in Ethiopia, travelling south through Debra Markos to Addis Ababa and then by Shashemene and Dilla down to Moyale and Kenya.

When I think of Ethiopia now, it is as though I am reading a book half of whose pages are missing. I am left with a series of images, ill-assorted and out of chronology. Images of landscapes of quite spectacular magnificence; of faces too, whose slender features, sharp eyes and full lips were of a beauty which it would be difficult to surpass. Yet most people were living in the depths of misery. Some without food; many afflicted by leprosy, elephantiasis, deformities of every kind, blindness, fever. Enormous contrasts were everywhere to be seen. Addis Ababa – large, modern, spacious: in the centre, a ludicrously well-appointed and heavily guarded American Library full of American propaganda and comfortable leatherette armchairs; and near by, the Italian cafés, run by exiled Italians and serving pizza, spaghetti and ice-cream. Then outside Addis, and on its outskirts, the miserable towns and villages with broken sewers, pit latrines full of rats and no medical facilities.

Rumour, suspicion, fear: one encountered them everywhere, particularly in the north. Intellectuals and students, the driving force behind the revolution, were being persecuted by the military. In the villages one frequently met students 'on campaign', teaching the illiterate to read and write. Some said they enjoyed it, they were doing it for the revolution. Others claimed it was the government's way of weakening the intelligentsia, by breaking up the student body and banishing them, in ones and twos and threes, into the countryside.

Brothels were our refuge. They were generally cheaper than the hotels and always more friendly. I spent four or five days in one at Bahir Dar, on the shores of Lake Tana. There were six whores and never any customers. The brothel was presided over by a fine old mama of enormous girth. What little hair she had was plaited tight across her skull. The brothel had a pleasant Italianate atmosphere. Its front door led into a bar, where one could sit at formica-topped tables drinking *tej*. The back door led into a square courtyard which was surrounded by small rooms, each with a single bed. Shuttered windows opened on to the courtyard, which on our arrival was occupied by a very sleek goat. One morning, just before dawn, I was woken by the sharpening of knives. I went into the bar and found a man slitting the goat's throat. Christian Ethiopia was celebrating the passover, and the goat's blood was daubed around the door. In the town a great slaughter was taking place – of goats, sheep, hens, pullets. That day we gorged ourselves on meat. It made a nice change from beans.

In Addis I was struck down by fever for a week. When I felt fit enough to travel I took a lorry south to Awasa, a small town by a lake, where I lay up in a brothel for several days. There were no food shortages, nor any civil unrest. I ate fish from the lake and there was a plentiful supply of fresh fruit. The climate was pleasant, warm during the day and cool at night. One of the girls befriended me (or perhaps it was the other way round). She was twenty, very beautiful and fluent in both Italian and English. She said her father, a wealthy landowner, had fled after the Revolution. She had graduated straight from university to the brothel. We spent the evenings drinking *tej* and chatting. I have often wondered what became of the girl. She was lonely then, and so was I. Brothels, incidentally, were often the only places to stay in in small villages. They doubled as hotels for travellers, most of whom, including myself, enjoyed them for their social and friendly atmosphere rather than for anything else.

My last glimpse of the Blue Nile was at Usiater, a small village perched on the lip of an immense gorge through which, almost indiscernible from the heights of the village, ran the river. A lunatic screamed and slavered when he saw me. He followed me through the mud village, walking on all fours and shouting garbled taunts. I stopped on a small knoll to look down the gorge. Below were small clusters of straw huts and peasants laboriously hoeing narrow terraces. The lunatic threw a rock at me and disappeared.

CHAPTER FIFTEEN

SWAMP STEAMER

Six weeks later I saw the Nile again, this time the White Nile, where it curled and twisted in diffuse strands through the jungle of northern Uganda.

I was in poor humour. I had spent two weeks in Mombasa, waiting for a charcoal boat on which I'd booked a passage to Madagascar, where I hoped to find work. News came that the boat had sunk. There were no other boats going in the near future and I was running very low on cash. I was forced to return to Europe, so I hitched back to Nairobi. The night I arrived I was mugged, though not seriously, and the next morning I witnessed the lynching of a thief, who was killed by a crowd near the bus station. Uganda was a mess (Idi Amin was in power) and I decided to splash out on an air ticket from Nairobi to Juba rather than risk crossing Uganda overland. I had three thousand miles to go before I reached Cairo and I was quite happy to cover the first leg in a matter of hours instead of weeks. The plane landed at Entebbe, where most of the passengers were stopping, but it failed to take off again – engine trouble, apparently – and the four of us bound for Juba waited four days for a Sudan Airways pilot (plus working aeroplane) to turn up. Late one afternoon he breezed into the plush hotel in which his company had put us up. He said we would be leaving the next morning. We didn't see him for another two days. When we did, he apologized for the delay and explained that he had felt compelled to visit a girlfriend in Kampala.

Sudan Airways is known by many who have flown with it as 'Inshallah Bokkra Mallesh Airways' (God Willing Tomorrow Never Mind Airways) and with good reason. Our pilot said that he had recently worked as a fighter pilot and we didn't doubt him. Our little Dakota banked, rose and fell like a drunken wasp. We overflew Juba and the pilot asked us all to scour the savannah below for some sign of civilization, a rather inappropriate description for Juba, where we landed half an hour later.

Two days later I left Juba. The Nile was grey and sleazy in the dawn gloom. Its sluggish waters slurped against crumbling mud banks and an ancient paddle steamer creaked beside a dilapidated concrete jetty. In a tin shack by the water's edge an official in an ill-fitting cotton suit was selling tickets for the seven-day journey from Juba to Kosti. A bare electric light hung above his head. The atmosphere was humid and malarial. Mosquitoes dipped down to feed on the queue outside the shack.

The dawn broke quickly, as always near the equator. The crowd swelled and with it the noise. The most ebullient were the young men – mostly Dinkas – who bantered among themselves and jostled in the queue for tickets. They were most impressive, very tall and thin, with all the men and many of the women well over six foot high. The men all had long knives hanging from their waists. Most of the women were bare-breasted. There was more luggage than there was human flesh. Bulging suitcases spewed cooking utensils and cloths, and many staggered on to the boat with charcoal stoves, bags of millet, bundles of sugarcane and bunches of green bananas.

I bought a third-class ticket with a student reduction. The official asked to see my student card. I didn't have one so I produced a piece of paper which I'd discovered in my rucksack the night before. It was a ticket, six months out of date, from a laundrette in Newcastle-upon-Tyne. The official copied down the name of the laundrette and the number of the ticket. I think I paid about £S2.

I clambered up the gangplank and made my way on to one of the third-class barges. The steamer gradually filled up. I imagine there were about six or seven hundred passengers, all but a handful on the three third-class barges. The sun rose above the rich green savannah and tropical birds in brilliant plumage descended on the river to feed. Half a dozen beggars had come down to the river to see us off. On the far bank a group of fishermen hauled a massive Nile perch, fully four foot long, into the lee of a small papyrus hut.

By eight o'clock the steamer was full. We were due to sail at nine. We left at twelve.

The paddle steamer was a contrivance of rare eccentricity, a floating shanty composed of six double-decker barges. Two second-class barges were lashed either side of the first-class barge, which housed the engine, the paddles and a solitary passenger, the Sudanese Minister for Weather. The three third-class barges were lashed together and led the procession downstream.

My barge, like the others, was little longer than a London bus and about twice as wide. It had no cabins and no benches. The roof was made of flimsy corrugated iron. There was a very public lavatory, a simple hole in an enclosure without a door. The bottom floor of my barge and two thirds of the top were reserved for men. The rear third of the upper deck was for women and children. The Arab steward, a vicious-looking character with a wall eye, ordered me into the women's section. Every square inch had been claimed by flesh, food and luggage, but I managed to make myself some space on the wooden floor.

The women's section gave me an excellent view of the second-class barges. The Arabs and the few negroes who could afford the price of a second-class ticket had arranged themselves with what seemed like affected decorum on the ample space of their upper decks. There was even a mosquito net, admittedly torn and useless, running round the deck. On the lower deck of one of the rear barges – the middle one, I seem to remember – there was a small restaurant. Third-class passengers were not allowed to trespass.

A few miles downstream from Juba we slipped past Gondokoro, the once great slaving town through which nearly all the captured negroes from the south were forced to pass. It was here that the slaves were loaded on to boats and ferried north to the markets of Khartoum and Shendi. All that remained of the town today were a few piles of rubble and the odd ruin. Long-horned zebu cattle grazed by the waterside and ox-peckers and cattle egret searched for insects at their feet.

When I awoke on the first morning out of Juba, my two neigh-bours were inspecting me with great wonder and concentration. Doubtless they had seen plenty of white men before, but this must have been the first time they had had one available for close scrutiny. Their expressions suggested that they were confronted by an object of rare and intriguing ugliness. The woman on my left had a shaven head and her pendulous breasts were cicatrized. A young baby hung from one teat and a two-year-old suckled the other. On my right sat a girl who greeted my awakening with a generous gap-toothed grin. She was no more than fourteen or fifteen and her breasts were firm and unscarred. Her skin was smeared with a thick oil which glistened in the early light of dawn. She was smoking a pipe. The girl handed me a three-foot length of sugarcane and its juices sustained me till we pulled into Bor, a hundred miles and a day north of Juba.

In a dusty marketplace soldiers slouched idly in the shade of some trees. Only the staple foods were available. There were no cigarettes for sale, only Sudanese grass.

A couple of hours after leaving Bor, and shortly before dusk, the steamer entered the vast papyrus swamps of the Sudd, an area the size of England and Wales. As far as the eye could see a monotonous green carpet stretched away to the flat horizons. The tedium was only occasionally lifted by the sight of a naked family eking out a precarious living on a dry hummock of land. These survivors of the swamps were greeted by silence. Crocodiles, on the other hand, elicited raucous shouts of derision from the safety of the boat.

The laborious journey through the Sudd was made all the more difficult by the steamer's steering system. There were only two directions in which it could go, straight forward and straight back. All the bends and kinks in the river had to be negotiated by accelerating into the bank (one good reason for having third-class upfront) and reversing off, hopefully to face in the right direction. A sulphurous stench would often rise from the reeds when we rammed the banks, and it accentuated the awful feeling of poverty which pervaded the third-class barges. Many of the negroes were travelling north to join the armies of cheap labourers in Khartoum, Port Sudan and the other big towns. They were heading for an empty promised land and most knew it. With every hour the barge became more foetid, the floor developing an ever-thickening scum of child's piss, spittle and discarded cane chewings. During the daytime there was no escape from the oppressive humidity and at night the mosquitoes because almost intolerable.

Midway through the third day the steward shouted across to me. He said I could use the restaurant if I wished. It had seen better days. The finely bevelled oak panelling had lost its varnish and large patches of mould had crept across the ceiling. There was a brass plaque asking passengers not to wear pyjamas at dinner. The food was simple but adequate: beans and dried fish.

I had caught glimpses of another white man over the last three days. Now he appeared. His name was Mohammed. He wore a white jellaba and a skull cap. He had an impressively hooked nose, pale skin and blue eyes. We shook hands and he explained why I had been allowed across. The Sudanese Minister for Weather, whom he had befriended, had insisted on it. The steward had stalled for two days – he didn't see why I should be allowed off third class (nor did I, though I was delighted to receive such favouritism) – but the minister had forced him to relent.

Mohammed was a Frenchman, one of that curious breed of travellers who had come to Africa in search of adventure and found Islam as well. Not only had he adopted the Arab's religion, but the superior attitude many show towards the negroes of the south. He said he found them boorish and depraved.

For those travelling first or second class it must have been easy to ignore the gulf between the back three barges and those in front. It came as a shock to return each evening, in the four days which remained before we reached Kosti, and smell the odours of overcrowding which at times during the night became so powerful that they woke me in a retching fit. Not that there was anything very special about the second-class barges. They had neither cabins nor bunks and the Arabs slept, as we did in third, on bare wood floors. But at least there was space. Space to sit without being jammed against human flesh. Space to lie down and sleep without being rolled upon, trodden underfoot or kicked. Space - just enough - to be alone, to sit slightly apart from others, on a rusty capstan or the blunt stern, and see nothing but one's own reflection rippling in the water.

After seven days, Kosti appeared on the horizon. The boat had to wait three hours to get through a new bridge, so Mohammed and I, loath to spend another minute cooped up on water, waded ashore and walked the last five miles across desert into the town. We ate breakfast - a bowl of hot milk in which we dunked bread - and found a lorry going to Khartoum. It should have been a four-hour drive; it took sixteen. With us in the back of the open Bedford were twenty Dinka men and a small Arab boy.

It was only afterwards that we realized that our lorry had headed west into desert for the first six hours, rather than north towards Khartoum. There were no roads and we were thrown about like rubbish in a dust cart. The Arab boy was unfortunate enough to be related to the driver, upon whom the Dinkas' wrath fell once they realized we weren't heading straight for Khartoum; and he was stupid enough to produce a knife and taunt the Dinkas, who had been teasing him. By then it was dark. The Dinkas drew their knives, and I thought they were going to kill him. I climbed over the side of the lorry and prepared to jump off. Mohammed pointed out that whatever happened in the lorry, it was a better place to be than the open desert. The boy put away his knife; the Dinkas followed suit. I climbed back in again. At midnight we stopped in a small village and took on twenty sheep. They leaked on our feet all the way to Khartoum. The Dinkas showed great restraint. I'd have been happy if they'd slaughtered the lot.

CHAPTER SIXTEEN
ROME

Men have left God not for other gods, they say, but for no god; and this has
  never happened before
That men both deny gods and worship gods, professing first Reason,
And then Money, and Power, and what they call Life, or Race, or Dialectic.

T. S. Eliot

'See this?' asked the lorry driver. He traced a thin finger along a
scar which ran from below his right ear to his chin. I nodded. 'From
the ambush,' he explained. He took me on a tour of the side of his
Bedford truck and pointed out the pock-marks in the metal. 'From
the bullets,' he said. 'From the bullets from the ambush.'

The driver's brother, another merchant, came to join us. We
shook hands. 'Yes, from the bullets from the ambush in south
Sudan. That's why my brother doesn't go to south Sudan any
more. We leave in three hours. Where are you going?'

'Rome,' I said, absent-mindedly.

'Italy?' he asked.

'Yes,' I said.

'We go to Wad Medani,' said the driver. 'OK?' I said it was.

We left Ed Damazin around midday. I sat in the front with the
driver, a fat woman and a young boy. Twenty others perched on
the merchandise in the back. In mid-afternoon we overtook the
steam train, which had left three hours before we had. It was a
hard, bone-shaking ride across a corrugated and unpaved track
which ran parallel to the rail track and never far from it. The skin of
water which hung from the side of the lorry split open soon after
we left, and every couple of hours we stopped at some tiny village to
drink tea. Our second stop was at a huddle of half a dozen *gesh* huts.

Two women, black, lanky and colourfully robed, served us, while their men lolled around in the fly-infested heat listening to an old radio.

A laconic and sleazy young man in a shabby suit obligingly turned to me. 'The man on the radio is saying Nasser was a bad leader,' he said in a soft voice.

'Why?' I asked.

He listened to the guttural and challenging Arabic which poured from the radio. 'He says Nasser wasn't interested in true Islam.' He grinned.

'Who is he?' I asked.

He lowered his voice still further. 'A religious man.' He rolled his eyes in mock piety.

In mid-afternoon we broke down. All the desert-tripping merchants take a mechanic with them, and ours was a wild character in a torn jellaba and a pair of trousers with one leg missing. He spent ten minutes wrestling with something under the bonnet, removed his headscarf to wipe the dip-stick and check the oil, and then stood back proudly to inspect his work. He grinned at us as if to say, 'That was quite a job!'

We stopped again around five o'clock. The mechanic set to work on the Bedford's engine. It was unbearably hot; hotter, I think, than I had ever known it. An old oil drum contained the only water here. It was a brown sludge. Some of the passengers wet their lips with it. I was stupid enough to take a small swig. My throat was so dry I could scarcely speak. I pined for sunset. An hour later I got it. It was magnificent.

We drove straight into the steaming crimson ball which fell in our path, stopping soon afterwards outside a small tin shack. There were six other Bedfords there, their bonnets up and open like yawning vultures. Everyone prayed except me. I bought a glass of tea and sat to one side on a charred log. A man tapped me on the shoulder and gave me quarter of a water-melon. I sank my teeth into pink and pippy flesh and the juice ran down my chin. The man had disappeared before I could thank him. It was a small thing, perhaps, but it was kindnesses such as these that lifted my heart most in Sudan.

During the day we had passed through three army checks. At the time I thought nothing of them, though they were tedious affairs. We had to open all our luggage and show their contents to the soldiers.

Late that night we pulled into Wad Medani. I found a hotel and went out in search of a café. I was famished. Everywhere was closed. I was about to give up and return hungry to bed when an elderly man asked me where I was going. I told him I was looking for food. He took me to a café and knocked up the owner, who gave me a bowl of beans.

Next morning I checked in at the police station. At Damazin I hadn't bothered to do so and I had had some trouble explaining to a policeman who accosted me in the souk why I hadn't. It took an hour for the Medani police to write down details from my passport. They couldn't work out why I had been down to Roseires.

There was an army roadblock just before we reached Khartoum. Everyone was ordered off the bus and I had to empty out the contents of my bag for inspection. The soldier who checked me over wanted to know what was in my notebooks. After half an hour we were allowed back on the bus and ten minutes later we arrived in Khartoum North, from where I took a taxi into town. Twice we were stopped by soldiers. They peered into the taxi before letting us through.

The taxi dropped me in UN Square. I walked over to the market. Groups of soldiers were kicking over stalls and flinging people into the back of a lorry. One of those arrested was a boy of eight or nine. He had been selling cigarettes. One man who refused to get into the lorry was pummelled over the head with a rifle butt. I made my way hastily to the hotel. Mohammed and Girma greeted me. I asked them what was going on.

'State of emergency,' said Mohammed. I asked what that meant. He shrugged.

I dumped my luggage in my old room. The other travellers had left, and I took Gerrald's bed. I was surprised to see copies of the *Sun* and *Daily Express* on my old bed. They were just two days old. Under the bed was a smart leather suitcase.

I ate a bowl of okra and potatoes in the café beside the hotel and played Mohammed twice at chess during the afternoon. I won one game and lost one.

I wanted to get on to the river, and I decided to leave Khartoum as soon as I could. My idea was to take the steamer from Karima to Dongola, and cover the rest of the journey to Wadi Halfa by truck. It would take me about seven days from Khartoum. In the early evening I went to book a ticket at the Nile Navigation Company's office. I was told that the steamer wouldn't be running again until the rains fell in Ethiopia and south Sudan in another six or eight weeks. I couldn't wait that long. But I didn't want to take the train, for the fourth time, through the Nubian Desert. I headed back into town and queued for an hour before I reached the counter in Egypt Air's office. All their flights to Egypt were fully booked for the next five weeks.

A ruddy-faced, pop-eyed German, his brow studded with sweat, his shirt clinging damp against his domed boozer's belly, pushed his way through the crowd to the counter. He got the same answer as I did. 'I must get out,' he muttered. The man behind the counter shrugged.

'Why?' I asked.

'You haven't heard?' he asked incredulously.

'What?' I asked.

'You are not well informed!' he barked. 'There's been a military *putsch*. And now – paff! One bullet and the whole country explodes.' He continued in similar vein for a few minutes. He said he'd seen 'huge army movements' in the east near Port Sudan; and that the army had tried to overthrow Nimeiri. He thought a civil war was about to begin in Khartoum. He scared the wits out of me.

'But we're safe enough, aren't we?' I asked, looking for reassurance.

'You joke!' he said, and left.

I walked down the street to Sudan Airways office. They said their flights to Egypt were fully booked for two months. I bumped into the German ex-pat again. 'It's these bloody Egyptians,' he said, tapping the side of his nose with a podgy finger. 'These Egyptian professors. They could smell trouble. They're getting out while they can.'

I wandered down to Athenae Square. There were hardly any soldiers on the streets; and in Casa Blanca the rich were ploughing their way through chocolate muds and banana splits without the bananas. It was reassuring. But back at the hotel the Ugandans in my room were uneasy.

The *Sun* and the *Daily Express* had been imported by a muscular Ugandan who'd flown in from England. He worked for the Red Cross in south Sudan and he'd just returned from a refugee conference at Oxford. His job was tracing missing Ugandans. He smoked a pipe and spoke the most perfect Queen's English. Another recent arrival was a sickly-looking youth of seventeen, also from Uganda. His skin was covered with white blotches. The Red Cross worker talked about the refugees in the south, British support for Milton Obote, and the state of English cricket. It was a depressing evening. 'Things in Uganda have got even worse since Amin went,' he said. 'Amin killed specific targets. Now the killing's indiscriminate. Amin claimed he was from West Nile province – which he wasn't: he was from Sudan – and so did many of his ministers. Obote is conducting a vendetta against the West Nile now. He's killing all the educated people. That's why so many doctors and teachers have fled. And it's the British who are keeping him in power.'

John – who still hadn't got through UNHCR's (United Nation's High Commission for Refugees) doors – nodded in agreement. 'Our people have even stopped growing coffee,' he said. 'They say that every kilo they grow buys Obote one more bullet with which to kill them.'

The Ugandans claimed that as refugees they received a much worse deal than the Eritreans. They believed that UNHCR was biased towards the Eritreans, as they were fighting a Russian-backed regime, and against the Ugandans, as they had fled a regime supported by the British. 'They think,' said one, 'that we should have stayed at home; and if we have left, it's because we are troublemakers.'

'Take that boy,' said the Red Cross worker, motioning with his pipe to the blotchy youth. 'He was in a camp near Juba. He's very sick, so they let him come to Khartoum for treatment. UNHCR have told him he can have an allowance of £S35 a month. That doesn't even pay for the hotel. How do they expect him to live?'

The boy let out a harsh laugh. 'I'll have to go back to Juba,' he said.

I asked what was wrong with him. He remained silent. One of the others told me later that he thought he was dying, possibly from cancer.

Apart from the Ugandans, there was one other man in the room, an Ethiopian. He talked little and slept most of the time. He had a bullet lodged in his back. He hadn't been able to get it removed.

I slept fitfully. Twice during the night I thought I heard aircraft passing overhead. Each time I left the room and peered into the sky. And each time I realized it was only the fan whirring above our beds. Just before dawn I had a curious dream. It repeated itself the following night. Colonel Gadafi sold me an air ticket to Tripoli. The pilot was the pop-eyed German. 'Such a nice place, Khartoum,' he kept repeating. 'Such a pity to leave.' He was shedding enormous tears, which ran down the side of his nose and splashed from his chin on to his fat belly. 'Such a shame! Such a shame!'

I reflected, when I woke, that I was running low on courage. I washed, drank a cup of tea and walked into town. The airline offices – I was going to try Ethiopian Airlines – weren't open yet, so I dropped into the British Embassy.

My contact there was amused at my consternation. 'Don't worry,' he said. 'I told you not to listen to rumours. There's been no *putsch*. Nimeiri has simply declared a state of emergency to tighten his grip on the country. Last night he sacked six of his top ministers.'

The army had taken over many of the powers of the police (and many soldiers in Khartoum seemed to have interpreted this as a mandate to beat up whoever they felt worthy of a beating), people's homes could be searched without a warrant, and suspects could be detained for fourteen days before being brought before a magistrate. The army had also been ordered to control transport and censor mail. (I was worried about my notes – more because of the postal service's inefficiency than fears about censorship – and the Embassy kindly sent them back to England in the diplomatic bag.) Demonstrations, strikes and public meetings had been banned, and the state of emergency had also paved the way for the imposition of curfews. Nobody seemed sure if there was one in Khartoum, but most people kept off the streets after midnight.

I spent a further week lingering in Khartoum. I went down with some sickness again, which I discovered, some two months later, to be giardia. I could have caught it anywhere, but the sludge-water I drank on the journey from Ed Damazin to Wad Medani seemed a likely culprit. There were only two trains a week to Halfa (there were four when I first came to Sudan) and I waited for the one which would connect with the Aswan boat. I spent most of my remaining time in and around the hotel.

The sick Ethiopian woman was carted off to hospital one morning. Her bed and her belongings were sprayed with insecticide and doused in disinfectant by Mohammed. (The hotel was exceptionally clean. One day a man appeared with a plastic canister on his back and a spray gun. He released an evil-smelling cloud of white gas from which we all fled. The Ugandans said it was DDT.)

Twice I went to Omdurman and both times I saw soldiers beating people up in the market. Mohammed introduced me to a house near by where I could get Ethiopian food. Most days I ate *injera* and *wat*, and most evenings I went to the *tej* joint.

After a few days the refugee worker left for the south, and a Ugandan student took his bed. One night he didn't return. He appeared the next morning. He was trembling. He had been arrested in Souk Arabi and dragged off to the police station, where he was crammed into a tiny cell with forty others. 'I thought I was going to die from the heat,' he told us. 'And the stench was unbearable.' Eventually he had managed to see the chief of police. 'Sorry,' the chief had said. 'They should never have picked you up. Maybe you should keep off the streets for the time being.' He stayed off the streets till I left.

At midweek a Swiss couple arrived from west Sudan. They had come from Jebel Marra, a range of mountains near Nyala, where they had built their own hut and lived a Robinson Crusoe existence for two months. Listening to Dominique and Patricia, I realized how little of Sudan I had seen, and what an unfair portrait of the country I was going to paint. They, too, were heading for Egypt. The night before the train was due to leave we packed our bags and prepared to leave. At midnight we said goodbye to the refugees we knew. Only once we were on our way out did someone warn us that we could be arrested. Apparently there was a curfew. So we waited. At four o'clock we woke Mohammed and Girma. I wouldn't,

I was sure, ever see them again. Girma was one of the few refugees who had papers to leave and I heard later that he went to Canada. Mohammed had no hope of escaping. I expect he is still there. We hugged one another and the three of us left for the station.

My notes describe the journey to Halfa.

5 a.m. Arrive at station. Train packed. Squeeze through window into 3rd class. Indescribable aggro. People fighting to get in.

8 a.m. Still here. Very hot. Can hardly breathe.

8.30 a.m. Feel faint. Get out of window. Faint on platform. Wake up puking. I'm not going. Dominique shouts at me to get on. I tell him I won't. He asks about my luggage – it's buried beneath others' in WC. Tell him I don't care. I plead with guard to let me sleep in guard's van. Still throwing up. Tells me to stand in sleeping-car corridor.

9 a.m. Ejected from sleeping car. Climb into 1st class corridor. Nearly as bad as 3rd. But I can squat.

9.30 a.m. Leave.

11.30 a.m. Conductor comes. Looks at my 3rd-class ticket. Someone tells him I'm sick. He says I can stay.

2 p.m. Arrive Shendi. Wailing women rush down to our carriage, weeping and imploring. First-class women begin weeping too. A first-class death, I suppose. God, the heat!

2.30 p.m. Conductor threw me out as we left Shendi. Running, I grabbed water pipe on side of buffet car and climbed on to roof. Black hands hauled me up. Wind, sun, dust. Snuff & grapefruit. Thirty of us on carriage. Camel-herder keeps me snuffed up. '*Kweiss* [well], John?' he keeps asking. 'Mrs Thatcher *kweiss*, John?' Sunset. Night. Blackness & wind. Feeling well & exhilarated.

10 p.m. Arrive Atbara. Everyone on roof climbs down before we get to station. I daren't. One slip and you're under wheels. Pull into station. Policeman arrests me. But he's greedy. He runs down train, leaping across gap between carriages after others. Escape into darkness. Power cut. I lose myself in crowd for an hour till train

leaves. Police watching for people getting on roof. Wait till it leaves and climb up on to third class (better footholds on 3rd class than 1st or 2nd; but roof less comfortable). Dominique, Patricia and American on same carriage. Tie myself on to water pipe. Sleep. Wind & flapping canvas.

3–6 a.m. Freezing cold. Fingers too numb to hold cigarette.

7 a.m. Sun again. Hot already.

8 a.m. Abu Hamed. Small market, beautiful. Four cups of tea, half water-melon, halva. Feel strong. Buy more fruit.

9 a.m. Leave. Roof again. Into Nubian Desert. Train goes *c.* 70 mph. Shaky and rough track. Cover head and body with Patricia's dress. Ankles sunburnt and raw. Lips ditto. Strong N wind.

Station 10, then 9, 8, 7, 6, 5, 4.5. (Why 4.5? Why not 4.3 or 4.65?) *Karkadee* at one. Dead bird in tank of drinking water. Odd how I don't mind squatting in desert with my white bum sticking out for all to see. Dominique says he hasn't used lavatory paper for three months.

4.00 p.m. Policeman appears from train (must have been there all along) and orders us off roof. Ten minutes out of station 3 he finds American still there. Orders him down. Mad! We're doing 70 mph. He gets down without falling. Desert, desert, desert. Nothing but vultures. Go into buffet and have tea. Ah, a seat! Bliss. Conductor wants to kick us out. Two distinguished Sudanese get us a reprieve. Man tells me: 'Weather's nice in Halfa. Only 39 degrees.' Bad joke.

9.30 p.m. 36 hours from Khartoum. Arrive Halfa. Filthy (me, not Halfa). I ate 18 grapefruit, drank 20 pints water, 5 teas, 2 *karkadees* & 1 coffee on journey. But only peed twice and meagrely.

I wandered round Halfa looking for a hotel. They were all full. We found a small café in the souk and ate some beans. A seedy Zanzibarean with close-cropped hair and tight, expensive jeans came to sit with us. We were too tired to talk. He picked up a chair, turned it round, straddled it and rested his chin on folded forearms.

'Hey man, I've got bad news for youse. You ain't goin' no place. No man, boat ees full.' He spoke in a carefully modulated trans-Atlantic drawl.

I wandered into the darkness, leaving the Swiss couple with the pessimist from Zanzibar. I found a charming policeman and asked him about tomorrow's boat. 'Yes, it's full,' he confirmed. 'Some people have been stuck here three weeks, waiting to get on. I'm afraid you'll have to wait.'

He told me where I should sleep. I retrieved Dominique and Patricia and led them out of town into the desert. About four hundred people were sleeping in the sand. I slept till dawn. Some people were packing up and walking into town. Others had lit fires and were cooking – they knew they wouldn't get on this week's boat. After we'd had breakfast in a small café, I asked around for Sheban, whom I was hoping might be able to get us on the boat. I couldn't find him so I went to the police station, where I found four other Europeans who had come by truck from Dongola. We waited two hours for the police to come. Some thought that *kawadjas* – the whites – would get special treatment and be taken on the boat. Others said we'd have to wait our turn, like the Sudanese. That meant a week or more in Halfa. Two men suggested that we should walk to another police station some five miles away; but fortunately one of the Europeans had the sense to take a taxi down to the dam. He came back with the news that we might get on if we went straight away. We rushed down on the first Toyota we could find. And we did get on. In fact, all the non-Sudanese were allowed on first: English, American, Egyptian, Chadians (of whom there were three), and the man from Zanzibar.

I was filling out forms on the customs barge when Sheban appeared. He looked tired and morose. 'You're lucky,' he said. 'Some Sudanese have been waiting three weeks.'

I found a space to lie down on the lower deck of the starboard barge. For company I had the whites who'd come from Dongola: two English teachers, and a Swiss journalist and his girlfriend. The boat left at midday. I felt euphoric. One of the teachers produced a bottle of *aragi* and we celebrated our departure. Someone rolled a joint.

I liked the journalist. He was in his mid-thirties, yet he looked a good ten years older. He was stocky and muscular with a strong bony face covered with black stubble, and he walked with a pronounced stoop, nodding his head continually like a felt poodle on the rear window ledge of a Cortina. His hobby was covering African guerrilla movements. I say hobby because I don't think he made much money at it. He had just been down to Ed Damazin, from where guerrillas had smuggled him across the border to visit the Oromo Liberation Front. It was his fourth trip into Ethiopia over the past two years. He had been in with both the Eritrean People's Liberation Front and the Tigrayan Liberation Front. And once he had flown to Addis masquerading as a tour operator. He'd spent six weeks contacting urban guerrillas, and had the true purpose of his visit been discovered he would undoubtedly have been killed. The friend who had accompanied him on that mission had recently been kidnapped by the Sudanese People's Liberation Army.

I asked him if he was ever scared. 'No,' he replied, 'I would never do it if I was.'

His girlfriend scoffed. 'He'd love to be captured and spend a while in jail,' she suggested. He replied with a crooked grin.

He was frank, fearless and obsessive. One day he would come to Africa – he was planning another visit in the autumn – and he wouldn't return. I think he knew that.

The boat didn't stop that night. We reached Aswan at five o'clock the next afternoon and moored a mile off the harbour. We spent the night on board. Next morning a small motorboat brought six customs men out to us, and they took the whole morning to check our passports.

I was back at the Aswan Palace by two o'clock.

I ate a late lunch in a café in the souk. A rat kept waving its long scaly tail out of a hole a few feet from where I sat. No one seemed to notice it. An ancient Nubian came to sit with me.

'Aswan is so, so rich,' he announced unprompted. He drew heavily on his *shisha* and exhaled a blue stream of smoke. It drifted out of the café and into the sunlight. 'So, so rich!' He nodded to the market stalls outside the Aswan Palace. 'Look there! Beautiful red tomatoes! Beautiful green cucumbers! Lovely potatoes! Juicy orange oranges! Fat pigeons! Ah! It's so good here!'

The poorest man in Aswan is a king compared to an inhabitant

of Khartoum. He is surrounded by brilliant colours, water, vegetables, flowering trees, rich scents, rushing people, donkeys, dramatic music, electricity, beautiful buildings.

'I miss Sudan,' said Patricia. 'The west was so fine, the people so
friendly. In two months we never saw one policeman. I miss that.'

'Yes,' mused Dominique. 'But it was hard. Here I'm standing
with one foot in paradise. I move five steps and I say "Come, have a
tea with me"; and there's always a café. Always people smoking
shishas. Then I go another five steps and what do I see? The Nile
fringed by palms. Flame trees in blossom. I turn round. Look! There's
a man on a donkey. And there's a man selling coffee from a beautiful
silver urn. Real beauty . . .'

I spent six days drunk with the loveliness, the lushness of Aswan.
Rarely have I felt such happiness as I experienced here – partly a
reaction to leaving Sudan; but more an inner celebration of beauty.
I saw the pigeon-seller squirting gruel from his mouth into those of
his birds; I listened to the shoe-shiners addressing one another as
Ya Rayeez! – 'Oh! Mr President'; I spent hours sitting in cafés and
watching egrets circling over the palm-covered islands. I saw
everything as though for the first time. I was dazed, almost feverish.
Even the simplest and most commonplace sight transfixed me, as
the rudest object will transfix an autistic child: a man frying spiced
liver; a woman suckling a baby; a policeman directing traffic. And
the wonderful indulgence of solitude. For the first time for over a
month I had a room of my own. No refugees. No arrests. No quiet
despair.

We stopped at every station between Aswan and Luxor in 1975.
Nobody bothered with the doors in third class. They simply
hurled luggage, goats, children and chickens through the open
windows and piled in after them. If they couldn't get past you
they'd bash you until you moved aside and made way for them. At
every station beggars climbed on and worked their way from one
end of the carriage to the other and they'd pull at your sleeve until
you gave them something. Four hours and half way to Luxor a
man climbed on with a lunatic on a lead. A table was cleared and
the lunatic was hoisted on to it. He was a stunted, crooked creature

who moaned and shrieked like a monkey. His master gave him some six-inch nails. The lunatic took one and stabbed it through his cheek. Then he speared his other cheek. Passengers howled their approval and encouraged him to stick more into his body. His skin was already a mass of scars and scabs. He plunged another four, at an oblique angle, beneath the skin across his belly. The passengers loved it. People threw money at the lunatic and he gathered it up. His master took it from him. They got off at the next station. There was nothing odd about this. Mutilation was considered an excellent form of entertainment.

My companion on that journey was a burly Sudanese who took it upon himself to act as my bodyguard, for which I was grateful. He was a great hand at belting any Egyptian imprudent enough to knock me on his way through the window. He spent a good deal of his time berating the Egyptians for their lack of manners and he was brave enough to condemn in the loudest possible terms the barbaric display with the lunatic.

This time I took the first-class sleeper from Aswan to Cairo. The train was made by Messerschmitt (Helicopters and Transport Division). I don't think there were any Egyptian passengers on it. It certainly wasn't the sort of place where you would wear a jellaba or kneel down and pray. Each compartment was a masterpiece of high-tech planning, a neat space-age plastic and metal module with wall-to-wall carpets, a washbasin, monogrammed linen sheets and more lights than you would find on a whole train in Sudan.

My companion was a small, plump and bespectacled Colombian psychiatrist who worked in New York. He was a compulsive talker and a Marxist. It was enough to drive a madman sane.

'You hear this escalator music all the time in America,' said the Colombian when Julio Inglesias was piped into our carriage. 'But not because they like it. In America people only play music to test the quality of their stereos.'

Airline dinners were dispensed by waiters dressed in natty beige uniforms. The meal consisted of courgette pie, lamb, processed cheese and Marxist theory.

'Doesn't being an ecologist make you a revolutionary?' asked the psychiatrist.

I motioned to the countryside which slipped past our window. From our air-conditioned capsule it was like watching a marvellous sunset on television. The sun was falling over a mud village and a grove of date palms. A mule and a she-buffalo were grazing by a canal. Young boys were diving from the banks and swimming. 'I like this sort of ecology,' I replied. 'People, animals and houses – all together.' I added that I would prefer it if I could smell the country as well as see it. It was no answer.

'Yes! Yes! That's it!' enthused the Colombian. 'Cultures spring out of peasants and the workplace. America doesn't have any culture. Just propaganda.'

The stewards woke us with airline breakfasts the next morning.

'What are those towers?' asked the Colombian as we passed a pigeon house.

'A pigeon house,' I told him.

'Oh! They eat pigeons!'

'Yes,' I replied. 'You must have seen them selling pigeons in the markets.'

'I haven't been to any markets.'

I felt sorry for him. He had spent six days in Egypt and seen almost nothing. He had paid $500 for a four-day excursion, which had taken him from Cairo by air to Luxor, where he had stayed in the Winter Palace; then from there to the Cataract in Aswan. He had ridden on a camel and sailed on a felucca. Shortly before we reached Cairo he pointed to a concrete water-tower. 'What's that?' he asked. A water-tower, I said.

'Aha! Very interesting! It must be some sort of public works.'

I nodded.

'That's good!' he exclaimed.

A limousine was waiting for him when we arrived in Cairo.

The sun was setting when I took the bus from Tahrir Square to the airport. The city was shrouded in smog. Looking back from the outer suburbs I could just make out the Cairo Tower and some of the skyscrapers in the city centre. They were a hazy vermillion.

Near the airport hotels, groups of Egyptians, Saudis and negroes were having picnics, sitting with their plates and rugs and radios on the central reservation of a dual carriageway. Traffic raced past them on either side, but they seemed unperturbed by the noise and the fumes. The bus pulled into the car-park outside the main terminal – a modest shed – and I threw up on one of the flowerbeds. I sat down for half an hour until I felt better, watching the last tatters of pink and purple cloud darken and then fade into the black night. Cairo was prickly with light.

I went into the main foyer of the airport. I had twelve hours to wait for my flight and £E1.60 to spend, which would have bought a third-class train ticket from Cairo to Aswan, but not a beer. The bar overlooking the runways was empty except for the barman. He gave me a beer, even though I was 20 piastres short. I sat and watched the planes come and go. The wind came straight through the open windows and blew my cigarette ends out of the ashtray on to the carpeted floor. I spent an hour drinking the beer. The barman left the bar and went to the W C. Through the open door I watched him remove his purple jacket and tie, then his shoes and socks. He ran some water into a basin and washed his hands and feet. Then he knelt down and prayed.

I spent the night on a hard seat in the foyer. It was impossible to sleep. If you lay down on the floor someone came and woke you up. Planes came and went through the night. Two to Nairobi, one to Karachi, one to Oman, one to Riyadh, one to Germany. I felt thoroughly disoriented. At eight o'clock we took off. Below I could see the two branches of the Nile, one going north-west towards Alexandria, the other north-east towards Damietta. We bisected the green delta.

After breakfast I went to the back of the plane for a smoke. An American joined me. 'I used to be in real estate,' he announced. 'But I'm retired now. I'm a great one for travelling. Last year me and the wife went to the Far East. This year we're doing Europe. You like Egypt?'

'Yes,' I said. 'I love it.'

'Yeah,' he said after some thought. 'Yeah, it's kinda interesting. But it's dirty. Now, take my wife: she won't even leave the hotels. Sometimes she doesn't even know what town we're in!' He roared with laughter and clapped his hands. 'But me,' he continued. 'I like to mix with the people. I been all over Egypt.'

I asked him how long he'd spent in the country.

'Four days.'

I stubbed my cigarette out and fell asleep.

By mid-afternoon I had crossed by bus from Athens to Patras, a small port in western Greece. I slept in a park until early evening, then went to catch the boat to Italy. A customs official pulled me out of the passport queue and led me into a small room. I was told to strip, and I was left naked for five minutes under the watchful eye of a uniformed man with a droopy moustache and sad watery eyes while two more men were summoned. It took them an hour to look through all my bags, my notes, my pockets, up my rectum and under my arms. They never said a single word during the search. They didn't bother to apologize either.

I slept on deck. It was wonderfully cold and it rained hard in the middle of the night. I was sick again but I liked the rain. By the time I reached Brindisi I was feeling too weak to travel and I lay up in a hotel for three days before taking the train north. Two events stand out in my memory. On the second night in Brindisi I was woken by screaming below my window. It continued for over half an hour, with one man systematically beating up another. He was trying to get information out of him. Nobody in the square could have slept through it. When the police arrived they threw the injured and badly beaten man in the back of their van. The assailant chatted to the police for a while and went his way.

Two days later I spent a night in Pescara, a small town on the Adriatic coast, some hundred miles east of Rome.

An Italian befriended an Austrian girl who had travelled north on the train with me, and he found us a hotel and invited us to eat with him. We met him in a bar later that evening, drank a beer and followed him to a small and simple café. The girl and I ordered a single dish each. He ordered a litre of wine and explained that he had eaten a five-course meal in mid-afternoon – he couldn't face a single mouthful tonight. However, he would watch us eat. We had a very pleasant meal, and he was excellent company. When the girl and I ordered coffee, the Italian announced that he was feeling peckish again. He then proceeded to order four dishes – spaghetti with mussels, a vegetable stew, roast rabbit and a salad – and we watched him shovel them down his throat.

What appalled me most, in these first few days back in Europe, was the gluttony. Of course, my sickly state of health may have had something to do with it; and within a week or so I was over-eating as much as those whom I now censured. All I could see was food: shops full of the most elaborate pastries, cakes, ice-creams; every imaginable sort of meat and vegetable and fruit; people everywhere eating to excess and spending much of their days doing it. It disgusted me.

R ome was cold. Storm clouds were gathering in the hills beyond Tivoli when the bus pulled clear of the city. By the time I reached the ruins of Hadrian's Villa they were obscuring the peaks and rolling down the valleys like a grey wash across a watercolour. Wild thyme soaked up the first heavy splashes of rain and a pair of whitethroats sang from a golden-flowered broom bush. Runnels of water ran down the chipped and weathered statues beside the pool of Canopus and a stone crocodile slavered from its serrated jaws. I sat down beneath an oak tree. The hill behind Tivoli became blurred and spectral and water slithered past my feet in sinuous gullies.

I wandered round the ruins, past the Canopus with its broken statues and architectural memories of Egypt, through a bank of oak and a thicket of dog rose, and into an olive grove. Below I could see Hadrian's columns and arches brooding beneath the dark cypress trees like wrecked hulls beside a deserted river wharf. Had things turned out as I had intended, I should have been in Juba by now. It would be raining down there too.

However aimlessly I have travelled in the past I have always had to give myself a target. When I left England in 1975, it was Khartoum. Once I had reached Khartoum, it was Nairobi; in Nairobi, it became Madagascar. I don't think I ever really intended to stop and work at Khartoum, although I made a desultory and half-hearted search for jobs; or in Nairobi, where I did the same. As for Madagascar, I never got there. I needed, I realize now, to fool myself into thinking that I was travelling for a purpose; that I was never leaving one place purely because I felt like leaving, but because I had to get elsewhere. I was searching for something but I never found it; not surprisingly, as I never knew quite what it was.

I envy Waugh, who could write once his travelling days were over, 'I never aspired to be a great traveller. I was simply a young man, typical of my age; we travelled as a matter of course.' I envy him partly because he was, if not a great traveller, a much better one than I was; but more because he travelled, as he put it, as a matter of course. I suspect that had Waugh been to Africa in 1984 he would not have been content, as I had been, to reach the dam wall near Roseires and turn tail. His inquisitiveness might have driven him further south. It could have been done. The Swiss journalist would have had no qualms about going to south Sudan had he felt like covering the civil war. Maybe Waugh wouldn't have gone south; instead he might have struck out west towards Central Africa; or perhaps he would have taken up the offer which I turned down to make the forty-day trek by camel from Darfur to Egypt. All this he would have done 'as a matter of course'. I had admitted defeat when I reached Roseires, but only partial defeat. Having forsaken plans to go further south I could not accept that this trip up the Nile could end so abruptly. If I could not end it in Juba, then why not in Hadrian's Villa? Sitting in the souk at Ed Damazin, waiting for a truck back to Khartoum, it had seemed to make sense.

I had believed, and it took me some time to recognize both the futility and the intellectual self-indulgence of the idea, that from Hadrian's Villa I could stand back from Africa, observe her from a distance and make some sense of what was happening in that continent. The denouement to my trip would be a short reverie, here in the home of a man for whom I had enormous admiration, about the terrible happenings in Africa today. It was a ludicrous idea.

Nevertheless, I sat in the shade of a brick arch while the rain beat down and scribbled some notes. I cringe as I read them now, but through them I find some explanation of why I made a beeline from Roseires to Rome.

'Evil is hydra-headed. No sooner do we rid ourselves of one tyrant than others rise up, decked out in different uniforms, proclaiming new ideologies, to continue the slaughter. The disasters which befall Africa today, disasters as much the making of the white nations as they are the fault of her own rulers, are the merest puff of wind beside the typhoon which will overtake the continent during the next decades. There will be more and bigger wars, famines which slay as never before, a march of refugees from country to country which will make the exoduses of today seem like pleasant seaside jaunts. There is inconceivable cruelty in many countries; torture is talked of as a way of life for those who dissent. It will become more refined, more sophisticated, more widespread . . .'

And so the rain-splattered notes continue. I am tempted to laugh, reading them again. Not because these views (when extracted from the cant in which they are couched) differ from what I believe now; But because I thought it worth saying. It did not require any great prescience to see that wars, famines and refugees – the triptych of Africa's misfortune – would not go away. By the end of 1984 Sudan was facing a famine every bit as serious as that which afflicted Ethiopia and which the West was belatedly recognizing. And by Christmas UNHCR was predicting that over 400,000 people would flee from Tigray to Sudan between autumn '84 and spring '85.

When I left for Alexandria I was determined that I should make some sense about what was going on on the banks of the Nile. I had no intention of writing an anthropological travel book, nor one which was solely preoccupied with my personal experiences while travelling. I wanted to understand how the river worked, how its waters were used and how the countries were feeding themselves. This was a modest aim, and perhaps I came some way towards understanding the river as a piece of geography. But much more, I wanted not just to see but to understand how people survived in unsewered slums, in overcrowded dwellings with no clean water, and in villages where malaria and bilharzia affected, at one time or another, every family. I am stunned, now, by this arrogance. How could an Englishman brought up among the English in England, speaking hardly a word of Arabic, understand how the Egyptians and Sudanese felt about what it was to be poor, when my concepts of poverty and suffering and theirs must have differed enormously?

Ohe first time I travelled through Africa I gave little, if any thought
to the leaders of the countries I passed through until I reached
Uganda. My knowledge of the political situations in Egypt and
Sudan was sketchy. I knew the handsome Sadat presided over
Egypt and Nimeiri over Sudan; but little more than that. Mengistu
was already in power in Ethiopia, but I heard more about Haile
Selassie than this military upstart. I came out of Ethiopia believing
that anything was probably better than Selassie, but my real
concerns lay elsewhere. My memories of the country reflect my
preoccupations then – a collage of high peaks and mud villages
of armed men and beautiful women; of hours spent picking lice
from shirt seams. I never made any effort to understand the
country's politics. I was a self-indulgent traveller, happy to take
adventure when adventure came, and pleasure when pleasure
beckoned.

In Kenya, Jomo Kenyatta was still in power. I saw him once, or
rather I saw one of his hands once. He was being driven down
Nairobi's Kenyatta Avenue in a large limousine with smoked-glass
windows. One of the back windows was wound down and a hand
appeared, a black hand with an enormous stone – an emerald, I
think – on one finger. The hand waved mechanically to the populace. I enjoyed the spectacle.

Only once I reached Entebbe did I give much thought to an
African leader. There was no pleasure to be had and little adventure;
we were confined to the grounds of the hotel. Every evening we sat
down to eat in a large dining-room with linen tablecloths and good
silver. The only whites apart from myself and the three other
stranded travellers were four Russian pilots. They wouldn't talk to
us. Some evenings, during dinner, the radio was turned on. Idi
Amin talked at the people, mostly in Swahili, sometimes in poor
English. One of the bell hops, a frightened man, would come into
my room at night and tell me what had happened over the past few
years. He asked me to smuggle a letter out of the country, but I was
too cowardly to do so, believing that I might be searched on the
way out – it was the time of the 'Hills Crisis'. (Dennis Hills, a white
teacher who had written unflatteringly about Amin, was in prison,
and it was to take the intervention of the British Prime Minister to
get him released.) Nothing untoward ever happened to us in

Entebbe, but it was impossible not to dwell on what Amin was doing to the country.

In 1984 Mubarek was leading Egypt towards some form of democracy. He intrigued me. As soon as he had come to power the Western press had castigated him as a weak man, forgetting, I suggest, that there is much to be said for weak leaders. But it was the current fashion for denigrating their dead Big Brothers, Nasser and Sadat, that fascinated me most.

Once I reached Sudan I became obsessed by Nimeiri. I would spend hours lying on my bed staring at the president's portrait above the Mad Rwandan's bed; and I would try to imagine how this man passed his days in the Palace. Of course, these thoughts led me nowhere, other than into fantasy.

With the exception of Iran, no other country in recent years has made the leap from secular to religious government so quickly as the Sudan. No need to reach up for God; just haul him down among the people and allow his spokesmen to dispense justice as they think fit (but in his name, of course).

The sudden transition from paternalistic feudalism to state communism in neighbouring Ethiopia – which was infinitely more bloody – was a step in the other direction. Ironically – for the Dergue was waging its own war against God: it wished to stamp him out – I did not find this secular jihad particularly blasphemous, even if it was thoroughly distasteful. The Ethiopian government will continue to persecute the Christian church and to install its own puppets as bishops and dignitaries, but there is not the slightest chance of them turning the people against God, even if the state proclaims itself to be godless.

Nimeiri, on the other hand, appeared to be guilty of a monstrous blasphemy. He was not only spitting in the face of the Christian God and the river gods of the negroes in the south; he was writing God into his own sordid little melodrama. Act 1 didn't work very well: like Lear he found that those around him were prepared to challenge his omnipotence. 'They told me I was everything,' said the demented Lear: ' 'Tis a lie, I am not ague-proof.' Nimeiri, in his pre-emptive bid against the ague, brought on a convenient cure. Act 2: Enter God.

What saddened me most this time in Sudan was the institutionalization of intolerance. Islam, by tradition, and unlike Christianity, makes no attempt to convert members of other religions, only pagans. But now Nimeiri was attempting to impose the mores of Islam on those who subscribed to other religions. I had never met, on my first visit, with such kindness as I received in Sudan. I remember, for example, climbing off the train roof after the two-day trip through the Nubian Desert to Khartoum. I was dishevelled and filthy. A uniformed policeman welcomed me and asked me where I intended to stay. I said I didn't know. He took me to a hotel a mile away, waited while I checked in, then escorted me to the police station near by. He showed me to the showers, took me to meet the police chief and then organized a simple meal for me. One took such hospitality for granted in the Sudan. Never once did anyone suggest I turn to Islam. It was simply accepted that I was of another religion or of none at all, and that was my affair. This time I met with much kindness too; but there were occasions when I sensed and experienced religious bigotry.

Act 3 the Sudanese melodrama will begin shortly: Exit Nimeiri.

None of this leads me back to Hadrian. It would have been just as logical to end my African journey in Albania, on the grounds that Mohammed Ali came from there, or at Sandhurst, where Amin and one or two other African leaders received their training. Certainly, Hadrian had had strong ties with Egypt and the Nile – it was part of his empire; he had travelled up to Luxor; and his lover had drowned in the river. I thought, when I left Khartoum, that I would stand Hadrian among the gruesome pantheon of leaders – black, white and Arab – who determine what happens in Africa today, and see one light at least shining from the darkness. But to compare Hadrian with today's leaders – whether African or European – would be impossible and meaningless. I was at the villa under false pretences.

Nevertheless, I was glad to be sitting here in the rain. At the villa I realized that my admiration for Hadrian had little to do with his qualities of leadership or his prowess as a soldier. Around me lay the ruins of the villa – which he had designed. In the city down the hill stood the Pantheon – which he had designed. He was a lover of poetry and music. He was said to have read every important book on philosophy and science. He went to Egypt not as a conqueror bent on forcing the Egyptians to adopt the mores and religions of

Rome, but to learn from them. He worshipped Egyptian gods and in the villa the Canopus remains his memorial to Egypt. ('The villa was the tomb of my travels,' says Yourcenar's Hadrian, 'the last encampment of the nomad, the equivalent, though in marble, of the tents and pavilions of the princes of Asia.') In short, he was a man of culture, an appreciator of beauty, a respecter of diversity; and his beliefs and actions were untrammelled by 'ideology', in whose name anything goes now.

I left Hadrian's villa in the early evening. It was half a mile to the bus-stop on the main road. Water dripped from the oak and olive. The rain had beaten flat a field of barley. Sweet pea, campion and herb robert glistened purple, white and pink in the half-light. Blackbirds chattered in the hedge-backs and worms oozed up from the sodden turf.

'The rain! Yes, that's it!' the camel-herder had proclaimed in the desert. 'That's the big difference between our countries.'

That, at least, made some sense.

BIBLIOGRAPHY

There must be many hundreds of books about the region which I have never heard of, let alone read, and the list below includes only those which I have mentioned in the text or found particularly useful and interesting. Anyone who wishes to keep up with current affairs in that part of the world will find four magazines of special interest: *New Africa, Africa Now, African Business* and *The Middle East*. All are monthly, and they can be obtained both in Britain and in Africa.

Bovill, E. W., *The Golden Trade of the Moors*, Oxford, OUP, 1978.

Cavafy, C. P., *Collected Poems*, London, Hogarth Press, 1984.

Chitty, Derwas J., *The Desert a City: An introduction to the Study of Egyptian and Palestinian Monasticism under the Christian Empire*, New York, St Vladimir's Seminary Press, 1966.

Durrell, Lawrence, *The Alexandria Quartet*, London, Faber, 1968.

Edwards, Amelia B., *A Thousand Miles up the Nile*, London, Century, 1982.

Evans-Pritchard, E. E., *Nuer Religion*, Oxford, OUP, 1977.

Flaubert, Gustave, *Flaubert in Egypt*, translated and edited by Francis Steegmuller, London, Michael Haag, 1983.

—— *The Temptation of St Antony*, translated by Kitty Mrosovsky, Harmondsworth, Penguin, 1980.

Forster, E. M., *Alexandria: A History and A Guide*, London, Michael Haag, 1982.

Frankfort, Henri, *Kingship and the Gods*, London, University of Chicago Press, 1948.

Hoagland, Edward, *African Calliope: A Journey to the Sudan*, Harmondsworth, Penguin, 1978.

Ikram, Khalid, *Egypt: Economic Management in a Period of Transition*, Baltimore, Johns Hopkins University Press, 1981.

Kapuscinski, Ryszard, *The Emperor*, translated from Polish by W. R. Brand and K. M. Brand, London, Quartet Books, 1983.

Lane, E. W., *An Account of the Manners and Customs of the Modern Egyptians*, 5th ed., ed. E. S. Poole, New York, Dover, 1974.

Marnham, Patrick, *Dispatches from Africa*, London, Sphere, 1981.

De Monfreid, Henri, *Aventures de mer*, Paris, Grasset, 1932.

Moorehead, Alan, *The Blue Nile*, Harmondsworth, Penguin, 1983 (first published 1962).

—— *The White Nile*, Harmondsworth, Penguin, 1973 (first published 1960).

Parrinder, E. G., *Africa's Three Religions*, 2nd ed., London, Sheldon Press, 1976.

—— *African Traditional Religion*, 3rd ed., London, Sheldon Press, 1974.

Seton-Williams, Veronica, and Stocks, Peter, *Blue Guide: Egypt*, London, Ernest Benn, 1983.

Waugh, Evelyn, *When the Going Was Good*, Harmondsworth, Penguin, 1951 (first published 1946).

Wikan, Uni, *Life Among the Poor in Cairo*, London, Tavistock Publications, 1980.

Yourcenar, Marguerite, *Memoirs of Hadrian*, Harmondsworth, Penguin, 1959.

INDEX

Index

Tamiya, 57
tej parlour, Khartoum, 165–70

Uganda, 11, 13, 17, 169
United Nations High Commission for
    Refugees, 215, 229
Usiater, 203

Venus Hotel, Luxor, 97

Wad Medani, 189, 213
Wadi Halfa, 147–8, 219–20
Waugh, Evelyn, 9, 11, 13, 52, 53, 78, 197,
    228
Wikan, Unni, 74

zabalene, 73
Zafarana, 43, 44, 51